Queer St Ives and Other Stories
Ian Massey

Queer St Ives and Other Stories

Ian Massey

Ridinghouse

For David – and for Lydia, all these years later...

Acknowledgements

I first dipped my toes into the research waters for this book in 2013, and, as a friend said recently, it has had a long gestation. It would never have reached fruition without the generosity of the many people who have helped along the way. Firstly, my sincere thanks to the following for granting interviews, and for engaging in conversations and correspondence: the late Keith Barron, Mary Barron, Peter Durkin, Christine Farrington, Jan Green, Lesley Hassey, Michael Hunt, Bryan Illsley, Geoffrey Key, David Lindsay, Valerie Lowndes, Marguerite McWilliams, Rachel Nicholson, Victor Sayer, Reg Singh, Jane Val Baker and Brian Wall.

While talking with those who knew John Milne and his circle has proved enlightening, access to archives, both public and private, has also been a crucial element in my research. Here, particular mention must be made of Tom Sargant's archives; his unbounding kindness has been unparalleled. Likewise, several visits to the St Ives Archive were of enormous value. Thanks also to Professor John Cave, for granting access to his collection of Richard Blake Brown's journals. Documents held by the Tate Archive and in the collections of Manchester Art Gallery, Manchester Metropolitan University, Salford Art Gallery and Salford Local History Library have all proven invaluable. My thanks to staff at all of these institutions.

Many individuals have been consistently supportive of my project. Chief among them I wish to thank Janet Axten, Michael Bird, Chris Booth, Sophie Bowness, Gloria Carter, John Charles Clark, Richard Dubieniec, Robert Harbin, Martin Harrison, Victor Ktori, Jason Lilley at Penwith Gallery Archive, Felicity Mara, Guy Milne, Carey Moon, Jessica Nicholls, Nancy Patterson, Linder Sterling, David Tucker, Jon Lys Turner, Dickon Tyrrell, Rupert White and Hephzibah Yohannan.

My thanks also to Lauren Adriana; Sue Astles; Clare Barlow; Rob

Barnard; James Barron; the late Trevor Bell; Sean Benbow; Stella Benjamin; Yorick Benjamin; Poppy Bowers; Michael Bracewell; Ivor Braka; Staff of the Special Collections Research Centre, Brotherton Library, Leeds University Library; David Butler; Toni Carver at the *St Ives Times and Echo*; Dell Castogly; Stephen Chambers RA; Edward Clark; Ken Clay; Shirley and Chris Cocklin; Deborah Cohen; Cathy Corbett; the late Adrienne Corri; Fiona Corridan; Jonathan Xavier Coudrille; Vincent Dowd; Patrick Elliott at the Scottish National Gallery of Modern Art; John Emmanuel; Gizzi Erskine; Maria Erskine; Stephen Feeke; Andrew Fletcher; Dr James Fox; Naomi Frears; John Frears-Hogg; Patrick Gale; Adrian Glew and staff at the Tate Archive, London; Mike Goldmark; Derek Guthrie; Nigel Hall RA; Gerard Hastings; Anthony Hepworth; Andrew Hodges; Annabel Hodin; David Horbury; Lucy Howarth; Andy Hughes; Daniel Illsley; Lucy Jackson; the late Colin Jellicoe; Andrew Kalman; Mary Lambert; Andrew Lambirth; Andrew Lanyon; Gail Levin; Rachael Levine; Wendy Levy; Margaret Lovell; Duncan McCormick at Salford Local History Library; Milly Massey; Sara Matson; John Maybury; Paul Moon; Alice and Bill Mumford; Clare Nadal; Peter Oglivie at Salford Art Gallery; Mark Osterfield; Peter Parker; Beryl Patten; Michael Pick; Stella Redgrave; Matthew Retallick; Mark Rimmell; Alban Roinard; Tommy Rowe; Jonathan Riley; Tony and Barbara Russell; David Sayer; Geoff Senior at the Northwest Film Archive, Manchester Metropolitan University; Mike Shepherd; Tony Shiels; Jeanie Sinclair; Alistair Smith; Ian and Vivien Starr; Chris Stephens; Elizabeth and Morvah Stubbings; William Summerfield; Maria Summerscale; Paul Swann; Jonathan Thomson; Selina Todd; Ken Turner; Martin Val Baker; Nigel Van Wieck; Andrew Waddington; Chris Waters; David Whittaker; Phoebe Wild.

For photography, scanning and provision of image files, many thanks to: Georgia Atienza at the National Portrait Gallery, London; Jean-Luc Brouard; Miles Clemson at Whitechapel Gallery Archive; Richard Coles at Godson & Coles; Elizabeth Comba at Roseberys; James Flower at Bonhams; Michael Gaca, Richard Blackborow and Dominica Williamson at Belgrave St Ives; Ben Harrison at the Estate of Francis Bacon; Pippa Jacomb at Christies; Charlie Minter at Sotheby's; Stephen and Sylvia Paisnel at The Nine British Art;

John Rastall; Graham Rees; Mike Shepherd; Chris Sutherns at Tate Images; and Anthony Tran at Trunk Archive.

My sincere thanks to all at Ridinghouse: Sophie Kullmann, for her unending support and guidance, Aimee Selby and Linda Schofield for their superbly rigorous editing, and Mark Thomson for his excellent book design. Production was greatly aided by a major publication grant from the Paul Mellon Centre, for which I am immensely grateful.

Finally, I wish also to dedicate this book to my late friend Elizabeth Diamond (the artist Elizabeth Finn, 1933–2019), and to my darling late mother Gwen (1936–2021).

Ian Massey, 2022

Note on Sources

Text quoted from original documents has been transcribed as closely as possible; however, underlined text has been rendered in italics. Unless otherwise noted, quotations from unpublished materials are from the following sources and reproduced with permission:

Richard Blake Brown, journals: Collection of Professor John Cave
Michael Hunt: Conversation with the author, St Ives, 1 May 2015
David Lindsay: Telephone conversation with the author, 13 July 2015
Julian Nixon, diary: Collection of Professor John Cave
Julian Nixon, journal: Collection of Tom Sargant
Julian Nixon, letters to and from: Collection of Tom Sargant
Julian Nixon, *Tapestry of Innocence*, handwritten manuscript: Collection of Tom Sargant
Victor Sayer: Conversation with the author, Manchester, 15 August 2013
Reg Singh: Conversation with the author, London, 20 April 2016
Byron Temple, diary: Collection of the Emmanuel Cooper Estate
Byron Temple and John Milne letters: Collection of Victor Ktori
Jane Val Baker: Conversation with the author, St Ives, 3 March 2015
Brian Wall: Telephone conversation with the author, 30 June 2015

Introduction: Shadow and Light

We read the past by the light of the present.[1]
—Siegfried Sassoon

The UK heatwave of 1976 began in the last week of June and continued until late August. Recorded temperatures were the highest of the century so far, with day after day in the mid-80s Fahrenheit, occasionally reaching the mid-90s. Nobody spoke of global warming then. The negative results of weeks without rain were grass fires, droughts and hosepipe bans. There were plagues of ladybirds, too, although what one remembers most is the sheer gorgeousness of such untypical weather during what was to become a legendary summer.

That August, I first visited and fell in love with St Ives. I was 20, and had previously travelled no further from my family home in the north-west of England than to Blackpool and North Wales. Whose idea it was to have a holiday in St Ives I cannot quite recall, although my interest in the artists associated with the place – particularly Barbara Hepworth and Ben Nicholson – certainly had something to do with it. Four of us made the journey: my mum Gwen, her boyfriend Roy, my 12-year-old sister Lydia and myself. We set off in a rented caravanette on a Sunday afternoon, with Roy, the only driver among us, at the wheel for the journey of 350 miles or so. I remember keeping an eye on him from the passenger seat, quickly nudging him awake at one point as we sped along A roads in the darkness of the early hours. The diary I kept then records how we stopped on Bodmin Moor at around seven in the morning, soon after passing Jamaica Inn, so that Roy could take an hour's nap. The bleak moor appeared otherworldly in the early morning light: 'a huge, weird, quiet place with unfriendly sheep', according to my diary. There were small trees, stunted and bent into shape by the wind, the likes of which we had not seen before; and abandoned tin mines, relics of a bygone industry. We arrived in St Ives a few hours later and camped on the Ayr caravan park above the town.

If you have visited St Ives you will know of its distinctive geography, of its location in the far south-west of England at the heart of West Penwith, on the northern coast of the Cornish peninsula. And you will know how the old town, with Fore Street and The Digey its main arteries, ranges between the two largest beaches, Porthminster and Porthmeor. Descending towards the town by road, you suddenly see below you the harbour and stone jetty of Smeaton's Pier, with behind it the grassy raised outcrop of The Island, topped by the tiny granite St Nicholas Chapel. If the day is clear enough you can also see the glittering white thumb of Godrevy Lighthouse perched on its rock miles out in the sweep of the bay. Arriving by rail is equally magical, if not more so. You board the branch line train at St Erth station for the ten-minute journey, passing en route the salt marshes of the Hayle Estuary, the dunes at Lelant Sands, then Carbis Bay, where the train sometimes stops at the little station before setting off again. From that point on, glimpses of St Ives harbour and The Island flicker like a lantern show between the trees that line the track, as the train curves along the way, soon arriving at its destination and terminus high above Porthminster beach, where you then alight and take the short walk into the town itself.

Warmed by the Gulf Stream, St Ives seems to exist in its own blue bubble, its climate quite different from that of the rest of Cornwall. There are palm trees there, which were wondrously exotic to visitors from the north-west of England in 1976. The Barbara Hepworth Museum had first opened to the public that April, and my sister and I were among its earliest visitors. There are photographs of us in Hepworth's garden, with its canopy of clear blue sky: Lydia with *Four-square (walk through)* (1966) and the six-part sculpture *Conversation with Magic Stones* (1973); myself with *River Form* (1965). At the Penwith Gallery I saw for the first time work by artists including Alan Davie and Ben Nicholson, and at the Wills Lane Gallery gouaches by Roger Hilton and William Scott, the latter of two lemons painted on a spare white background. Lydia and I entered the open door of the Puffin Studio, where we talked with the artist Lily Barnard

(1902–1980) – her name, I later realised, a reminder of the painter Lily Briscoe in Virginia Woolf's *To the Lighthouse* (1927) – about her paintings, some of which, I seem to recall, were of coastal rock formations.[2]

We travelled out of St Ives that week, driving in the caravanette one evening through Penzance to Mousehole – 'quite a nice little place' – and 'then to Lands End – a bit disappointing – it's become terribly commercialised with lots of trashy gift shops etc. We came home via Zennor in the dark and had a late meal of egg and chips.'

Our holiday was brief: we arrived around 10am on Monday 16 August and, after another drive through the night, were back at home by 9am on the Friday. But since then, magnetised, I have returned to St Ives countless times, in all seasons.

More than any other English county, Cornwall exerts a particular hold on our collective imaginations, the potency of its mythology stemming in no small part from its presence in literature and film, where it forms the backcloth for narratives of mystery and romance, of old-time religion and the derring-do of smugglers. One thinks of the supernatural atmosphere of Alfred Hitchcock's 1940 film version of Daphne du Maurier's novel *Rebecca* (1938), with its opening line, 'Last night I dreamt I went to Manderley again', read in voiceover by Joan Fontaine as the camera twists and turns towards the house along its overgrown drive, the scene swirling in mist. Manderley was based on Menabilly, du Maurier's home at Fowey, the fictional house being both a stage set and a character in itself, whose very walls hold the secrets of its turbulent history. Enid Blyton's 'Famous Five' books greatly stirred my childhood imagination and invaded my dreams, in which I would join the Five on some adventure, waking with a sense of loss and longing in my pale suburban bedroom. While Blyton's source for Kirrin Island (the setting for several adventures in the novels) was in Dorset, the twelfth book, *Five Go Down to the Sea* (1953), is set in Cornwall. The back cover of my paperback edition reads: 'Why does a light shine out on stormy nights from the ruined Wrecker's Tower overlooking the rocky Cornish coast? This is the mystery the Five set out to solve.' One yearned – still yearns – to solve it with them.

It is, though, rather too easy to sentimentalise Cornwall, to ignore its history of often dangerous toil in fishing and tin mining, to bypass the present-day poverty of many of its inhabitants. Better instead to concentrate on its ever-seductive mythologies of place, on the pagan mystery of its landscape, with its standing stones and megalithic dolmens. The county has long been considered a haven for non-conformists, a place of self-imposed exile far from the madding crowd. In this respect, the romantic notion of Cornwall as 'other' – both part of England while at the same time 'Celtic' and therefore intrinsically foreign – is fundamental to its allure. So, too, is its close relationship to the surrounding seas, for its coastline is longer than that of any other English county. The beauty of much of Cornwall's landscape is indisputable, stretches of its coast being among the most dramatic in England. While it has long been a cliché to remark on the particular clarity and translucency of the light in St Ives, it remains that the light is indeed transformative, certainly in the way it affects colour, notably that of the sea, which takes on hues – aquamarine, mauve, turquoise – more redolent of the Mediterranean than the Atlantic. Generations of artists have been drawn to the town because of this defining characteristic of light. At Porthminster beach, less celebrated than Porthmeor though equally beautiful, sand and sea often appear delicately opalescent, certainly in the mornings and early evenings, when the curve of its beach becomes a bleached Naples yellow, the sea pale eau-de-nil. One thinks of the evanescent watercolours made by James Abbott McNeill Whistler during his stay in 1884, and also of the wonderfully atmospheric canvases of Julius Olsson (1864–1942), who loved to paint the sea beneath a big sky in moonlight or as dusk descended.

The atmospheric mystery of Cornwall continues to cast its spell. The art historian J P Hodin (an émigré from eastern Europe, of whom more later) first visited the county in 1946. Subsequently he wrote of the 'unforgettable impressions' he was left with, and of:

> The strange Cornish landscape with its white china clay dumps near St Austell, the disused mine shafts scattered here and there in deserted places which remind one of the temples of a forgotten religion, and the granite shores, with their picturesque harbours ... beaten by the waters of the Atlantic and the Channel, the moors between, and the regular pattern of small square fields and grey stone houses stretching from sea to sea.[3]

Then, 64 years later, the dashing art historian Dr James Fox presented a television documentary about the St Ives artists. It begins with him standing on a Cornish clifftop in full sunshine, intoning the irresistible opening words of his narration against a backwash of swooping strings and urgent violins:

> Ancient and mysterious, romantic and remote: Cornwall stands at the very edge of our world, yet it exerts a magnetic pull on our imaginations. Coincidence, curiosity and crisis drew a string of great artists to this remote region. Responding to each other and the dramatic landscape, they went on to produce some of the most exhilarating art of the twentieth century. The history of British painting and sculpture would be redefined in this distant and forbidding place.[4]

The artists Fox goes on to describe working in that distant, forbidding place are those now firmly ensconced in the St Ives pantheon, their lives inextricable from the region's geography. Their individual and collective biographies, sometimes embroidered with anecdotes of indeterminate authenticity, have entered the historical record. And while these stories continue to fascinate, what we understand of St Ives can, conversely, somehow seem as if preserved in aspic, the place as though a cosy middle-class theme park; Bloomsbury-sur-Mer but without the homosexuality. In fact, the queer history of St Ives is an important one, integral to the development of twentieth-century modernism in which the town is so significant. For while the majority of those artists considered canonical to St Ives were heterosexual, or ostensibly so, there are other figures associated with the place who were homosexual or whose sexuality was more fluid. And as visibility and understanding have increased in recent decades, queer lives have gradually been written into the histories from which they were previously excluded. One thinks of such figures as the art critic Adrian Stokes (1902–1972) and the painter Christopher Wood (1901–1930), whose stories have now been told without eliding their sexuality. Among others with St Ives associations are the artist Frances Hodgkins (1869–1947), who lived and worked there from 1914 to 1920, where she befriended the queer couple and fellow painters Cedric Morris (1889–1982) and Arthur Lett Haines (1894–1978). Outside the immediate locale were artists with connections to St Ives, such as the Lamorna-based Marlow Moss (1889–1958) and Gluck (1895–1978); and in Newlyn the couples Max Chapman (1911–1999) and Oswell Blakeston (1907–1985), and Charles Breaker (1906–1985) and Eric Hiller (1893–1965). Among other queer residents or visitors in the twentieth century were the writers Virginia Woolf, Katherine Mansfield and Hugh Walpole. There was also D H Lawrence – permanent seeker of an idyll of self-imposed exile – who lived together with his wife, Frieda, in a cottage at Higher Tregerthen, above Zennor, for a period during the First World War. Lawrence recounted his experiences there in his autobiographical novel *Kangaroo* (1923), in which he wrote of himself under the guise of 'Richard Somers' and included references to his real-life homoerotic friendship with local farmer John Hocking.

This book does not set out to detail the queer history of St Ives in full. Rather, it focuses on the lives of queer inhabitants and visitors during key decades of artistic production in the town, from the early 1950s to the late 1970s. At its centre is the sculptor John Milne, who was, like me, a gay working-class lad from the north-west of England.

1 The Boy from Eccles

> The Jungian analyst Marion Woodman posits that unwanted or superfluous children have difficulty in becoming embodied; they remain airy, available to fate, as if no one has signed them out of the soul store.[1]
>
> —Hilary Mantel

Tucked away in St Ives, not far from its main shopping streets and just around the corner from the Barbara Hepworth Museum, is Trewyn Gardens, a small public park that first opened soon after the coronation of Queen Elizabeth II in June 1953. Its well-maintained garden comprises a rectangular lawn bordered on three sides with a footpath and edged with dense plantings of trees and shrubs, among them palms, japonica, euphorbia, holly and hydrangea. There are flower beds planted with dahlias, begonias, marigolds and suchlike, the stuff of municipal gardens. And sheltered among trees and bushes at the furthest end of the park stands *Megalith II*, a quietly imposing sculpture in bronze made in 1974 by John Milne. The artist presented it to the town as a memorial to his recently deceased mentor, friend, neighbour and fellow sculptor Barbara Hepworth; it is in fact the only public sculpture in St Ives not made by her. Almost 2 metres high, it surmounts a slender granite plinth over a deep concrete base. Set into the plinth is a small metal plaque engraved with the words: 'Megalith – For Dame Barbara Hepworth – 1976 – John Milne'.[2] *Megalith II* – its title suggests a monument – is a sophisticated work, more complex in design than might at first appear. Its structure is that of a rectangular box, its four sides angled to flare outwards from the base, its top a shallow dome. On the front of the sculpture are two vertical forms of equal length. That on the left is in negative, recessed in a triangular wedge that widens as it ascends; that on the right protrudes and is rounded, baton-like. These two forms are opposites, reminiscent of symbols for female and male, yin and yang. Over the years, the sculpture's lightly abraded surface has become gently weatherworn, patinated in verdigris. Mysterious and inscrutable, it has something of the vault or tomb about it, and, situated as it is in close proximity to Hepworth's former home, it reads not solely as a memorial to her but as a discreetly positioned sentinel.

Trewyn, the large house in which Milne lived and worked, is a matter of footsteps from *Megalith II*, on the other side of the narrow lane that runs alongside the little park, and immediately behind the high perimeter fence of Hepworth's garden. It was there, quite hidden behind tall granite walls, that he lived for over two decades, and where he died in 1978 at the age of 47, little more than three years after his neighbour. And while her career and reputation far eclipsed his, the two were closely connected; in his case, one might go so far as to say fatally so.

*

In the summer of 1975, Milne discussed with the art historian J P Hodin (1905–1995) the idea of a book about his life and work. By now, Hodin (his first name was Josef, although he was known to friends as Paul) had high repute as a writer on art, and was trusted by artists, having previously written on many British and European sculptors and painters, including Henry Moore, Ben Nicholson and Hepworth.[3] He had also written an essay for Milne's most recent show of sculpture, held the previous October at the Marjorie Parr Gallery in London. The two had first met seven years earlier in St Ives, at the opening of a Penwith Society exhibition at which Hepworth was also present, and where she had praised Milne's work to Hodin, indicating that she felt he had the potential to capitalise further on the advances he had already made. In preparation for the book, Milne made a number of visits to Hodin at his flat at Carbis Bay, where the art historian made copious written notes during their discussions.

In the resultant book, published as *John Milne: Sculptor* in 1977, Hodin wrote that Milne's work was 'best understood when we realise that its one root reaches into his personal conflict'.[4] The conflict was one that Milne had discussed openly with him, explaining how when growing up he felt at odds with his family, and how from a young age he had felt an emotional turmoil that had never left him. That he confided in Hodin in this way indicates the degree of trust he had come to have in him. Not only that, but in reading the book one gains an impression of the writer enacting the role not merely of art historian but of therapist or father confessor. Perhaps by now Milne felt it was time to put on record aspects of his life he had previously been guarded about, for those who knew him in St Ives recall that he never spoke about his family. It was, says his friend Lesley Hassey, 'as though he had been found under a bush; you know, *nothing*. I think he had that insecurity of not being accepted by his family. Because he never talked about them.'[5]

While working on the book, in a move that can only have been made with his subject's agreement, Hodin asked the London-based Jungian psychologist Marianne Jacoby to draw up Milne's horoscope. When she subsequently posted the chart and notes to Hodin, in her covering letter Jacoby described Milne as 'A very uneasy man, as you will see.' Following on from this, at her request Hodin sent a sample of Milne's handwriting, and after examining it, she wrote in reply:

> I only wanted to have a look at it as a sort of safeguard for my horoscope. The handwriting confirms what I gathered from his creative shapes that he masters single units of expression, but that on the whole, or with regard to overall perspectives, he is confused. He is not really aware of it, perhaps not yet. A prognosis, if one should make one at all, is not very good.[6]

The horoscope chart was illustrated on a page of Hodin's book, Jacoby identified only by the initials 'MJ', with the stipulation that she had no personal knowledge of Milne beyond his date of birth. Her notes, also included in full within the book, begin thus: 'According to this horoscope the native is an artist of conflict. Nothing is easy for him or gives clear perspectives of solutions. What is left to him is to state and re-state the thousand and one facets of ever the same basic discords.'

She goes on to include the following insights:

> There is an undertone of pain, a sensitivity to the feeling of lack, of never having been chosen. But it is this emotional pain which is the very spur to his artistic creativity.
>
> ... He claims an artist's need of freedom. But there will be much in life, or in particular, in personal relationships, that he shuns. However, it is not a simple flight, he is by no means a luxurious escapist, he meets here with something tricky and bewitched that is beyond his control. It is not so much that he runs away from personal relationships, but more that they run away from him.

In her final paragraph, Jacoby concludes:

> The conflict is very deep in him. He grew up in disharmonious conditions. Temperaments at home did not compensate each other but clashed, and perhaps cancelled him out. There is a deep pain in him ... of not being loved and of not being really important to any particular person. Nor is he inclined to bind anyone to himself. As a social phenomenon he is a loner, but as an artist he is one with the creators of our cultural history and with the never-ending stream of creative impulses and the endless variations of his artistic material.[7]

*

John Erskine Milne was born at Eccles, near Salford, Lancashire, on 23 June 1931. His father was James Alexander Milne (known as Jimmy), born on 14 January 1872 to Scottish parents: Anthony Milne, a journeyman tailor, and Anna, née Maxwell. James's birth was registered at Benholm, Kincardine, although by the time he was four years old the family had left Scotland and were living in Eccles. Like his father, James became a tailor. In 1924 he married a woman 19 years his junior named Lottie (née Leafe), born on 18 July 1891 and originally from Derbyshire. Five years before her marriage, Lottie had had a son out of wedlock named Harry. Before John, the youngest of their children, Lottie and James had two daughters: Audrey, born in 1925, and Jean in 1928.

There are in Hodin's book certain factual discrepancies about the family history that result from information that came from Milne.

One such relates to his father's age at the time of his birth: Hodin has him aged 63, whereas in fact he was four years younger. He writes also that James Milne was in his second marriage, and that John had a half-sister and two half-brothers from this first marriage. However, no record of a first marriage has been traced, and one suspects that the confusion may have arisen from the fact that James's father, Anthony Milne, had married for a second time: the 1911 census lists him as still resident in Eccles, by now with a wife named Lizzie Milne. And James did have a half-brother, Archable, eight years his senior; so along with Lottie's son Harry these two are perhaps the half-brothers to whom Hodin refers. The half-sister remains a mystery.

What is verifiable is that the family lived together at 24 Wellington Road, Eccles, in a substantial semi-detached house, one of many that were demolished in 1971 to make way for the M602 motorway. They were a working-class family: James Milne conducted his tailoring business from home and Lottie took in boarders, commercial travellers and the like, who each had their own room in the house. A couple of these men lived there long-term. The Milnes' combined income ensured that the family suffered no particular hardships. That said, due to austerity measures the war years meant certain deprivations for virtually everyone, including the rationing of foodstuffs. The measures were introduced by the government in January 1940 and only fully ended in 1954.

Less than 3 miles west of the centre of Salford, and under 4 miles from that of Manchester, Eccles lies close to the north bank of the Manchester Ship Canal. The town's industry was largely in engineering and textile production (still operative, although in decline, in Milne's childhood years). During the Second World War, the docks of the Ship Canal were a target for enemy bombing and received a particularly bad hit, with loss of life, in December 1940.

In comparison to the population of neighbouring Salford, many of whom lived in real poverty, the inhabitants of Eccles were generally quite well-to-do, and there were within its precincts areas of middle-class prosperity. Marguerite McWilliams, a distant relative of James Milne on the maternal side of her family, lived with the Milnes off and on from the mid-1940s until 1959. Asked about the town during the period she lived at Wellington Road, she describes it as:

> A village, very much a little village ... Trains went literally across the road from our house. The village itself was very compact, with a market down at what we call Eccles Cross. There were loads of cinemas; we could go to the cinema every night if we wanted to, there were about three or four within walking distance ... There were loads of shops along the main road. It was a close environment, little corner shops and things. It wasn't a village like in the country, but a villagey type of environment.[8]

Reading Hodin's account of Milne's early life one gains the impression of a rather sad childhood, for he describes him as 'a sensitive and very lonely child'.[9] McWilliams, who got to know Milne well while living at Wellington Road, concurs with Hodin's verdict – 'I would say that was probably true' – going on to remark how surprised she was when she first read the book: 'I found it very depressing. I just thought to myself, my God, I didn't realise he was so unhappy.' Yet at the same time, she remembers Milne – who was seven years her senior – as 'a very, very charming person, and he was also very giggly. He had a great sense of humour and giggled away at things. There was no nasty part of John that I was aware of. I was very fond of him.'

James Milne was a wayward and demanding man, and his marriage an unhappy one. Milne told Hodin that he had hated him, and recalled, 'When I was old enough to think, speak, he was like a grandfather.'[10] Out of loyalty, he often took his mother's side during her frequent arguments with her husband; she was very possessive of him, 'because I was the youngest and only son – that was the reason'.[11]

Milne and his mother were close, and he the apple of her eye. McWilliams remembers her with great affection as 'Auntie Lottie':

> She was one of those warm people who invited everybody to come to the house: waifs and strays. If anybody was stuck for somebody to look after the children, Auntie Lottie would look after them. Generally speaking, she was a wonderful person. She was a mother figure, a really warm mother figure. To me, she was second to none.

Milne suffered from insomnia for much of his life, a condition that may have begun in childhood, for, as he told Hodin, as a youngster he was frightened of sunlight and would go out on long walks alone after dark, losing himself in a world of shadows. In his teens he often found solace walking in the nearby Peak District and in the Lake District, and in 1949 he visited Scotland and the Isle of Skye with a group of friends.

From the age of five, Milne attended Clarendon Road Council School close to his home and later, on receipt of a scholarship, went on to study at the Royal Technical College, Salford.[12] He wanted to study art but was forbidden to do so by his father, who insisted he instead study for what was considered a reliable trade. And so it was that the 13-year-old enrolled as a student on the two-year Junior Building course in the Junior Technical School.[13] The college prospectus for the 1944–45 session states: 'The Junior Technical School is designed to meet the requirements of boys who desire to enter the Engineering, Building, Chemical or Textile industries as apprentices at about the age of 15.' It goes on to describe three courses, each commencing in September 1944: General Engineering, Building, and Textile, the latter introduced that year. The prospectus also outlined the curriculum for each course: the first-year Building curriculum comprised English, History and Geography, French, Mathematics, Geometrical Drawing, Building Drawing, General Science, Art, Workshop (Carpentry and Joinery), Physical Training and Games, and Assembly. In the second year, Building Drawing was replaced with Building Construction and Building Science, while the Workshop element expanded to include Painting and Decorating, Plumbing, Brickwork and Masonry. Study was for 30 hours per week and was intended to provide experience and skills to prepare graduates for employment as apprentices in the trade.

Although Milne applied himself to his college work as best he could, he was not happy with the idea of a career in the building trade, and in the end his mother, aware that her son wanted above all else to be an artist, was instrumental in helping him to make the transfer to the art department. The head of the college's School of Art, recognising Milne's ability, also helped persuade James Milne to allow his son to transfer to study Junior Art in the next academic year. There his subjects were Design, Illustration, Plant Drawing, Commercial Design, Lettering and Craft, with classes and exams also in English Composition, Literature, Geography, Arithmetic, Biology and French.

His exam results showed him strongest in art and design subjects, and weakest in Arithmetic, Biology and French; his overall average was 55.5 per cent. The rest of Milne's studies comprised Intermediate Art (1947–48), Senior Art (1948–50) and the National Diploma in Design (1950–51); then a year specialising in Sculpture (1951–52) followed by a final year of Postgraduate Sculpture (1952–53).[14]

Upon completion of his general training in art and design, Milne decided to specialise in sculpture, a choice resulting from his fascination with the work of the Romanian Constantin Brâncuşi, which he had come across in photographic reproduction.[15] There was, however, no specialist sculpture course or facility at the college, so he worked instead in the ceramics department. There, after first making some pots, he began to produce a series of figures based on life drawings: nudes, most of them female, modelled in accretions of terracotta clay and then kiln-fired. Both formally and technically they are highly reminiscent of nudes by the English sculptor Frank Dobson (1888–1963), an artist of whom Milne was very much aware (see, for instance, Dobson's *Noon* of 1936 and *Kneeling Figure* of 1935, terracotta works now in the Tate collection). There are similarities, too, with the nudes of the French sculptor Aristide Maillol (1861–1944), whose work Milne admired for its solidity and compactness; and with those of another sculptor whose work interested him, the German Wilhelm Lehmbruck (1881–1919).

Milne's developing awareness of both historical and contemporary sculpture is evident in his assimilation of ancient and modern forms in his student work. Much of his knowledge came from library books, and from magazines such as *The Studio*, although he also found inspiration elsewhere, citing for instance the collection of ancient Egyptian artefacts at the Manchester Museum. Among important exhibitions he is likely to have visited was *Henry Moore: Sculpture and Drawings, 1923–1948* at Manchester Art Gallery in June and July 1949, a substantial show comprising 53 sculptures and 73 drawings.[16] Further afield, Assyrian bas-reliefs at the British Museum in London excited his interest, evident in a dozen or so relief sculptures he produced, among them the sandstone *Fertility Figure* (1948) and the terracotta *Christ Carrying the Cross* (1950), subsequently installed at Eccles Presbyterian Church. There was also, towards the end of his studentship, *Minerva* (1952), a relief in pre-cast stone not unlike the relief works of Eric Gill (1882–1940). This last resulted from an approach from Lancashire County Council, which asked the college to select a suitable student to produce a work to decorate the exterior of Summerville County Primary School in Salford. (*Minerva* remains *in situ* at the time of writing.)

Milne was a good-looking young man with deep blue eyes and medium brown hair that he always kept nicely trimmed. There is a photograph of him taken at the art school in which he is shown with his *Reclining Figure* of 1948, made from carved plaster (for which he must have acquired some relevant technical advice). He appears to be working intently, holding a chisel and rounded sculptor's mallet, in a photograph probably made both as a record and for publicity purposes. Stylistically reminiscent of sculpture by the German Ernst Barlach (1870–1938), and again that by Gill, *Reclining Figure* is a highly competent work, certainly for a student of 16 or 17. Inventive in its abstracted formal rhythms, it was the largest and most sophisticated work he had made thus far, and redolent also of the stone or marble figures of Moore and Hepworth. Milne followed the work in plaster with a less refined version in Portland stone, his first ever direct carving, made for his college bursary.

A driven and productive student, Milne made the most of his opportunities and was proactive in getting his work seen. For example, in the same year that he produced the first *Reclining Figure*, he exhibited a drawing titled *Lyme Hall, Cheshire* in a Local Artists Exhibition at the City Art Gallery, Salford. A terracotta *Seated Figure* was later selected for inclusion in a Manchester Academy show in 1951.[17]

Milne was highly sensitive in nature, and early feelings of loneliness were surely exacerbated by the fact that he had nothing in common with rest of his family. They shared none of his interests in classical music and poetry and found themselves bemused by him. In feelings typical of those of a queer child, he must have known that he was different, that something unbridgeable and at times bewildering separated him from his family and most others. Marguerite McWilliams realised that Milne was homosexual when he was 17 or 18 years old; asked if she thinks that his parents knew of his sexuality, she replied that she does not know but that she believes it unlikely that his father, who died in 1950, was aware of it. She remembers James Milne working at the kitchen table, cutting fabric from which to make suits: 'He did used to get a bit wound up when John was playing his music, all his classical music. He used to get a bit annoyed about that on occasions. John didn't get on with his father, but I think it was more to do with the age gap than anything else.'

In common with the vast majority of homosexuals of his generation, Milne cannot but have internalised the widely felt homophobia of the period. The predominant tendency was to vilify and punish gay men, public suspicion and lack of understanding being magnified by sensationalist newspaper reports. As the historian David Kynaston has written:

> the moral panic of the late 1940s and early 1950s generated a sustained campaign to stamp out such wicked congress, with indictable offences (mainly for sodomy and bestiality, indecent assault and 'gross indecency') rising sharply. The Director of Public Prosecutions, Sir Theobald Mathew, was a zealous homophobe; successive Home Secretaries were disinclined to restrain either him or the police; and the men in blue now started using agents provocateurs to catch homosexuals, as often as not 'cottaging' in public lavatories.[18]

At the age of 17, Milne approached and then underwent analysis with a Jungian depth psychologist, Dr Franz Greenbaum. The analysis continued for two years, with the full approval of Milne's mother, who had become concerned by her son's troubled nature. Born in 1903, Greenbaum (his name anglicised from its original Grunbaum) was, according to his obituarist, 'a man of great personal charm, and a warmhearted colleague with a subtle, unteutonic sense of humour'. Importantly, certainly for Milne, he was also a connoisseur of the arts and had a 'particular flair for interior decoration, colour, and design'.[19] Analysis with the cultured and intellectual Greenbaum was to prove immensely beneficial; in his conversations with Hodin years later, Milne described how the analyst had greatly expanded his knowledge and thinking while actively encouraging him to be an artist. This positive affirmation of the Jungian approach might explain Hodin's decision to approach Marianne Jacoby when researching his book about Milne. In fact, Hodin had a long-established interest in Carl Jung and had interviewed him at his home in Switzerland in 1952, two years after which he delivered a lecture, 'C. G. Jung and Modern Art', at the Institute of Contemporary Arts in London.[20]

Shortly before the commencement of war in 1939, Greenbaum travelled as a Jewish refugee from Nazi Germany to Britain, settling in Manchester. When war was declared, he was interned for a short while and after his release went on to develop an extensive psychotherapeutic practice in the city. When the National Health Service was introduced in 1948, Greenbaum became a psychiatrist and analytical psychologist at both Salford Royal Hospital and Hope Hospital, the latter also in Salford. It is likely that Milne was referred to him as an NHS patient.

In Jungian analysis, the interpretive process begins with the 'amplification' of a dream, in which its atmosphere and mood are determined, along with details of its images and symbols. The goal is to use this amplification as a means of confronting the workings of the unconscious mind. As a Jungian, therefore, Greenbaum attached great importance to dreams and instructed Milne – who had drawn obsessively since childhood – to make drawings of his frequent nightmares, some of which terrified him in their highly sexual nature. While these drawings were retained by Greenbaum and seem not to have survived, they set in motion what became for Milne a lasting habit. He often drew while listening to classical music, its movements informing those of the marks he made on and across the paper: abstract expressions of his inner life that, in contrast with the formal containment and smooth surfaces of much of his mature sculpture, read as maps of his state of his mind. Usually made in his favoured materials of charcoal, pastel or crayon, many are of disorientating spaces: vortexes, tunnels and dead ends. That drawing continued to act as a form of release is evident from an anecdote told to a newspaper journalist in St Ives in the early 1970s, in which Milne recounted: 'once a decorator who was working in the house looked at one of my abstract drawings. He said he didn't know much about modern art but he got the feeling from it that he was the driver of a car just before a crash. And that's just what it was – a drawing of tension. That pleased me.'[21]

Although for much of his life he was a troubled man, there is nothing to suggest that Milne was unhappy about or unaccepting of his sexuality. Whether or not the subject was broached during his discussions with Dr Greenbaum is open to conjecture, but it seems at least probable. Intriguingly, in the autumn of 1952 Greenbaum began to psychoanalyse the mathematician, founder of computer science and wartime code-breaker Alan Turing (1912–1954), who had been convicted of gross indecency in March earlier that year. Turing was not imprisoned but was bound over on probation for 12 months, on condition that he agreed to a course of hormonal therapy treatment at Manchester Royal Infirmary as a suppressant and potential 'cure' for his homosexuality. Turing's biographer Andrew Hodges has stated, 'My impression is that Turing took a lot of trouble in summer 1952 to locate a psychiatrist whom he thought the right person, and I think this would certainly mean someone who did not regard homosexual desire as a disorder.'[22]

In fact, as Hodges identified, Greenbaum's liberal-minded philosophy resulted in him prompting Turing to live according to his true nature, and not to hide or otherwise try to suppress his sexuality. At Greenbaum's request, Turing wrote down his dreams, filling three notebooks with descriptions of them. In writing about Greenbaum, Hodges described how in the 1950s there was:

> a powerful come-back of psychoanalysis, and increasingly vocal claims to the effect that its techniques could eradicate homosexual desire. But Greenbaum did not take such a view; homosexuality was not a 'problem' to him. He accepted Alan as a 'natural' homosexual, and as a Jungian, he did not consider human activities in terms of displaced or unconscious sexuality ... His emphasis, as with Jung, was on the *integration* of 'thinking' and 'feeling'.[23]

In considering the reasons for Milne's initial approach to Greenbaum, one wonders if his sense of turmoil was intensified by worries about the imminent possibility of conscription for national service. Introduced in the year in which he first met with Greenbaum, the National Services Act 1948 changed the age range of conscripts from between 18 and 40, to 17 to 21, with the period of service itself lengthened considerably from six to eighteen months. This doubtless caused alarm for many young men of Milne's age. In fact, he was not conscripted, most likely exempted on medical grounds, for in a note on a postcard sent to his student friend Reg Moon, undated but probably written in 1952, he mentioned, 'I will not be going in the forces after all.'[24]

*

Manchester had a rich cultural scene in the postwar world of the late 1940s, outlined in a newspaper column by Tom Driberg from May 1948:

> The Hallé, last Sunday, was playing Shostakovitch and Tschaikovsky at its superb best. The twenty young artists of the Manchester Group have an interesting show at the Mid-day Studio[s]. The City Art Gallery has better moderns – Matthew Smith, Ben Nicholson, Maurice Lambert – than any other provincial gallery I know.

Driberg goes on to report that the dancer and choreographer Rudolf Laban, 'whom Goering sacked from his directorship of the Berlin State Opera', was now in Manchester working with Theatre Workshop, 'whose next production is now in rehearsal ... and will be staged there in July. Its title, "The Other Animals".'[25]

Milne certainly engaged with the city's cultural life during his student years, each week attending concerts by the Hallé and the BBC Northern orchestras, both of which performed regularly in Manchester. Some performances – including those by the contralto Kathleen Ferrier and violinist Ginette Neveu – affected him so profoundly that he found himself unable to speak of them afterwards. It seems that, 'more fascinated by music than by realities', he existed emotionally and spiritually elsewhere, in a mental space at one or two removes from everyday matters.[26]

Notwithstanding his underlying conflicts, Milne was a sociable being, making friends with a number of his fellow students at Salford. Marguerite McWilliams was not part of his social circle but recalls that a lot of these friends came to the Milnes' home. Among them was Katherine Dowd (1930–2006), a working-class girl who studied to become a teacher and later lived at Milne's home in St Ives. Another was the aforementioned Reg Moon (1930–2009), who trained as a ceramicist at Salford; like Katherine, he and Milne were to become lifelong friends. Milne was also part of a group of art students who congregated in cafés in the centre of Manchester, the most popular of which was the Kardomah Café.[27] This social world is brought to vivid life in *The Lights of Manchester* (1991), a first novel by Tony Warren (1936–2016), another of Milne's friends. In it he describes how one of his two central characters, the 14½-year-old Mickey, makes the acquaintance of a group of art students and through them discovers 'a whole café life; centred around making one cup of coffee last for hours. Its headquarters were down in The Kardomah, on Deansgate; a subterranean coffee house with arched and vaulted recesses.'[28]

It is clear that Warren based the character of Mickey on aspects of his own personality and experience, for as his friend and co-executor David Tucker recalled, 'From what I understand, Tony's escape from the confines of suburbia to Manchester bohemia was through hanging out with art students somewhat older than he was, in Manchester's coffee bars of the late 1940s and early 1950s (helped by the fact that his cousin Roy [Varndell] was at Salford School of Art).'[29]

Born Anthony McVay Simpson in 1936, Warren grew up in Eccles, where, like Milne, he attended Clarendon Road School. He too was gay, and as a youth he was drawn to the Manchester cafés, pubs, theatres and galleries, where he found a previously unimagined world in which bohemian and queer communities intersected. It was a world where otherness was accepted, where he could begin to enact his dreamed-of real self. Meeting the art students was his point of entry.

In all of this, proximity to central Manchester was crucial, for as has long been true, queer people were drawn to major towns and cities. In Milne's explorations of social and cultural life, he too found the haunts where fellow homosexuals congregated during the decade or so after the Second World War. One is able to map these places. Among them was the Café Royal on Peter Street, and the Princess Bar on Oxford Street. There was also the subterranean Long Bar beneath the Gaumont cinema on Great Bridgewater Street, featuring, as its name suggests, a long bar, one end of which was invisibly demarcated as a queer meeting place. Each of these venues was smart and respectable, and one could walk between them within a matter of minutes. Less salubrious was the Union, a gay pub on the corner of Princess Street and Canal Street (the latter later made famous as a queer epicentre), which Warren, talking years later of the gay scene of the 1950s, described as 'the tacky end ... but of course the tacky end was the most fun'.[30] The Union hosted drag shows during the war, and certainly by the 1950s was known to attract a gay clientele. At the time of writing, the pub, now known as the New Union, is all that remains of those early gay venues.

Warren wrote four novels in total, all of them drawn from his own experiences and containing invaluable insights into the bohemian life of the period, particularly in the aforementioned *The Lights of Manchester* and *Behind Closed Doors* (1995). In both books he writes of his youth in Salford and Manchester, and of the postwar gay world. David Tucker notes how Warren often combined traits of several real-life friends or acquaintances when creating each of his fictional characters. This applied, too, in *Coronation Street*, the famous television soap opera he originated, which was first broadcast in 1960 and which drew on his familiarity with working-class life in Salford. The feisty Elsie Tanner, for instance, portrayed by the actor Pat Phoenix, was based on a combination of his Aunt Lily along with two other women of his acquaintance.[31]

There is an intriguing echo of Milne in Barney Shapiro, a character first mentioned towards the end of a passage from *The Lights of Manchester*. It is set in 1951, the Festival of Britain year:

> The students tolerated them [Mickey and his best friend Sheila] in The Kardomah but suddenly became lofty nineteen- and twenty-year-olds when the children demanded to be taken to meet Magda Schiffer.
>
> Magda Schiffer was a Manchester bohemian legend. In fact, the word bohemian had gone out of fashion – and it was only outsiders who still called creative people 'arty'. Sheila and Mickey longed to be insiders. Friendship with Magda Schiffer seemed to be a prime qualification. Jewish, a painter, born in Berlin, survivor of the Buchenwald concentration camp – Magda Schiffer nightly held court in the nearest thing Manchester had to a salon.
>
> These gatherings took place in an attic flat, under the gothic eaves

> of some former cotton merchant's mansion, in the Victoria Park district. She was said not to have two ha'pennies for a penny, and to offer little more than a cushion on the floor and her famous cheese straws. Magda Schiffer nevertheless attracted the brightest young talents in Manchester. Her dusty attics were reputed to throb with vitality and new ideas.
>
> ...
>
> 'We'll get there,' said Mickey confidently. 'Barney Shapiro will take us.'
>
> 'Who's he?'
>
> 'Another art student. He comes back from St Ives next week. Barney Shapiro is the most beautiful man I've ever seen.'[32]

Here, the reference to St Ives suggests that Milne is among those from whom Warren devised the beautiful Shapiro. The character's physical appearance does not fully match that of Milne – again, one assumes he is a composite – although it does include a description of Shapiro's eyes, deep blue like Milne's: 'the colour of a sailor's collar' (a reminder of Milne's predilection for naval types); and this description of a face rings true: 'of great beauty yet it was a clown's face. Sad and comical at the same time.' Mickey's friend Sheila falls in love with Shapiro after first encountering him at Magda Schiffer's flat: 'Sheila saw Barney Shapiro for the first time and she would remember the moment for the rest of her life.'[33]

As for the character Magda Schiffer, she is based on the real-life artist Käthe Schuftan (1899–1958), whose soirées in her Victoria Park home Warren is known to have attended on at least one occasion.[34] According to her biographer Hephzibah Yohannan, whose artist father Eugene Halliday was among those close to her in Manchester, 'Käthe hosted soirées in her home, and had a following of young people.'[35] Her following included art students such as Milne, who later told Hodin that Käthe had been a strong and encouraging influence on him during his student years. She was also a friend of Franz Greenbaum, having like him arrived in Manchester as a refugee in 1939; she is known to have given him drawing lessons. It may well be that she forged an introduction between Milne and the analyst, too.[36]

A German Jew, Käthe had studied art in her home town of Breslau (now Wrocław) in the years after the First World War, going on to study in Munich under the photographer and graphic artist Hans Leistikow (1892–1962). She then pursued an artistic career while at the same time becoming active politically, initially with the Social Democratic Party and later with the Marxist Socialist Workers' Party. In 1933 she moved to Berlin, where she continued her involvement in underground political activities and where, that November, she was arrested and subsequently detained by the SA (the *Sturmabteilung*, the Nazi Party's original paramilitary wing), who tortured her brutally. Accused of plotting to overthrow the constitution by violent means, she was tried alongside others and sentenced to two years in prison. Subsequently, with the period in which she had been on remand taken into account, in late 1935 or early 1936 she was released. Her work, two examples of which had been acquired in 1927 by the Silesian Museum of Arts in Breslau, was included in a show of so-called 'degenerate' art at the museum in December 1933, an exhibition pre-dating Joseph Goebbels's notorious 1937 *Entartete Kunst* (Degenerate Art) exhibition of work deemed by the fascists to be an insult to Germanic values.[37]

Käthe's older brother Paul, a highly qualified chemical engineer and inventor, had arrived in England in 1936, and it seems likely that Käthe, along with her mother and maternal grandmother, travelled to England to be with him.[38] In Germany, Paul had been employed by the major gas producer Linde, which, concerned by the escalating threat to Jews, made measures to send certain of their highly qualified Jewish employees to safety abroad. Of these, Paul was the most prominent, having 'played a major role in overseeing construction of Linde-designed plants in several countries in the early 1930s, including the United States, the Soviet Union, and Japan'. Because of his classification as a Jew under National Socialist legislation, Linde sent him to England in 1936, on the pretext that his expertise was necessary to support its suffering business there. In fact, Linde reached a gentlemen's agreement with the British Oxygen Company to transfer his employment to them, initially for five years. In the end, Paul Schuftan was to work for the British company for the remainder of his career.[39]

Many refugees, certainly those from Germany, Austria and Italy, were detained as aliens in internment camps as a precautionary measure soon after their arrival in the UK. Although kept under surveillance, Paul Schuftan was exempted from internment, as was Käthe (their one other sibling, Lotte, emigrated to Buenos Aires). Käthe was to work during the war in a munitions factory in Eccles, but her first employment was as live-in housekeeper to Arthur Neville Rawlinson (1905–1983), who sponsored her when she first arrived in England.[40] Known to all as Neville, Rawlinson worked in a bank in central Manchester and lived with his partner Richard 'Dickie' Gardner at 10 Clifton Avenue, in the city's Fallowfield suburb. Records show that Käthe was resident at that address from September 1939 (when she first arrived in England), and also in the following year, while from 1941 onwards she lived at several other locations in Manchester. She spent the rest of her life in the city, forming supportive friendships with fellow artists and exhibiting her paintings. Her work, much of it in watercolour, is expressionistic and symbolic, reflecting the experiences of violence and degradation that haunted her.

From the time of her first arrival in Manchester, Rawlinson was highly supportive of Käthe, insisting she spend more time on her painting than on domestic duties. He was, in fact, a great supporter of the arts, and very much part of a circle of Mancunians keenly engaged with cultural matters. He was also a bibliophile and a devotee of Marcel Proust, reading his *À la recherche du temps perdu* (1913–27) in its original French. His book-crammed house became – as did Käthe's flat later – something of a meeting place for those with similar interests, including artists and fellow homosexuals (groups rarely mutually exclusive). Rawlinson supported young artists, among them Geoffrey Key (b.1941), whose work he bought when the painter was first trying to establish his career; he was also instrumental in arranging a show of Key's work at Salford Art Gallery in November 1966. Among other pictures in his collection were several by Julian Trevelyan and an Ivon Hitchens still life, *White Gladioli* (c.1940–42).

Rawlinson undertook research on the Manchester-born Rowley Smart (1887–1934), corresponding with many people who had known the artist but never completing a proposed book about him. Later, Rawlinson was involved with the Manchester Institute of Contemporary Arts (MICA), set up in 1958 by a group that included the poet Robin Skelton and painter Michael Snow. MICA published pamphlets by poets such as John Fuller and Glyn Hughes and organised art exhibitions, among them *Trend*, a 1963 show of work by Anthony Benjamin (one of Milne's friends in St Ives), Joe Tilson and Gwyther Irwin. In the following year, Manchester Art Gallery put on *Collectors' Choice*, a show of 112 works loaned from private collections, of which 11 belonged to Rawlinson; they included his Hitchens canvas, a Trevelyan, and Milne's *Growth (Head)*, which was probably a work on paper (no sculpture of that title is known to have existed).[41] Rawlinson also knew Franz Greenbaum, whom he likely first met through Käthe.

Jan Green, who worked from 1962 at the Tib Lane Gallery in central Manchester, knew Rawlinson, as did her husband Geoffrey, who had studied art at Salford and who had opened the gallery in 1959. She recalls that soon after she began to work there, Rawlinson started to call in every weekday. It seems that his visits offered respite from his job at the bank, which he hated:

> He used to come into the gallery every, but *every*, lunchtime. He couldn't stand his colleagues at the bank; he thought they were total philistines ... He was a very, very civilised, erudite and cultured man. He was most charming, very softly spoken and extremely well read. If not bilingual in French, he habitually read in French. He was extremely articulate. He spoke just beautifully. He was coherent and thoughtful: a natural intellectual without being an academic.[42]

The writer Ken Clay befriended Rawlinson later on in the 1960s, by which time he was living in a large semi-detached house in the Manchester suburb of Whalley Range. Clay later wrote of him thus:

> a homosexual, socialist, Gallophile with a passionate interest in the arts, primarily literature and painting ... Like most queers his age is hard to guess. He's nearly always suntanned, spending months abroad in places like Tunis, Corsica and the Canary Isles, and has thick grey black hair (a wig?). He's certainly over fifty, perhaps sixty, and although he did work in a bank, which he detested, he no longer does so.

He goes on to describe the contents and ambience of Rawlinson's house: 'Paintings, statues, bookcases, antique furniture pieces, wall lights, a solarium full of flowers and the regular attention of a Scottish cleaning hag (I have only heard her voice on the phone) maintain its atmospheric opulence. "It's like going into another world!" The ready cliché occurs to all those who tread there.'[43]

Another figure involved in the Manchester cultural scene was Rawlinson's great friend Matthew Haygarth (1909–1988). From a family of butchers in Bury, Haygarth had trained as a ballet dancer and during the war years became a leading light of the Manchester Ballet Club, both as a choreographer and a performer. Tall, with classical features, he cut an imposing figure. Geoffrey Key remembers him as: 'A very important player; a very big friend at one time of Neville. He began as a ballet dancer; he knew Diaghilev. When he entered an exhibition, when he entered the room, everybody knew he was there: he had the most amazing magnetism.'[44]

In or around 1951, his dancing days behind him, Haygarth bought the Whitethorn Cottage Café at Prestbury in Cheshire. At first an unlicensed tea room, under his ownership it was transformed into a restaurant of great repute whose wealthy clientele included stars of *Coronation Street* such as Arthur Lowe and Violet Carson; there were signed photographs of cast members on its walls. The restaurant became for Haygarth a stage on which to perform, as David Sayer, who along with his wife knew Haygarth from 1964 onwards, recollects: 'Matthew was outrageous – he loved to be outrageous. He swore copiously. A performance. Always wore the same outfit of full-length white apron, short-sleeved white shirt, and hand-tied bowtie, worn a bit askew.'[45]

Like Rawlinson, Haygarth supported young artists, Geoffrey Key among them. He also collected paintings by L S Lowry, who became a friend and regular visitor for lunch at his restaurant, as Key recalls: 'Lowry used to get in a cab from [his home in] Mottram to Matthew's restaurant every Wednesday, to have lunch with Matthew. Matthew had the most wonderful Lowrys from the 1928 and 1930s period.'

Käthe Schuftan made a watercolour portrait of Haygarth, who mounted a display of her work at Whitethorn Cottage (then still a café) in August 1951. It is clear from a rather critical review of the show in the *Manchester Guardian* that Schuftan had been able to bring at least some of the art she had produced in Germany with her when she travelled to England. The review was headed 'Refugee Artist':

> An exhibition of watercolours and pen drawings by Käthe Schuftan is being held at Whitethorn Cottage, Prestbury. The artist, who is German-Jewish, came to this country as a refugee in 1939 after being imprisoned by the Nazis. Most of the work done in Germany in the thirties reflects grimly that decade and the artist's experience of it, notably the harrowing 'Self Portrait' and 'The Witness' – the violent, bitter portrayal of a man who testified against her at her trial. Later work shows a confusing diversity of styles, and the unassimilated influence of Blake lies heavily on three of her most recent paintings – 'Creation of Light', 'Creation of Matter' and 'Birth of Man'. 'Human Being', an earlier study in a similar manner, is more satisfying. Miss Schuftan achieves a variety of unusually dramatic effects in her watercolours but the raw power which informs many of the paintings sounds too strident and personal a note, at its most aggressive in the rather hysterical 'Hatred'.[46]

Another important character – and, like Rawlinson and Haygarth, one whom Milne is certain to have come into contact with – was the immensely stylish and proactive Margo Ingham (c.1917–1961), a somewhat legendary figure in the Manchester art world of the 1940s and 1950s.[47] Ingham was a friend of Schuftan's and for a time her near neighbour in Victoria Park, when she too would have attended her soirées.[48] Born in Manchester, she studied art and practised as a painter. Like Haygarth she was involved with the Manchester Ballet Club, from 1942 to 1946 acting as its wardrobe mistress and art organiser, and coordinating regular exhibitions while also showing her own work as a member of its 'Seven Painters' group. By September 1943, the *Manchester Guardian* was able to report that the club was 'now established as a hive of creative activity in several arts', including ballet and drama classes, ballet performances and art exhibitions.[49] One of the club's patrons was the dancer, teacher and pioneer of modern ballet Marie Rambert.

Along with her first husband, the artist Ned Owens (1918–1990), who reviewed art for the *Manchester Evening News*, Ingham established Mid-Day Studios, a privately run gallery in the basement of 96 Mosley Street, opposite Manchester City Art Gallery.[50] The couple also founded the Manchester Group of local painters, for which the gallery acted as headquarters. Mid-Day Studios first opened in November 1946, and over the five years of its duration mounted many exhibitions. Lowry's first ever major one-person show was held there in October 1948. Presented in cooperation with the Lefevre Gallery, London, which then represented him, it proved an important milestone in establishing the artist's reputation in the north of England.[51] The working relationship with the Lefevre Gallery also facilitated Mid-Day Studios shows that included work by other artists, including Ben Nicholson, Keith Vaughan, Harold Gilman, Wyndham Lewis, John Minton, Duncan Grant, and the Roberts Colquhoun and MacBryde.

Like others associated with the Manchester Group, Ingham established links with artists in St Ives, among them Sven Berlin (1911–1999), who exhibited at Mid-Day Studios in the autumn of 1947. In 'Introducing Sven Berlin' in the gallery's November bulletin, Ingham wrote:

> Visiting London galleries last spring, I was interested in the work of several contemporary artists, among them Sven Berlin. In August, my holiday in St Ives combined business with pleasure and I saw more of this artist's work in a show with three other young members of the St Ives Society of Artists. In London I had only seen Berlin's paintings but here were also displayed drawings and carvings of a quality that confirmed and increased my estimation of his work: particularly fine were his sensitive drawings of birds and animals.

The show, in the gallery's annexe, comprised six carvings, three paintings and twelve drawings. Concurrent with it was a display of Ingham's paintings, including *The Wharf, St Ives*; *Studios, Porthmeor*; *Porthmeor Beach* and *Corner Shop, St Ives*.[52]

Although Mid-Day Studios lasted for only a relatively short time – it closed towards the end of 1951, following a notice to quit from the landlord – it proved a significant cultural centre; its exhibition programme was an important and educative one, certainly for art students such as Milne. Ingham continued to be active as an artist, and latterly also as a teacher of art, and from the mid-1960s acted as regional critic for the magazine *Arts Review*. After Ingham's death, her friend the Manchester gallerist Colin Jellicoe wrote of her: 'She was tall and elegant with a great deal of charm and charisma, all this was mixed with a forceful personality that once seen was never forgotten.'[53]

Another important venue for modern art in Manchester at the time was the Crane Gallery, which was opened towards the end of 1949 by Andras Kalman (1919–2007). From a prosperous middle-class Jewish background, Kalman first travelled to England from his native Hungary early in 1939 in order to study leather chemistry at Leeds University (one of only two European universities then providing courses in the subject: the other was at Lyon). His original intention was to return home once he had completed his studies and there set up a family business making gloves and shoes. In fact, he became the sole member of his immediate family to survive the war years: both of his parents died at Auschwitz, while one of his two brothers was beaten to death, the other dying from typhoid soon after liberation from Dachau.

Having realised he was unsuited to leather chemistry – he later told the writer Andrew Lambirth, 'I was the worst leather chemist' – Kalman eventually found employment as a labourer at a leather factory in Bolton, where he worked night shifts.[54] At the end of the war he returned to Hungary on family business; realising there was nothing left to keep him there, he returned in 1948 to the north of England, where he moved from Bolton to live in Manchester. When young he had been junior tennis champion of Hungary and represented his country in international tournaments. He continued to play tennis in England, making the early rounds of Wimbledon, and was able to earn a living by working as a professional tennis coach at weekends. Kalman dreamed for some time of opening a gallery and, while walking in the centre of Manchester one day, found his premises: a basement at 35 South King Street, which previously had been used as an air-raid shelter. A friend whom he met at the Northern Tennis Club in Didsbury not long after his return from Hungary agreed to back the venture financially. This was Joseph

Braka, Manchester-born and of Lebanese-Syrian Jewish descent. He had made his money in textiles, as a manufacturer of curtain fabrics, and married the daughter of a local ironmonger. His son Ivor, a prominent art dealer himself, recalls that his father saw the gallery 'as a gateway into a more colourful life.' In speaking of Kalman, Ivor Braka describes his 'cultural depth. He was charismatic and had a vision about what art could do in your life'. More prosaically, the gallery premises in the disused air-raid shelter were, at £2 per week, 'about the cheapest space you could find'.[55]

In order to get hold of stock to form his first exhibition, Kalman wrote to a number of artists asking if they might each lend two or three works for his opening show. They included Henry Moore, Augustus John and Jacob Epstein. All agreed, and so from the outset he was able to show a range of pre-eminent contemporary British artists; his subsequent exhibitions featured many from mainland Europe.[56] Another of those who agreed to send work for the inaugural show was Ben Nicholson (1894–1982), whose paintings Kalman admired enormously; the two were to bond over a shared love of tennis. Altruistically, Nicholson persuaded Kalman to exhibit work by his first wife, Winifred Nicholson (1893–1981), while other artists with St Ives connections included Christopher Wood and the naïve painter Alfred Wallis (1855–1942). Kalman came greatly to prize Wallis's paintings, which were very much in keeping with the passion he developed for English folk art; he gradually formed the large collection now housed at Compton Verney in Warwickshire. Referring to this interest in folk art, Braka describes Kalman's 'love of Englishness' with its 'representations of individuality, liberty, a beacon of hope'.

Kalman was to develop a particularly strong friendship with Lowry, whose work he also exhibited; their friendship was forged when, on first visiting the gallery, the artist saw that Kalman was struggling to sell work, so bought two paintings from him. While sales were never healthy – Braka states that there was a 'total lack of response' to the gallery, describing it as 'a complete flop' – Kalman did manage to lure actors such as Michael Redgrave, Mai Zetterling and Richard Attenborough to the gallery when they were working in the city, several of whom became long-standing clients after the business relocated to London in 1957, when it was renamed the Crane Kalman Gallery.

Among the regional artists Kalman showed in Manchester was Alan Lowndes (1921–1978), a working-class painter from Stockport who was to become one of Milne's great friends, both in Manchester and then later on in St Ives. How they first met is unclear, although it may have been at the Crane Gallery, where Lowndes held his first show in 1950. Alan was one of five siblings, their father a local railway clerk, their mother a blacksmith's daughter from Kilmarnock. She died when Alan was only three years old in 1924, soon after giving birth to the last of her five children. Apprenticed to a decorator on leaving school at the age of 14, Alan was largely self-taught as an artist, although after war service in Italy and the Middle East he attended evening classes at Stockport College, where he was taught by the painter Emmanuel Levy (1900–1986). He worked also as a textile designer in Manchester.

Lowndes's show, from 31 March to 22 April 1950, was the fourth at the Crane Gallery. It formed part of *Five Painters*: the accompanying catalogue lists John Craxton, Lucian Freud, Allan Milner, Stephen Gilbert 'and First Exhibition of Paintings by Allan [*sic*] Lowndes of Stockport'. Lowndes showed ten oil paintings, while there were seventeen works by Craxton, ten each by Freud and Milner, and seven by Gilbert (these other four artists were each shown 'by arrangements with London galleries').[57]

Lowndes was by all accounts a rather obstinate, often argumentative man, although also highly sociable and an animated conversationalist. The gallerist Reg Singh worked for Kalman at the Crane Gallery in Manchester and got to know Lowndes well: 'Alan had lots of poet friends. And we liked the same jazz clubs, so we used to go to the same jazz clubs on Friday nights.'

He remembers that Lowndes made sketches at these clubs, where everyone assumed he was an art student:

> I was quite young, about 16, 18. And there were these kind of romantic people, you know, poets and people, going to bed with people while having affairs and things; and it was all kind of the 'real world', you know, to me ... This was in Manchester, and with the countryside all around, so we would go up into the hills to somebody's place. We had a fantastic time.

In 1951, Milne had what proved to be a life-changing encounter, with a man 16 years his senior whom he later described as 'the biggest influence on my life'.[58] His name was Cosmo Rodewald (1915–2002), and he was a lecturer in classical history at Manchester University. There are different versions of how they met: one is that Rawlinson introduced them; the other that Rodewald initiated a conversation with Milne while both were at Manchester Art Gallery. It may well be that all three were at the gallery at the same time, and that Rawlinson, already friends with them both, forged the introduction. The exact date of their meeting is unknown, although in the light of subsequent events it is tempting to imagine that it might have occurred during the show of Barbara Hepworth's work at the gallery in September and October that year.[59] What is certain is that Rodewald immediately found Milne entrancing and that they soon became lovers.

Rodewald was born in Spring Lake, New Jersey, on 17 August 1915. His parents were cousins: Carl Adolf Rodewald, born in Bremen in 1868, and Anna Fredrika Rodewald, born in New Jersey in 1880. Rodewald's paternal grandfather, Leo, had amassed a fortune on the American Stock Exchange during the nineteenth century and presciently sold all of his shares, with the exception of those in General Electric, before the 1929 stock market crash, so avoiding financial ruin. He subsequently set up trust funds for family members, including Rodewald, who was to have a very substantial inheritance. Following his parents' divorce, the four-year-old Cosmo and his mother settled in England, where he attended Stowe School, then studied at New College Oxford, graduating with a First in Greats (Classics). Between 1938 and 1939 he was a student at the British School at Athens, where he researched the Greek colonies on the Black Sea coasts of Bulgaria and Romania.[60]

First employed at Manchester University in December 1947, Rodewald became a greatly respected teacher at the institution. He felt that he should use his wealth to benefit others, and so became a lifelong and discreet philanthropist. A highly cultured man, he was an avid follower of the arts, especially music, with a keen interest also in painting and sculpture. Both Rawlinson and Haygarth were among his social set. Former director of the Whitworth Art Gallery Alistair

Smith met him in the 1960s, when he became 'alerted to his quiet passion for contemporary art'.[61] Over time, Rodewald formed a collection of works by British artists, including Nicholson, Hepworth, Peter Lanyon, William Scott, Terry Frost, Tony O'Malley, Keith Vaughan, Wilhelmina Barns-Graham and Bryan Wynter. He also owned work by Paul Klee and Marino Marini. Much of the collection he bequeathed to the Whitworth.

In 1955, while still in his relationship with Milne, Rodewald met Victor Sayer, a teenager 25 years his junior who later became his life partner. Sayer's parents were circus people and on the stage; his social background was therefore entirely different from that of the 'almost frighteningly intellectual' Rodewald. Sayer describes how meeting Rodewald provided an entrée to the gay world, a world of tacit understanding and support largely operating outside the usual strictures of class, in which 'nobody asked questions; you were always welcome.' The same applied to his best friend at school, David Lindsay, who grew up in the working-class district of Levenshulme in south Manchester; for him, too, Rodewald introduced a world of which he was totally unaware, and became for him 'a role model ... somebody who lived in a world which interested me'.[62] Lindsay left Manchester at the age of 17 to study chemistry in London, where he was able to immerse himself in the city's gay life, before then going on to study at Cambridge. He never returned to live in Manchester, although he continued to see Sayer and Rodewald outside term times and was introduced to Milne, who later invited him to spend a few weeks at Trewyn in St Ives.

For young gay men from less privileged backgrounds then, figures such as Rodewald and Rawlinson were significant, facilitating an introduction to a necessarily covert society. The book about gay identity had yet to be written, and, faced with illegality and the bewildering homophobia of the 1950s, there was nowhere readily apparent where one might seek guidance. But initiation into the gay world, where nobody asked questions and you were always welcome, presented role models and opened doors to alternative ways of living. It was also educative, a fact expressed rather poignantly by an anonymous interviewee in the book *A Minority*, published in 1960:

> As a boy from a very poor home, homosexuality has been a great help to me. Not only have I met many excellent people that I couldn't have met if I had not been homosexual, but also my homosexual friends have helped to educate me. It's been like going to university, except the university has come to me.[63]

And for Milne, Rodewald presented a hitherto unknown life, far removed from the one he led in Eccles. Rodewald fell in love with him – he was, remembers Lindsay, 'totally besotted' – and was from the outset immensely generous in supporting him financially, support that continued well beyond the years of their intimate involvement.

*

Upon being awarded a bursary in 1952 – his student records state that during the academic year 1952–53 he was studying postgraduate sculpture[64] – Milne decided to go to Paris in order to study at the Académie de la Grande Chaumière in Montparnasse. There is no available record of the dates when Milne studied there, but it cannot have been any later than June of that year. En route to Paris, he and Rodewald stayed in London, from where he wrote to his friend Reg Moon. The undated letter is written on the notepaper of Browns Hotel, Dover and Albemarle Streets, W1:

> Dear Reggie,
> We have been spending a few days at Cosmo's family hotel [the hotel at which the Rodewalds always stayed when in London; they did not own it], prior to my departure for Paris. I must say that, in this atmosphere, I feel as far removed from the impecunious art-student en-route to study abroad, as it is possible to imagine. What with shopping in the Burlington arcade, lunching at Claridge's (yes we really did!), dining at the Caprice, midst London's 'smart set'. Concerting at the festival-hall and meeting a french-millionaire for tea, followed by dinner again at the Etoile (the leading restaurant for those who really know how to eat) sitting at a table next to Robert Helpmann and Katherine [*sic*] Hepburn.[65] All this makes me feel

tremendously comfortable but, as usual, also tremendously guilty – ah well – !!

...

All my love, John
My address is HOTEL BREA Rue Brea Paris[66]

Whatever guilt Milne felt in this new life of luxury did not last very long. For, as Victor Sayer says, 'John was spoilt rotten by Cosmo', and he recalls how there were sometimes scenes between them as the indulged younger man became yet more demanding.

At the time Milne arrived in the French capital its reputation as the centre of Western art remained intact, and as such it was a magnet for those embarking on an artistic career. The city retained the bohemian glamour of its association with such figures as Pablo Picasso, Henri Matisse, André Malraux, Jean-Paul Sartre and Simone de Beauvoir. Sculpture classes at La Grande Chaumière were under the direction of Russian-born Ossip Zadkine (1888–1967), who was appointed to the role in 1948. Zadkine described his class at the Académie as 'a meeting point for international youth who are investigating the new world of forms'.[67] One can imagine Milne's excitement, as he first entered the building, to meet and work alongside students of different nationalities and backgrounds. In fact, he quite soon became disappointed, frustrated and disheartened by what he felt were the limitations of the teaching, which proved very traditional, with little recognition of modernist approaches. Students were tasked to produce copious life drawings and anatomical studies, with a view to better understanding the human form. In sculpture, Milne's main tutor was Emmanuel Auricoste (1908–1995), whose work arose from the same classical tradition as that of his own teachers, Antoine Bourdelle and Charles Despiau. Auricoste had his students sculpt the figure from direct observation in front of the life model, using a technique of clay modelling.[68] The aim was for naturalism, and although Milne engaged with this work as a discipline, he did not feel that he was able to capitalise on the advances he had already made in forging his own sculptural style at Salford. One is left wondering who had recommended the institution to him and what he had been led to expect of the place. What is more, Milne made no friends in Paris and found his time there lonely and depressing. There were, though, certain compensations, such as taking French lessons at the Berlitz School, and although disappointed by the Académie, he was able to further his education in art elsewhere. He frequented the Musée du Louvre, where he studied ancient Egyptian artefacts and other antiquities, and also made trips beyond the capital, including to Chartres Cathedral, where the monumental Gothic architecture and sculpture impressed him deeply. When visiting exhibitions, he more often found inspiration in work by painters, and among those he particularly appreciated were Paul Klee, Picasso, Georges Braque, Marc Chagall, Hans Hartung and Pierre Soulages. In sculpture there was Auguste Rodin, whose statue of Honoré de Balzac, close to his hotel on the Boulevard Raspail, he passed each day. There were also Henri Laurens and Alberto Giacometti; years later, Milne remembered a particular sculpture that he saw in Paris, Giacometti's *Figurine dans une boîte entre deux boîtes qui sont des maisons* (Figure in a Box between Two Boxes which are Houses) of 1950, the simplicity of which belies a psychological resonance that clearly struck a chord with him. Most of all there was Brâncuși, whose carvings in marble and wood he was able to see for the first time. They entranced him, further consolidating his desire to abandon modelling in order to concentrate solely on carving when he returned to England.

There are a handful of black-and-white photographs from this time in Paris, taken by Rodewald during a visit he paid while Milne was studying there. In them, the 21-year-old is fresh-faced, with neatly combed side-parted hair, and dapper in flannel trousers and a wool gabardine blazer with an embroidered crest on its breast pocket. In one of the photographs he perches on a balustrade by the Seine; in another he stands by a fountain in the Place Edmond Rostand, with the Panthéon in the distance behind him. Yet another shows him standing on a lawn, with the Château de Bagatelle in the Bois de Boulogne in the background. There are also a few photographs of Rodewald, including one in which he strides along the bank of the Seine, smiling at the camera held by his young lover.

*

> There are three places I wanted most to see when I was young and which did not disappoint me: Greece – Persia – Morocco.[69]
> —John Milne

That summer of 1952, Milne's education continued – thrillingly so – when Rodewald took him to Greece, to witness at first hand places and artefacts he had until then known only from books. It was an extensive tour during which they visited many of the most renowned sacred sites of the classical world. They travelled first on the Simplon Orient Express to Venice, where they stayed for a while before setting sail through the Adriatic, landing at Brindisi and Patras and stopping off for a time on the islands of Cephalonia, Zakynthos and Ithaca. They then continued through the Gulf of Corinth to Piraeus, the port of Athens. From Delphi the pair went south to Itea, exploring the Peloponnese before staying at Pilos, a small harbour. Next they journeyed northwards to the mountains of Andritsaina, where they visited the temple of Bassae. The islands of Delos and Hydra also formed part of their itinerary, all of it doubtless planned in advance by Rodewald.

From Athens, Milne sent a postcard to Reg Moon, by now living in Norfolk and working at the Holkham Hall pottery:

> British School of Archaeology,
> 52 Odos Souedias,
> Athens, Greece
>
> Dear Reg,
> I am at last in Athens and comfortably established here at the above address. If you should write to me, and I would be glad if you would because it is very pleasant receiving letters from home[,] write to me here. I shall be going away pretty soon to some of the islands and probably to Turkey but this address will always find me, if your *letters*? arrive here before the 21st of July. The journey here from Italy was beautiful. We sailed from Napoli last Thursday and sailed past STROMBOLI and CAPRI through straits of Messina and the gulf of CORINTH, which is called the most beautiful view in the world; into

the Salonique sea and so to PIRAEUS. The Acropolis is the main feature which I have visited so far, but also we have seen a beautiful Byzantine church at DAPHNI, which contains the most wonderful mosaics I have yet seen, they are reputed to be the finest in Greece.

Love, John[70]

Years later, Milne typed up notes from diary records made during this visit to Greece that document his revelatory and baptismal arrival and which show an existent knowledge. The following is an extract:

One of my first impressions was awakening at dawn as we sailed through [the] gulf of Corinth. Standing on deck, in a light more brilliant and clear than I had ever experienced, was breathtaking. On the right stretched the rolling coastline of the Peloponnese – to the left, towering cliffs ablaze in the morning sunlight making a great, upsurging curve towards the area where I knew Delphi was situated. That mysterious place of which I had heard so much and was yet to discover. The mountain ravines and crevices were still deep in shadow and cool looking at that early hour; there was an overall impression of great majesty and grandeur. Overhead the sky was a dazzling turquoise and below, the hundreds of shades of blue which constitute the Aegean. I knew I had at last arrived in Greece, with its eternal landscape and romantic mythology. *There* was Delphi, and beyond lay Mount Olympus, the home of the Gods. I was entering a new phase in my life; awakening to a new era.

DELPHI:

The long winding road from Athens begins over a vast, flat plain. It is a route steeped in legend. At one point we passed the point where Oedipus, unknowingly, killed his father Laius. I was dreaming of Delphi, the ancient sanctuary situated at the foot of mount Parnassus; the most ancient and sacred in all of Greece. Where the monuments, long since ruins, stand testimony to the states [men whose administrators and warriors] had made their pilgrimages to consult the Oracle on matters of important policy and prior to going to wars. Where the youth of the country had participated in all manner of sports, discus throwing, wrestling, chariot racing, all of which have

> been recorded in the sculpture of the time. We left the low flat plain and began the steady climb. Increasingly slowly and seemingly never ending as the bus snaked around the mountains, hugging the cliff face at each precipitous bend with the road dropping away steeply into gorges far beneath, filled with acres of olive trees as they had been for hundreds of years. I was constantly aware of the massive strength of the mountainside to which we clung and the frightening chasms below. There was a physical emptiness in my stomach but elation in my mind as I looked upwards at the towering peaks. Suddenly, there was Parnassus. An eagle soared overhead and I thought of Icarus. At last we rounded the final bend and saw Delphi, minute in the far distance, the small flat roofed houses clustered around the mountainside almost as if they were about to slide off. And the ruins ablaze in the setting sun. We were on top of the world. There is a sculpture in the museum at Delphi representing the navel. An ancient offering presented in the belief that Delphi was the centre of the world. I think it was at Delphi that I first became *really* aware of my passion for mountains. Of their dominating masses, their architectural splendour and the minuteness of the human figure in comparison. It was here also that I became familiar with the early (archaic) Greek sculpture. The massive Kouroi for example, with their strong influences of Egypt and Mesopotamia.[71]

Among the many artefacts that bewitched Milne during that summer in Greece were the Calf Bearer at the Acropolis Museum, some very early Cycladic carvings, and Cretan Minoan bronzes. But it seems the most resonant of all was the famous bronze Charioteer of Delphi from 470 BC, displayed by itself in a room at the Archaeological Museum of Delphi. Years later he recounted how it had been possible to spend hours alone communing with the life-size statue of the young athlete, marvelling at the almost abstract folds of his garment's drapery, the texture of his hair, his inlaid onyx eyes with their individual bronze eyelashes, the full, sensual mouth and the wonderfully lifelike modelling of his feet. Perhaps, immersed in the ancient light of Greece, he saw in this personification of male beauty a symbol of possibility.

From Greece, Milne and Rodewald travelled to Turkey, of which Milne later wrote:

> Here I explored the coast of Asia Minor, visiting Istanbul and such ancient sites as Ephesus and Pergamum journeying as far south as Antalya on the so called 'turquoise coast'. It was my first introduction to the world of Islam and the religion of Mohammed; something I was to be much more deeply involved with later in Persia and Morocco.
>
> I was not greatly impressed with the mosques of Istanbul, which I found heavy and dour outside and crudely ornate inside. The Turkish landscape and the sites of the Greco-Roman ruins of such places as Ephesus and Pergamum held more appeal for me echoing, as they inevitably did, what I had seen before on visits to Greece.[72]

In fact, Milne disliked Turkey quite intensely, and in a change to what must have been their original plan he and Rodewald returned to Greece, as he outlined in a card to Reg Moon sent from Athens on 28 July:

> Dear Moon,
>
> Yes, still here. After we returned from Constantinople I persuaded [Cosmo] that another week in Greece was needed to rid ourselves of the unpleasantries of Turkey. To my surprise he was not *really* averse to the notion of prolonging our stay in this glorious country. Every day the weather becomes hotter; you know, I think that, after several months of this weather one would actually begin to long for a grey sky and the rain. I agree that it would be very good indeed if you could join us on one of these trips.[73]

Eventually the pair returned home, Rodewald to commence teaching in the new academic year at Manchester and Milne to prepare for his next move. That winter he made his way down to St Ives, to begin working as an assistant to Barbara Hepworth, little realising that he would live in the town for the rest of his life.

2 At Trewyn

Sculpture, to me, is primitive, religious, passionate, and magical – always, always affirmative.[1]
—Barbara Hepworth

For Milne, the prospect of working with Hepworth was in reassuring contrast to his disappointing experience at the Académie de la Grande Chaumière, for it presented an opportunity to gain invaluable experience of the mechanics and processes of carving in the workshop of a highly regarded contemporary sculptor. How the initial introduction was made is unclear, although it may simply be that Milne wrote directly to Hepworth, who was always receptive to approaches from young artists.[2] He could doubtless rely upon an enthusiastic reference from his college tutor, recommending his talent, hard work and ambition.

By now Hepworth was firmly ensconced at Trewyn Studio, the small house at the foot of Barnoon Hill that she had acquired at auction in autumn 1949. It had two floors, each with a single room. At ground level Hepworth had a kitchen installed, plus bathroom and dining area, while the upstairs room served initially as a studio space, with the carving yard immediately behind the property. One imagines Milne turning up on that first day with a combination of excitement and trepidation, and how unlikely it was that he had previously encountered anyone remotely like Hepworth. Then nearing her 50th birthday, she and her sculpture were as one: poised, highly articulate, intensely focused. She was also very demanding, no more so than of herself, for she worked every day of the week. As her great friend and sometime patron Margaret Gardiner (1904–2005) wrote, 'Barbara totally redefined the meaning of the word "work" for me. Work was at the centre of everything for her; it was what sustained her through all the stresses and strains of her life.'[3]

Given Milne's limited experience of direct carving, Hepworth initially agreed that he could work for her for three months on an approval basis, as a pupil and therefore without pay. He did so in the mornings, leaving the rest of the day to concentrate on his own work, which he made in a series of rented rooms that served as both accommodation and studio space. Quite soon Hepworth began to give him a small wage, an indication of her appreciation of his application and skill in responding to instructions. Working alongside Milne was the more experienced chief assistant Denis Mitchell (1912–1993). Initially a painter, Mitchell went on to become a sculptor in his own right. He had begun his employment at Trewyn Studio in 1949, and was to continue there for ten years, the longest serving of Hepworth's assistants. During the war years he had worked at Geevor tin mine in Pendeen, where he learned how to use tools and manipulate heavy loads, skills that proved immensely useful in Hepworth's studio. The third member of the workforce during Milne's time was Roger Leigh (1925–1997), who joined the team in 1953. Originally trained as an architect, Leigh also went on to forge a career as a sculptor.[4]

Hepworth taught her assistants a great deal – certainly the younger, less practised ones such as Milne – and that of course was why they wanted to work for her. Fundamental to her approach was that one should never attempt to impose oneself upon the sculptural material, but should recognise and work in harmony with its inherent qualities; in this respect, each block of wood or stone was unique. This ethos, of the sculptor in communion with their materials, was central to both modernist production and that of the ancients. Milne was to gain experience of working with a wide range of materials: different types of stone, metal and various woods, including elm, lignum vitae, oak and Nigerian guarea. The sculptor Tommy Rowe (b.1941) worked part-time for Hepworth for a period in the late 1950s, and then on a full-time basis in 1963–65. He later wrote of the experience, providing an insight into what it was like to work with her:

> Barbara taught me to carve marble and work with Plaster of Paris. She showed me how to work forms and purify them. She would caress

> the form with her hands and mark surfaces with a cross for a hollow and a circle as a high, or what she would describe as 'an invisible hummock'. In the morning you would find your piece of work covered with circles and crosses, and arrows indicating which way the form should be worked. This went on until she was satisfied the form was perfect.[5]

Hepworth's granddaughter, the art historian Sophie Bowness, has noted how she would draw outlines of the forms for her assistants to carve, 'using a brush tied to a long bamboo stick and ultramarine paint, or with chalk'.[6]

By the time of Milne's first arrival in St Ives, Hepworth's artistic reputation was on the ascendant, her work having been shown in the British Pavilion at the Venice Biennale in June 1950, the year in which the Tate Gallery bought her *Bicentric Form* (1949), the first of many of her sculptures acquired for its collection. However, the early 1950s were also marked for her by profound personal loss. Having towards the end of 1949 agreed reluctantly to separate from her second husband, Ben Nicholson, their marriage was dissolved in October 1951. Hepworth never got over it, for, as the art historian Penelope Curtis has written, Nicholson was 'the man who – without sentimentality or excess – can be called the love of her life'.[7] Then, only months after Milne began working for her, Paul, her son with her first husband, John Skeaping, was killed at the age of 23. A flying officer with the Royal Air Force, he died when his aeroplane crash-landed in Thailand on 13 February 1953. His father later wrote in his autobiography of being told the news of his son's death, and of how 'Someone had placed a bomb in his plane which blew up ten minutes after take-off from Bangkok, killing him and his navigator. Only his charred and unrecognisable remains had been found.'[8]

Hepworth's relationship with her oldest child had not been an altogether easy one; she and Skeaping were separated in 1931 and then divorced when Paul was only three years old, by which time she and the boy were living with Nicholson in London. Two years or so later, in October 1934, Hepworth gave birth to the triplets she had with Nicholson. Gardiner wrote of how when Paul was nine years old his mother asked him where he felt his real home was, in London with her or with his father, and of how Paul chose to live with the latter: 'At the time I was puzzled; I thought it too much to ask a child to make such a choice. But perhaps Barbara realised that life in the studio with her was too constricting for him and with Jack [John Skeaping] he would have an outdoor existence with horses and dogs and masculine pursuits.'[9]

Gardiner goes on to write of how Paul later often spent holidays with his mother in Cornwall, although in time he reacted strongly against her home and working environment. Gardiner also describes how his death became a source of lasting grief for Hepworth: 'She wrote to me soon afterwards, "The vitality & radiance in Paul, the light he always brought into a room ... seemed impossible to associate with an early death. And yet, always, at all times when I regarded his special quality which so warmed me – some sadness and shrinking seemed to twist my heart."'[10]

Hepworth wrote of her son's death to her friend and champion the writer Herbert Read:

> I expect you will have heard by now that my darling Paul lost his life last week flying over Thailand. These last days have been almost past bearing – he always had a radiance upon which I, and all of us, seem to depend, but which in some way foretold the end, always twisting one's heart. Rilke best describes it. I cannot find any consolation except perhaps that he cannot now be taken 'prisoner'. Px. [her great friend the composer Priaulx Rainier] came down and has looked after me.[11]

*

As a young and ambitious fledgling sculptor, Milne had arrived in St Ives at an auspicious moment, for the 1950s were to prove the years when the town's artistic reputation was at its zenith. Many other artists were drawn to St Ives, too. By mid-decade, the painters Paul Feiler (1928–2013), Patrick Heron (1929–1999), Roger Hilton (1911–1976) and Karl Weschke (1925–2005) were living within striking distance. The painters Anthony Benjamin (1931–2002) and Trevor Bell (1930–2017) and the sculptor Brian Wall (b.1931) – all three contemporaries of Milne – were either in the town or nearby. Both national and international curators and art dealers were also drawn to St Ives. They included Charles and Peter Gimpel – it was Charles Gimpel who had first introduced Heron to the influential American art critic and writer Clement Greenberg in 1954 – and Leslie Waddington, from their respective London galleries. From further afield came Willi Sandberg of the Stedelijk Museum in Amsterdam, and New York gallery owners, including George Dix of Durlacher Bros (who had in 1949 exhibited both Hepworth's work and that of Nicholson; the latter also showed with the gallery in 1952 and 1956); Catherine Viviano (who gave shows to Peter Lanyon and Trevor Bell); and Martha Jackson, a visitor on several occasions, who considered opening a gallery space in St Ives (in New York she presented exhibitions of Hepworth, Nicholson and William Scott). There were also visits by highly influential figures from British institutions, such as Lilian Somerville of the British Council, Philip James from the Arts Council, and gallery directors such as Norman Reid of the Tate Gallery. And famously, the Abstract Expressionist painter Mark Rothko visited in 1959, as did Greenberg, who stayed with the Herons at Zennor.

Although long established as an art colony, St Ives's renown was rooted in no small part in the avant-garde modernism of the 1930s, in which Hepworth and Nicholson were key figures. The couple had travelled with their four-year-old triplets from their home in Hampstead in September 1939, only days before war with Germany was declared. They had been invited by their friend the writer and artist Adrian Stokes to stay at Little Parc Owles, the house he shared with his artist wife Margaret Mellis at Carbis Bay. Other friends, the Russian sculptor Naum Gabo and his wife Miriam, soon joined them there. Following Nicholson's departure for Switzerland in 1958, only Hepworth of these six remained in Cornwall: Stokes and Mellis had left shortly before their divorce in 1946, by which time the Gabos were living in America.

In an article entitled 'The Cornish Renaissance', published in 1950, Paul Hodin wrote of Cornwall as:

> the living ground from which one of the oldest European cultures has grown ... But Cornwall has voices of the present as well: there are new

> creative forces arising from the old soil. Sponsored by its good geniuses, the peculiar landscape, a strong cultural background and a new cosmopolitan consciousness of human values, they have already begun what might be called a Cornish Renaissance.

Hodin makes reference in his article to many artists associated with the county, among them John Wells, Bryan Wynter and Peter Lanyon. Of Hepworth he states that she had 'established her fame amongst the few great names of contemporary sculptors', before going on to write: 'It is her belief that "at the moment we are creating a new mythology", and her deep affinity to the art of the Neolithic builders of stone monuments "standing throughout Cornwall and Brittany as memorials to long-forgotten dead", which makes her one of the pillars of this Cornish Renaissance.'[12]

Coming so soon after the Second World War, Hepworth's reference to 'memorials to long-forgotten dead' had a particular resonance, of which she was doubtless acutely aware. Framed within a broader context, the idea of renaissance – the drive to regenerate – was hardly confined to Cornwall in the postwar era, but part of a more widespread social endeavour in which those from all walks of life would have a role to play. It was fuelled by the need to rebuild, both physically and spiritually, in a bid to reconnect with the utopian ideals of the interwar years. In Britain it could be seen to form a continuum of a strain of propagandistic myth-making prevalent during the war years themselves. It was found in the so-called neo-Romantic artists – Michael Ayrton, John Minton, John Piper, Graham Sutherland, among others – whose work of the 1940s drew on 'a projected past which found its myth in origins of the land itself ... an organic myth of rocks, hills and Arcadia'.[13]

It was with this deep, mythologised history of landscape, and of the sculptor's place within it, that Hepworth felt a strong and lasting connection. Given to making statements in which she, her work and the landscape of Penwith were effectively symbiotic, she sought to draw upon a Neolithic past in the creation of an idealistic future. It was a narrative in which she cast herself in a central role, one that proved intrinsic, and indeed essential, in the formation of her own myth.

Within the weaving of this myth, Milne, like all of Hepworth's assistants, was a subservient thread, a factor implicit from the outset of their employment. She doubtless appreciated their wholly necessary input – and they of course gained much from the experience – but she remained at all times the sun around which they orbited. During the years in St Ives she had only one female assistant, Angela Conner (b.1935), in 1963; the rest were men, and Hepworth, forging a career and reputation in a male-dominated field, was understandably keen to give the impression that she and she alone realised every stage of each sculpture. Therefore, when important visitors arrived to see her work, her assistants were told to hide away. Living and working within the 6-metre-high walls of Trewyn Studio made her a subject of intrigue in the town. Her daughter Rachel Nicholson has described how Hepworth 'was a sort of mystery to the locals – because she didn't go out'.[14] To her neighbours and the wider community, the signs of her success were evident in the large sculptures that quite regularly left her studio, creating a spectacle as they were transported through the town's narrow streets.

The initial agreement between Milne and Hepworth was that he would work for her for two years, but after 18 months or so he decided to focus solely on his own work. He went on during 1954 and 1955 to produce a number of highly competent, sizeable carvings in wood, in both walnut and Nigerian guarea (the latter a gift from Hepworth), for example *Vertical Form* (1954) and *Torso* (1955). Though lacking in formal elegance, there is in these pieces a level of design and craftsmanship that signals the beginnings of his mature work. Informed technically by what Milne had learned while working for Hepworth, there are also stylistic affinities with her sculpture: for instance, *Torso*, carved in walnut in 1955, bears a resemblance to her Spanish mahogany *Figure (Churinga)* of 1952, which Milne probably had a hand in making. He is likely also to have worked on her limestone *Monolith (Empyrean)* of 1953, a memorial to Hepworth's son Paul and his navigator. Both represent abstracted figures, each like Milne's *Torso*, with hollowed-out forms.[15] *Gnathos*, carved in Nigerian guarea in 1955, was the first of Milne's sculptures to show a maturity and sophistication of style identifiably his own. It was also the first of his entirely abstract pieces. Ostensibly simple, it is in fact a work of great poise and subtlety. Its title is from the ancient Greek word for jaw; Milne described it as an action of 'biting into ... perhaps predatory – a theme that appears often in the sculpture and drawings'. Made from a rectangular block, each of its sides – both exterior and interior – curves in finely judged gradations to end at two slender pointed wedges. The hollowed-out interior, a truncated teardrop, changes size and shape as one walks around the sculpture. Milne returned to it 12 years later, producing versions in both polished and patinated bronze. There is a related drawing, *Study for Gnathos*, in coloured chalks and pencil, which shows a similar form but with seven tensile strings within the open shape, very much like one of Hepworth's stringed sculptures. Milne was to consider *Gnathos* to be among his best work, certainly according to a newspaper interview published in 1972, in which he stated: 'It's a key work in my career. Most works are experimental. Some you grow tired of but some you stay satisfied with. *Gnathos* is absolutely right.'[16]

Milne and Hepworth remained entirely amicable after he left her employ, and it was partly at her urging him 'to put down roots' that he made the decision to remain in St Ives. He continued to step in and help in her studio occasionally, and she often advised him about his own work; Rachel Nicholson recalls that they would telephone one another if either needed help.[17] Hepworth was clearly fond of Milne, perhaps seeing in him something of a surrogate son, to whom she was able to provide her own brand of nurture and encouragement. She and Milne had a number of things in common, including their comparatively humble backgrounds in the north of England. He, with his passion for Brâncuși, would have discussed the Romanian sculptor with her, she recounting her visit with Nicholson to Brâncuși's studio in Paris in the spring of 1933. She had written of that visit in quasi-mystical terms, as an encounter with 'the miraculous feeling of eternity mixed with beloved stone and stone dust'.[18] Milne is likely to have told her about his experiences in Greece, where she travelled for the first time in the summer of 1954. Margaret Gardiner accompanied her on the trip, having first suggested it in the hope that it would alleviate the depression Hepworth felt following the death of her son. The visit was to prove revelatory, affecting her both physically and spiritually, and she subsequently named some of her sculptures after sites she had visited: *Oval Sculpture (Delos)* and *Curved Form (Delphi)*, for instance, both made in 1955. Still later, she produced a series of nine lithographs entitled *The Aegean Suite* (1971).

One wonders how much Milne confided in Hepworth, whether for instance he told her of his psychoanalysis with Franz Greenbaum. If so, she would have been fascinated to discuss it with him, not least because she had developed an interest in Jungian philosophy long before Milne's arrival in St Ives, and during the 1940s made references to the psychologist in correspondence with Herbert Read, who subsequently edited a volume of Carl Jung's collected works.[19] A letter Hepworth wrote to Read in late December 1946 includes the following: 'If Jung is right about the shadow fight (& I think he is) we can only live and create in equilibrium by facing darkness from time to time.'[20]

Milne, with what was to become a lifelong battle for mental stability, would have related strongly to such a sentiment. On a more prosaic level, Milne and Hepworth both loved cats, each doting on them as pets. And symbols of their friendship were in the birthday and Christmas presents they exchanged. There is a letter from Rodewald in which he responds to Milne's request for advice on what to buy as a Christmas gift for Hepworth. Dating from 13 December 1955, quite early on in Milne's life in St Ives, it is indicative of the solicitousness he felt towards her, and his desire to please:

> A small present for Barbara? Apart from things that one could have lit on only by chance by wandering around the stores while we were in London, I can suggest only a book or something of the scent or toilet water class. Knowing her, as I do not, you can guess, as I can't, what might be the right one & either – looking through *Observers* and *Statesmans*, if you haven't burnt them all, might suggest the right book. In a city you might find the right piece of costume jewellery, but hardly in St Ives or Penzance. Conversely, the products of St Ives craftsmen, however estimable, would be hardly the thing for her. And from what you tell me, liquor wouldn't do. If you think there is any delicacy to which she is addicted which St Ives doesn't provide, I could try for it here and send it to you. Otherwise I revert to scent or book: the former you could perhaps get locally (but if you think

> of some particular one that you can't get I could seek it here and send it) – for the latter you had better turn to some friend or shop in London.

Milne and Rodewald continued to travel abroad during those early years in St Ives, Rodewald as ever providing the necessary funds. In May 1953 they were again in Paris, from where Milne sent a postcard of the Seine and Notre-Dame to Reg Moon:

> Dear Reg,
> Surprise! Surprise! Here I am again.
> Just in Paris for a few days (actually, probably a week)
> We had a gorgeous, champagne lunch on the plane coming over and are now eating delicious steaks. I can't think why you don't come to Paris at this time of year!
> Tomorrow the Vienna State Opera, and a new work by Strauss (RICHARD)
> Love, John

In July there followed another postcard to Reg, this time from Athens: 'It seems hard to believe that it is a year ago today since I was last here. When I wander down the streets in the shadow of the Acropolis it feels as if I had never been away from it. Really I think Athens must be the world's most beautiful city. We flew here from Cyprus yesterday.'[21]

Both together and apart, Milne and Rodewald were to revisit Greece many times over the years, there forming a number of acquaintances and friendships, as is evident from this extract, taken from the same letter in which Rodewald had offered Milne advice on a gift for Hepworth:

> Though my international correspondence is a thin trickle against your flood, I did hear unexpectedly yesterday from Demetrios, that ardent boring youth from Halkis, who spoke of being about to set out, in the brilliant sunshine, on an all day walk with his friends, first along the beach and then 'into the green hills, where we shall do many crazy things'. How pleasant to be in a country where one can do crazy things in the green hills in December. *Green* hills are, I expect, not what

> figure in your dreams of Greece, but green is what they would be now, and again still more from February ... Have you heard anything lately of Brian de Jongh – or of Robert [Liddell] – to whom I ought certainly to write?

The full identity of the ardent boring youth is unknown. Brian de Jongh (1912–1977) was a writer on Greece, as was his friend Robert Liddell (1908–1992). Often known as Jock, Liddell wrote prolifically, including works of fiction, literary criticism, travel writing – Milne had a copy of his *Aegean Greece* (1954) on his bookshelf at Trewyn – a biography of the queer Alexandrian poet Constantine Cavafy and several volumes of autobiography.[22] He had studied at Oxford, where he afterwards worked as an assistant at the Bodleian Library. Liddell developed long-term friendships with the English writers Ivy Compton-Burnett, Elizabeth Taylor and Barbara Pym, all of whom he wrote about. In 1940 he became a lecturer for the British Council in Athens, but after the German invasion of Greece moved to Cairo, where he was a lecturer in English literature at Fuad I University. There he lived with his dog Sappho and the flamboyant Hon. Edward Gathorne-Hardy (1901–1978), son of the Earl of Cranbrook and former member of the Bright Young Things of the interwar period. Liddell returned to Greece in 1953, where he taught in the English department of the University of Athens. He never returned to England, but maintained friendships with English friends such as Rodewald and Milne, who visited him in Greece.[23]

*

During his first few years in St Ives, Milne formed a number of local friendships, not least with Mary Redgrave (1923–2002), wife of the sculptor William Redgrave (1903–1986) and known to all as 'Boots'. She was eight years his senior and they remained great friends, she his most loyal confidante. The artist Tony Shiels (b.1938) lived in St Ives from 1958 and soon got to know Boots. Of her he remembers:

> Boots enjoyed throwing parties. She had opened a restaurant, Dauber's, on Island Road, off Back Road West, and was an excellent

> cook. By the way, Dauber was the name of one of her Dalmatian dogs. When I first knew Boots, she was still married to Bill Redgrave and they ran St Peter's Loft, along with Peter Lanyon, a kind of 'atelier-style' painting school, on Back Road West. Terry Frost did some tutoring there, too. Anyway – back to Dauber's – at the end of the summer tourist season, the party season would begin. Boots was very generous with the Scotch, which she handed around in half-pint measures. The place would be packed to the gunnels. Regulars included Patrick Dolan, Nancy Wynne-Jones, Tony O'Malley, Sydney and Nessie Graham, Alan Wood, Anthony and Stella Benjamin, Vernon Rose, Robert Brennan, and many more.[24]

Sympathetic to artists, Boots was sensitive to the fact that many endured long periods of penury. She had a reputation for kindness and readily provided help or advice to those in need, although you first had to pass a test, in which you were quizzed to ensure that she approved of you. Her friend Nancy Wynne-Jones later described No. 1 Island Road as 'the unofficial club of the St Ives community'.[25]

The Penwith Society of Arts in Cornwall (more usually known as the Penwith Society) played a highly significant role in the postwar history of St Ives. Formed in February 1949, the society had 19 founder members, and its first show, of 36 artists, was held that June on the first floor of the Public Hall on Fore Street. Nine years later the society relocated to premises elsewhere on Fore Street, before then moving into a former pilchard-packing factory on Back Road West in 1961. Milne was elected a member in 1956 and exhibited in the annual exhibitions of members' work thereafter. According to Brian Wall, who joined in the same year as Milne, 'As an artist down there, if you weren't a member of the Penwith you didn't exist.'[26] The society was, as Chris Stephens has written, 'the main route to agencies such as the Arts and British Councils as well as the main showcase and saleroom of the town'.[27]

Within the society's membership there developed both strong allegiances and venomous divisions. Jostling for position resulted at worst in some members becoming sidelined or frozen out. Within this febrile environment one of its founder members, the stalwart Denis Mitchell, appears to have remained on friendly terms with everyone, although he was a comparatively rare exception. The most famous feud was that between the painter Peter Lanyon and Nicholson and Hepworth, both of whom he accused of overbearing self-interest and duplicity. The row came about after the newly formed society's committee proposed that members be divided broadly between representational and abstract practitioners. However, Hepworth and Nicholson managed to manipulate the proposal, so that an altogether more rigid system was applied, resulting in exclusive groupings of representational art (category A), abstract art (B) and crafts (C). At this Lanyon, instrumental in setting up the society in the first place, resigned. The situation was made all the more unpleasant given the fact that he and Nicholson had been friends. Not only that, but in the autumn of 1939, at the suggestion of their mutual friend Adrian Stokes, Nicholson had given art lessons to Lanyon. Twenty-four years older than Lanyon, he had proven something of a father figure to him, crucial in helping him steer his work towards abstraction, in forms radically different to those of the traditional paintings he had made thus far. Following their falling out, Lanyon's resentment and distrust of Nicholson and Hepworth continued undiminished.

Effectively frozen out from the Penwith Society was the Constructivist painter and sculptor Marlow Moss. A radical lesbian, her carefully assembled physical identity was at one with the austere elegance of her work: she kept her hair severely cropped and side-parted *à la garçonne*, and wore cravats paired with mannish tailored jackets and jodhpurs. Born to wealthy Jewish parents in Kilburn, London, in 1889 and named Marjorie Jewel Moss, she adopted her gender non-specific name at the age of 20. She trained at St John's Wood School of Art and then at the Slade School of Art; in 1927 she went to live in Paris where, during the following two years, she studied with Fernand Léger and Amédée Ozenfant at the Académie Moderne.

Moss had her champions, though few in Cornwall, where she and her partner the Dutch novelist Nettie Nijhoff lived from 1940 onwards at Lamorna, a small village about 12 miles south-west of St Ives. There she is likely to have crossed paths with another openly lesbian artist, the painter Gluck (1895–1978), born Hannah Gluckstein, who had established part-time residence there in 1916. It is clear that Hepworth and Nicholson saw Moss as an interloper, a threat to their primacy, both in St Ives and beyond, for her links to the European avant-garde were every bit as strong as their own. Although Moss is known to have exhibited with the Penwith Society on at least one occasion, due to their opposition she was not invited to become a member. Hepworth – who had met Moss in Paris – perhaps felt her pole position at risk, as a female artist who had also effectively queered herself so that she could compete with men on their own terms. What is more, Moss had made her first purely abstract works a couple of years before Nicholson produced his first entirely abstract reliefs and Hepworth her first abstract sculptures. There was additional displeasure in Moss's connection with the Dutch artist Piet Mondrian (1872–1944), for while their own friendship with him gave them legitimate claims, Moss's predated theirs. Mondrian had evolved a form of abstract painting that he named Neo-Plasticism, in which he used only the three primary colours, always unmodulated and set within a grid of vertical and horizontal black lines on a pure white ground. Moss had become Mondrian's disciple after seeing one of his paintings for the first time in Paris, in either 1927 or 1928. Electrified by it, its geometric purity held a mirror to her self-presentation while also proposing a way forward in her own work, and in 1928 she changed direction to become a non-figurative artist. Nettie Nijhoff and her husband, the poet and essayist Martinus Nijhoff, knew Mondrian, having met him in the Netherlands before the First World War; like them he was now living in Paris, and Nettie invited Moss to meet him at the Nijhoffs' apartment in the Rue du Bac. This introduction took place in 1929 and, while Mondrian tended to avoid personal friendships, it seems that the two were immediately empathetic towards each other. Moss went on to make her first Neo-Plastic works a year or two after her first encounter with Mondrian's painting. In 1931 she took part in the formation of the Abstraction-Création group, which Lucy Howarth, who has undertaken major research on Moss, describes as follows: '*Abstraction-Création* was set up by members of *De Stijl* as well as others – Jean Arp and Auguste Herbin – and represented the unification of many factions of international non-figurative art ... It ran until 1936, and published five annuals – Moss was the only woman and the only British artist to feature in all of them.'[28]

Hepworth and Nicholson joined Abstraction-Création in April

1933, the year in which Nicholson first met Mondrian, who in the following year invited him to visit his studio in the Rue de Départ. Hepworth also visited, and like Nicholson was awed, not merely by the artist's paintings, which they took some time to understand, but by the studio itself. Nicholson later described it in terms not unlike those of Hepworth's hallowed account of her visit to Brâncuşi's atelier:

> Rectangular pieces of board painted with the primary colours, blue, red, yellow, white and neutral grey covered the walls. His room was very high and narrow, a very strange shape; out of the window one saw the railway lines running into and out of the Gare Montparnasse. The quality of Mondrian's thought in his room and the silences in between the things he said made a deep impression on me.[29]

After the Munich Crisis, and believing that Paris would be targeted by German bomber aircraft, in early September 1938 Mondrian wrote to a friend in New York, requesting a formal invitation to travel to America that he could present to immigration authorities. Later that month he left for London assuming it would be a stopping-off point for onward travel, with Nicholson's first wife, Winifred, accompanying him across France. Nicholson, along with Hepworth and their friends Naum Gabo, Henry Moore and Herbert Read, were then all living in close proximity in Hampstead, where they found a studio for Mondrian. He remained there until September 1940, by which time the group of friends had moved out of the capital. Conditions became ever more dangerous because of the Blitz – ironically, it was London rather than Paris that was bombed – and after a bomb destroyed the house next door Mondrian left for New York, where he lived until his death in February 1944. He and Moss kept in touch, and in a letter of May 1941 Mondrian provided her with Nicholson's address, suggesting that she write to introduce herself to him. There are three extant letters from Moss to Nicholson. The first, dated 2 July 1941, begins thus:

> Dear Mr Nicholson,
>
> I am taking the liberty of writing to you as advised by Piet Mondrian, who I know is a good friend of yours.

> As we are both Abstract Painters and at one time were both members of the group 'l'Abstraction Création', I venture to ask you if you can give me some information if there are any galleries in London or any group organising exhibitions in which I can send some work?
>
> Of course I should prefer to talk with you on the possibilities for Abstract works in England at the moment, would it be possible to meet?
>
> I had the pleasure in Paris of having tea with your wife and would be very pleased to see her again, could you both come over one day?

Moss goes on to provide information about the bus service from St Ives to Lamorna, inviting Nicholson and Hepworth to visit her at home there on a day and time to suit them. It is clear that she received no reply, for in her second letter dated 5 August of the following year, she writes that she fears her first has not been received. The third letter, dated 24 May 1943, in which she once more invites the couple to visit (they never did), makes it plain that there had been at least some form of communication from Nicholson, for in it she writes, 'Unfortunately I cannot get hold of any of the publications you noted down for me.'[30]

The influential French critic and writer Michel Seuphor included Moss in his *Dictionnaire de la peinture abstraite* (Dictionary of Abstract Painting, 1957). The entry informs the reader that she was 'the first and purest disciple of Mondrian in Paris' and that she exhibited in group shows in Paris, London, the Netherlands and Switzerland and in the Salon des Réalitiés Nouvelles.[31] In 1953 she had a solo show at the Hanover Gallery in London, which was run by the German lesbian Erica Brausen (1908–1992), who had given Francis Bacon his first solo exhibition. Moss died in August 1958, a couple of months after a cancer diagnosis. She had held her second exhibition at the Hanover Gallery earlier that year.[32]

Three or four months after Moss's death, Hepworth wrote in a letter to Herbert Read:

> I think sometime it would be nice (historically) if somebody paid tribute to Ben's (specially) and my contribution to the international link in England via Paris. In the early days Ben forged links with Paris

long before any other English artist and we both had contacts which eventually brought about the general influx in the middle 30s. It is not possible to attribute this to HM [Henry Moore].[33]

Posing no threat, mild-mannered Milne was never involved in feuds with other artists, nor was he on the receiving end of the kind of sidelining to which Moss was subjected. He continued to focus on his work, steadily gaining in confidence and prowess, and regularly exhibiting drawings and sculpture in group shows with the Penwith Society and at Newlyn Art Gallery. In 1956, Andras Kalman showed his work at the Crane Gallery in Manchester, and in spring 1959 he took part in an open-air exhibition of sculpture at Trewyn Gardens, which also included work by John Hoskin, Roger Leigh, Denis Mitchell, Bruce Taylor, Barbara Tribe and Brian Wall.[34] Earlier that same year came his first American exhibition, with his inclusion in *Eleven British Artists* at the Jefferson Place Gallery in Washington DC. Barbara Burton, an American painter who had studied at St Peter's Loft School of Art in the summer of 1958, assembled the show, which comprised gouaches, drawings and prints. Milne showed four drawings in charcoal, described in a newspaper review as 'clean geometric forms in angular compositions of great vitality'.[35] Also taking part were Sandra Blow, Terry Frost, Patrick Heron, Roger Hilton, Peter Lanyon, William Redgrave, John Wells, Karl Weschke, Nancy Wynne-Jones and Bryan Wynter. The catalogue introduction was by Read; Lanyon was present at the opening reception.[36]

Milne continued to carve in both stone and wood. In 1957 he produced *The Kiss* in Portland stone, a work that pays homage to Brâncuși, referencing as it does his sculptures of the same title, of which there are four versions. Among them, that of 1916 in the collection of Philadelphia Museum of Art is perhaps the best known; Milne is likely to have been aware of it in photographic reproduction. He may also have seen the 1909 version when he was in Paris; it is sited on the grave of Tatiana Rachewskaia in the cemetery at Montparnasse. His own sculpture takes the same premise, of a male and female figure fused in intimate embrace, but makes it yet more abstract and detached, without any indication of the facial features seen in Brâncuși's works. And in contrast to Brâncuși's rough-hewn primitivism it appears mechanistic, its planar precision and lunar paleness akin to an industrial prototype: closer, in fact, to the Romanian sculptor's immaculate polished marble pieces, such as *Bird in Space* (1923). While atypical in Milne's output as a whole, its curved geometries, and reliance upon a particular definition of shape and edge, point forward to future work.

*

For those who travelled to St Ives from the north of England in the 1950s and early 1960s, the contrast must have been comparable to that between grainy black-and-white and Technicolor film. The difference was not only in the quality of light but in the very air that one breathed. Writing while in Manchester, having returned to the north-west to visit his family in January 1963, Milne described the city as 'black and dismal – I have not, even after seven days, seen the tops of the buildings (which are already black) – because of the dirty fog'.[37]

Mancunians lived for years under a permanent haze, caused by the extensive use of coal in both industrial and domestic settings: one thinks of Lowry's city and townscapes with their soot-blackened buildings, their mill and factory chimneys emitting endless plumes of smoke. In Manchester's 1945 Redevelopment Plan, the city surveyor had claimed that its citizenry had in many respects enjoyed a healthier life in 1650 than that of the present day, and described how its inhabitants lived in an environment of 'perpetual smoke ... which enfeebles the health-giving property of the sun's rays and lowers our general vitality and ability to resist infection'.[38]

The problem was not confined to Manchester but affected many British cities. It led to the introduction of the Clean Air Act in 1956, its legislation including powers to establish smokeless zones, and with subsidies provided to households converting from coal to cleaner fuels. The catalyst for the Act was the London smog disaster of December 1952, when a combination of air pollution and weather conditions led to the descent on the capital of a thick yellow-black smog. It lasted for four days and caused severe respiratory diseases that led ultimately to many thousands of deaths. There followed a second Clean Air Act in 1968, yet it was only during the 1980s that city skies were deemed to have cleared sufficiently to reduce the health hazards associated with air pollution.

A fellow escapee from the north-west of England was Alan Lowndes, who, from the early 1950s onwards, began to spend part of each year in Cornwall, living at one point in a barn at Tremedda near Zennor, and in the summer of 1956 sharing Milne's accommodation at The Old Bakehouse in St Ives. It was to that address that Milne sent him a picture postcard from St Tropez, on which he reported to his resolutely heterosexual friend:

> We would all feel quite at home here if we moved from St Ives, and not look out of place. The only difference is that nobody ever stares – at least, not because you look different – only if you look queer. Tremendous weather scorching heat during the day. On the public beach *everyone* wears nothing – Paradise. Am now in Cannes quite different! Love to JAN
>
> Love, J.[39]

During that same summer, Lowndes painted Milne's portrait. The result, in oils on canvas board, with pigment put down with both brush and palette knife, is typically direct in application. Milne stands against a deep terracotta background, his skin lightly tanned, his hair sun-bleached, in a pose that appears both highly considered and determinedly casual. With his head angled slightly upwards, he looks pensively to his left, his right forearm resting on his raised knee and his left hand held against his side at waist height. His costume, of rolled-up denim jeans and deep blue T-shirt, its sleeves also rolled up a little, is that of both the young artist and the young gay man. In considering what kind of image both the painter and his 25-year-old subject sought to project, one thinks of contemporaneous representations of youthful masculinity within the mass culture of newspapers, magazines and films. The sexiest and most potent models came most often from America. There was the 21-year-old sensation Elvis Presley, whose first record, 'Heartbreak Hotel', entered the UK Hit Parade in May 1956. There were also certain film stars with whom Milne may well have identified: beautiful, often emotionally vulnerable young men of ambivalent sexuality, such as Marlon Brando, Montgomery

Clift and James Dean, the last of whom had died in a car crash less than a year before Lowndes painted Milne's portrait. Lowndes often painted from preliminary sketches, and one wonders if the painting was made from life or from a working study; such a drawing is not known to have survived. While not an immediately recognisable likeness of Milne, it is the only known portrait of him and serves as a record of the friendship between two working-class men from the north-west finding themselves as artists in the heady environment of 1950s St Ives. A few years after the portrait was made, the friends had a two-person show at the Crane Gallery in Manchester.

When Milne made the decision to remain in Cornwall, Rodewald offered to buy a property for him to live in, and so bought Trewyn. The sale was completed in December 1956 and Milne moved in soon after, as too for a time did Lowndes, who helped to decorate the house in exchange for lodgings. By then well over a century old, Trewyn has an intriguing history. Local lore has it that Whistler had visited the house: the writer Denys Val Baker (1917–1984) referred to it as 'a stately building ... from whose elegant porch Whistler used to sketch'.[40] It was built around 1840 by James Halse – described by St Ives historian Cyril Noall as 'the local solicitor, mine adventurer and politician' – on a site he had acquired in 1807.[41] At first the house was named Halse's Court. Subsequently, in 1878, it was renamed Brunswick House, and then finally, when the Trewhella family acquired it 14 years later, the house became Trewyn, said to mean 'the fair place' or 'the place of innocence'. (Milne was to express his amusement at the latter, given the antics that took place there during his tenure.) In fact such meanings were erroneous. 'Tre' is both Cornish and Welsh, and 'Trewyn' in Cornish means 'White House' or 'homestead' rather than 'place'.[42] The Trewhellas owned the property for at least 50 years. Janet Axten, the doyenne of St Ives historians, has written of it in some detail:

> Sir William Trewhella made many alterations to the main property. Buildings at the foot of Barnoon Hill, perhaps an old stable block, were demolished in 1908, and he was able to incorporate the additional land into his garden. He then constructed a large retaining wall to prevent his newly acquired land from slipping down the hill.

> It is believed that in about 1910 he built a small house at the lower end of the garden for his children's use. It was this property that was to become Barbara Hepworth's house and studio.[43]

Trewyn is a large, double-fronted house on three floors. Its entrance is through a central porch, leading into a hallway off which is a room at either side, with a kitchen adjoined to one of them. From the hall, a broad, angled staircase sweeps upwards, opening on to a spacious landing on the first floor, where there are five rooms. A small open balcony positioned immediately above the front door of the house has views of the harbour and Smeaton's Pier, with Godrevy Lighthouse visible far out in the bay. A circular staircase leads to the two rooms of the second floor, one of which Milne established as his own private space and sleeping quarters. Running along the front of the house is a paved terrace, from which half a dozen steps slope down to the lawn. The garden is a substantial one, well stocked with flowers, shrubs and trees including small palms; it contains a sculpture studio designed by Henry Gilbert that was built specifically for Milne to work in. Photographs from the 1970s show pieces of his sculpture sited on the lawn, with smaller ones set on plinths at the edge of a rectangular pond.

Not long after Milne moved in at Trewyn, he began to offer accommodation to paying guests, placing advertisements in upmarket publications such as *The Tatler*. The idea had been agreed with Rodewald when he first undertook to buy the property and was seen as a means for Milne to secure some income, independent from his ongoing reliance on Rodewald to fund him so extensively. Centrally located, private and spacious, the house was an ideal place for visitors, including those who were in town to see Hepworth, who, given her own space limitations, quite naturally recommended they stay there. Along with bed and breakfast, Trewyn guests had the option of an evening meal on three nights of the week, for which they pre-booked. To facilitate all of this, Milne relied on friends and local acquaintances to help out. He had definite ideas about the kind of food he wished to offer, and was himself a good cook, his sensual appreciation of food and repertoire of dishes undoubtedly influenced by visits to Mediterranean countries and by the exclusive restaurants to which Rodewald had taken him. Friends remember lots of garlic in his dishes, something still quite unusual in English cuisine of the 1950s.

Hidden behind its high perimeter walls, Trewyn became a private oasis in which Milne was able to create his own 'House Beautiful'. His innate good taste resulted in distinctive interior decor, combining a truth-to-materials aesthetic of simple wooden tables and plain white walls with modernist furniture by designers such as Harry Bertoia and Ernest Race. All of this made the place additionally attractive to visitors and guests. William Redgrave described its interior design as 'an example of modernity unmatched in St Ives'.[44] Others remarked in similar terms. David Lindsay was invited to spend a few weeks at Trewyn one summer in or around 1958, and while equally impressed by its decor recalls that Milne had some very good art in the house, including what he describes as 'a wonderful Keith Vaughan'. This was the artist's oil on canvas *Two Figures in Sequence (5th Assembly)* (1957–58). There was also a lithograph by the French Tachiste painter Pierre Soulages, whose work Milne had admired while in Paris in 1952, and ceramics by both Bernard and Janet Leach.[45]

Two years after he had bought Trewyn, Rodewald acquired the flat beneath the house, known as Trewyn Flat, and then another downstairs flat, Hanter Chy, formed from what had once been the kitchen, dairy and scullery of the main house. This flat was self-contained and had a separate entrance on Ayr Lane. Later, in the spring of 1965, Rodewald gave the whole property to Milne in a deed of gift.[46] He quite regularly stayed at Trewyn, often bringing Victor Sayer with him. While Brian Wall does not recall meeting Rodewald he remembers his visits: 'We knew he came down. But he kept very separate; he kept very private. Cosmo had a blue Mercedes convertible, which was really quite exotic in the 1950s. He would come down to see John. I just assumed he was a very rich benefactor.'

*

On 21 February 1958, not long after she received financial reparation from the German government for her maltreatment during the 1930s, Käthe Schuftan died from cancer at the age of 58. A few days later, Margo Ingham's appreciation appeared in the *Manchester Guardian*. There she wrote of how she had exhibited the artist's work in her studio above the Manchester Ballet Club in 1945, in a show entitled *Seven Painters*:

> Of her your critic then said: 'Käthe Schuftan shows a brilliant portrait drawing, but prefers to subordinate her talent to satirical comment and emotional expression. One can readily understand why the Nazis dared not leave at large such a mordantly graphic expositor of human indignity ... Since then she had held two one-artist shows in Manchester and had earned her living at commercial art. Her technique as a painter in watercolour was superb and this combined with her fiercely independent creative spirit made her a unique figure among artists of the North of England.'[47]

Salford Art Gallery mounted a small retrospective of Schuftan's work in June 1958, just months after her death. In St Ives, Milne made a delicate and sensitive drawing, simply titled *Drawing for Käthe Schuftan*, in memory of her. Compositionally it is formed of a complex sequence of interwoven arcs, which gradually diminish in scale and tonal density as they funnel inwards and rise upwards towards what reads as a striated beam of light. There is something strongly architectural in this drawing, and one wonders if Milne's visit to the cathedral at Chartres was on his mind while making it. He was profoundly aware of, and moved by, the power of such places to evoke matters of the human spirit. And of Schuftan, who had been such a strong influence on him as a student, he remembered how she bore no resentment towards others, no matter how greatly she had suffered.

3 Tapestry of Innocence

A man who feels an attraction towards other men is a social misfit only; once he gives way to that attraction, he becomes a criminal.[1]
—Peter Wildeblood

Julian Nixon first visited St Ives at Easter 1958, driving to Cornwall from London with Edward Moulton Barrett, a lawyer with whom he was then intimately involved. Moulton Barrett was the latest in a string of older men with whom the 22-year-old had formed attachments, and it was he who had proposed the trip and arranged for them to stay as guests at Trewyn. Soon after his visit, Nixon wrote to his friend and mentor, the novelist Richard Blake Brown in Bristol, telling him that Milne was prepared to let him have a room at Trewyn for two pounds and ten shillings per week, for which he could also have the general run of the house. Then renting a flat shared with its male owner in Chiswick in west London, Nixon had been working at a nearby swimwear manufacturer, probably in a clerical capacity. Often in debt, he owed a substantial amount in rent and was keen to move on: St Ives appealed to him as a place in which to make a fresh start. By the second week in May he was living at Trewyn and working at Pat's Kitchen, a restaurant on The Wharf opposite Smeaton's Pier. There he did some of the cooking while also waiting on tables.

Brown had accompanied Nixon when he made his return train journey to St Ives, and had stayed for one night at Trewyn. Nixon wrote to him soon after he had left St Ives, ending his letter: 'P.S. So glad you liked John – we are very great friends – especially when he has no mistresses from Paris about the house to distract his attention.'

The 'mistress' from Paris is likely to have been the photographer Michel Ramon, who was in St Ives in 1958, when he made photographic portraits of both Milne and Hepworth. He and Milne had first met in Paris four years earlier and became good friends; it may be that they were also lovers for a time. Ramon paid fairly regular visits to St Ives, certainly up until the early 1960s.

Precocious as a child, the adult Nixon was given to self-dramatisation. There is a black-and-white photograph of him, shown in profile looking pensively out of a window at Trewyn, on the back of which he has written: 'Me as an artist. St Ives'. The note is probably purposely ironic, especially as Nixon was now living at an artist's house in a famous art colony. He very probably sent the photograph to Brown, who was, like him, a theatrical personality given to role-play. The idea of artistic identity, though, with its inbuilt mystique, certainly appealed to Nixon. He was not an artist; nor, despite what were to become long-held literary pretensions, did he ever become a professional writer. He left indelible impressions on many of those who encountered him in St Ives. David Lindsay met him while staying at Trewyn and took a dislike to him, later describing him as 'living in a delusional world'. Long-time resident Michael Hunt, himself gay, dismisses him as 'just a camp little queen', and Reg Singh, who first visited St Ives in the 1950s, remembers: 'Julian was a very flamboyant gay, which was quite unusual then. He was so flamboyant he embarrassed John. He was blond, but I'm not sure if it was real or out of a bottle.'[2]

Nixon was in fact naturally blond, as is evident from childhood photographs. He was a rather handsome, fresh-faced young man, with blue eyes and a capacity to charm, a skill he had developed from an early age. Denys Val Baker and his wife Jess got to know Nixon through their friendship with Milne, and in a volume of autobiography published in 1963 Denys wrote of him thus:

> The first time I ever saw Julian I think he was wearing an astrakhan overcoat and carrying a silver-topped cane. That was, of course, in winter-time, but the advent of summer merely offered Julian a wider variety of choice for vivid and dramatic clothes. Julian in gay continental shirt and bright blue jeans, Julian in green corduroys and beautifully careless angora sweater, Julian in diminutive beach shorts, Julian in startling striped beach gown ... Perhaps of all these pictures

> that come to mind the most delightful is of Julian wearing tight crimson trousers and silk shirt and an enormous black cloak with a scarlet lining: dressed in this delightful Beau-Brummel fashion he would stalk around St Ives to the delight of most, the amusement of some, and the consternation of a few of the more strait-laced.[3]

St Ives had, then, found its own Bright Young Thing, delivering both amusement and consternation to a seaside town already known for its bohemian contingent. In an era when for a man to wear a green necktie might raise questions about his sexuality, Nixon's sartorial flamboyance – not to speak of his behaviour – surely made his predilections screamingly obvious. He must also have unnerved those locals quietly living under little or no suspicion of their queerness; one imagines them avoiding him like the plague. And in Denys Val Baker's description of his colourful attire, Nixon comes across as though modelling for the Vince Man's Shop mail order catalogue. First opened in Soho in 1954, the shop's proprietor was Bill Green, aka 'Vince', a pseudonym adopted shortly after the war for his work as a photographer specialising in homoerotic studies of muscle boys, which he sold to male physique magazines. His shop advertised slender line slacks, jeans, beachwear, shirts and swimwear 'Inspired by the Continent', and became a magnet for queer men and those with a taste for clothing that drew attention to the masculine physique. Milne is known to have bought from the shop; Nixon surely must have, including perhaps those diminutive beach shorts.[4]

In terms of the characters whose stories are recounted within the pages of this book, Nixon was an identifiably queer presence at a time when such figures were rare, and not only in St Ives. What is more, by the time of his first arrival in the town he had a particular history, worth recounting for what it adds to our knowledge of queer experience in the years leading up to the Sexual Offences Act of 1967.

The eldest of three brothers, Nixon was born in Gloucester on 8 July 1935 and christened John Capper Humphrey Nixon; his father's name was John Capper Nixon.[5] 'Julian' was a self-invention, an adopted name that he deemed appropriate to the sophisticated persona he sought to project. His childhood home was in Chester, and it was there that he first developed theatrical aspirations, acting in several amateur productions. Among the first was a Chester Theatre Club staging of Terence Rattigan's *The Winslow Boy* (1946) in May 1948. Several press cuttings, kept with the programme in his scrapbook, describe the 12-year-old's performance as Ronnie Winslow in glowing terms. Keen to establish a stage career, Nixon later wrote to a number of professionals to ask their advice on entering the acting profession; among the replies was a letter from Laurence Olivier, who in September 1951 wrote to suggest he might try to get some work in repertory.

In 1953 Nixon began a journal, writing his first entry on 1 October. Nearing his 18th birthday, in May of that year he had begun his period of national service, joining the RAPC (Royal Army Pay Corps) Training Centre at Devizes in Wiltshire. Based subsequently at Nunsfield Camp in Taunton, Somerset, he was able to take part in further amateur theatrical productions. He took the role of Freddie in a Taunton Thespians staging of George Bernard Shaw's *Pygmalion* (1912) in November 1953, then shortly afterwards began rehearsals with the same group for Talbot Rothwell's *Queen Elizabeth Slept Here* (1949).

In a journal entry of 1 December, Nixon makes no mention of his duties at Nunsfield Camp. The focus is instead on how busy he has been in his work at the theatre, and on the impact he has made locally:

> I have progressed considerably, both socially & otherwise since descending on Taunton. People find me strange, amazing, novel, in fact different people find me different altogether. One half hate me & the other half love me, but the 'have-nots' are always jealous of the 'haves'. I've barged right in and been accepted straight away, whereas other people have had to wait years before they even got their nose in. Of course I have to be careful from now onwards, I'm much too forceful a person, with too great a tendency to stage manage events *and* peoples [*sic*] lives,[6] well if the bloody fools will let me it's not my fault. People are already frightened of me as a result of this ... Since arriving here I've risen socially to the extent that I can now count a Knight, & Earl & Countess amongst my friends, in Taunton I mean. I am an unmitigated little snob as far as the social ladder goes, but who isn't these days.

> My programme seems fairly full for the next 2, 3 months, one play after another, interthread with dances, Balls, parties, etc. But it is so much better to take things at a faster pace while your [*sic*] young & have the stamina.
>
> I'm dying to pull everyone to pieces, but while I'm still in Taunton would prove far too dangerous. Taunton is a hotbed for scandal & gossip, & my being newly arrived here have been a sitting target for it all. I unfortunately have not always taken it with the required grain of salt.
>
> Since arriving here I have been very well controlled as regards 'affaires de Coeur'. I have only had one little flirtation, & one that was unrequited. Such hell, but fun. Half the fun is the chase, & anyway I soon lost interest.
>
> I am an Escapist, I came to this conclusion over the weekend. Most of us are but I appear to be to a much greater extent than most.
>
> One of the reasons perhaps that I shall never really fall in love is because I am in love with myself, subconsciously when I meet new people I compare them with myself which is entirely the wrong thing to do. This no doubt accounts for the schoolboy crushes I sometimes get on older men – it's a form of hero worship. I subconsciously see part of myself in them. It's all very complicated at times, & I often wonder whether or not I am such a complex character at times, or whether I just try to be ...

Less than two months later, Nixon's buoyant tone has changed dramatically:

> Jan 22nd [1954]
>
> Dear Journal – so much I wish to write but can not whilst I remain in Taunton. Oh God – how can people be so cruel. They have very nearly made my life unbearable ... If I was not so fond of life I would be inclined to kill myself. It is a satisfactory feeling knowing that I always have the PB's in a necessity.

One can only guess at the exact nature of the unpleasantness referred to here, and one assumes that the 'PB's' Nixon mentions were a lethal drug, perhaps phenobarbital, bleakly coincidental in the light of what soon followed. For in February 1954 he was arrested on a charge of gross indecency and detained in what he described as a mental hospital while awaiting trial. He was then one of 15 men brought before the judge at Somerset Assizes on 26 May; all were charged with the same offence, and all were found guilty. The case was particularly shocking because one of them committed suicide immediately after the judge's verdict. It was reported in *The Times* on the following day:

> MAN'S DEATH AFTER SENTENCE
> 'VICE THAT SPREADS LIKE PESTILENCE'
> A few minutes after being sentenced at Somerset Assizes at Wells yesterday to 12 months' imprisonment on a charge of gross indecency, Gilbert Andrew Nixon, aged 37, company director, of West Kirby, Cheshire, was found dead in a cell where he had been placed. An autopsy is to be held.
>
> In passing sentence, Mr Justice Oliver had said: 'It is a terrible thing to see a man like you with a gallant military record standing as you are.'
>
> Nixon was one of 15 men, some with Taunton addresses, who had pleaded Guilty to charges of committing or attempting to commit unnatural acts and acts of gross indecency between November, 1951, and March this year. Nine of the men received prison sentences ranging from one to four years.
>
> The Judge said that it was an appalling thing for him that an ancient, historic, not very large town like Taunton should at one single Assize exhibit as many cases of homosexual crime as in the ordinary way he met with in a whole year. The answer, as he saw it, was not that the population of Taunton was more debased than other groups of the community, but that once that vice got established in any community it spread like a pestilence and unless held in check threatened to spread indefinitely.
>
> It was stated during the trial that Nixon retired last year, with the rank of Lieutenant-Colonel, from the command of the 1st Battalion of the Liverpool Scottish Regiment, TA. He was on active service during the war and received the MC for gallantry in Sicily.[7]

Gilbert Nixon had in fact swallowed a cyanide tablet that he had secreted on his person. (Just 12 days later, Alan Turing took his own life by biting into an apple dipped into a cyanide solution.) Nixon was married with a child and had a previous conviction for 'improper conduct' – probably cottaging – a fact he had managed to keep secret from those close to him. He and Julian Nixon (their shared surname merely coincidental) had had sex in the officers' mess at Nunsfield Camp.

The case of those men brought before the court came as the result of an episode on 20 February that year. Geoffrey Williamson, a 17-year-old boarder at a public school in Taunton, had solicited a man for sex during a train journey from Exeter to Taunton. The man, an off-duty railway policeman, engaged with Williamson in what he subsequently described as an improper conversation and, when the train arrived at its destination, placed him under arrest. At the local police station, Williamson named many men, including his lover Private John Nixon, aka Julian Nixon. In a detailed account of the case, historian Patrick Higgins wrote of Nixon:

> Nixon it turned out had an even more active sex life than Williamson. Several of their partners blamed the young men for enticing them into sex ... Private Nixon had many admirers across the country, some of whom foolishly wrote to him. He preserved their letters. Walter Sexton, forty-five, a civil servant, was terribly smitten, telling policemen that they had met in Chester when Nixon had been sixteen. He thought he had met a soul-mate. 'My interest in Nixon', he insisted, 'is not limited to one aspect. He has a lively, deep and precocious interest in other things. He was interested in amateur dramatics.' Sexton had advised him not to 'become over-zealous in sexual matters', advice that was probably the product of bitter experience.[8]

The trial at Somerset Assizes came a little over two months after the highly publicised Montagu case, when on 24 March, subsequent to their arrest that January, Edward, Lord Montagu of Beaulieu, his cousin Michael Pitt-Rivers and the journalist Peter Wildeblood were all found guilty of gross indecency and imprisoned at Winchester Castle. In 1954 there were 2,034 recorded offences of gross indecency. The case in which Nixon was involved was just one of many 'chain' prosecutions that resulted from the arrest of a number of men after they had been named by others. Police often urged those arrested to name their homosexual contacts, implying that doing so would result in leniency by the judiciary (it did not). Williamson named several men, as indeed did Nixon; among them was Howard Kent-Jones, his 38-year-old friend and lover, referred to as 'Kent' in his journal, who was tried alongside him at Taunton. Nixon was not one of the nine men sent to prison after the trial but was returned to the hospital for a further 12 months. Williamson and Kent-Jones joined him there.

Nixon recorded a full account of his experiences in his journal, from his arrest and initial period in the hospital, to the trial, verdict and subsequent return to the same hospital. Here are extracts from his entry of 30 May, made four days after the trial. Though subject to some of his usual dramatic flourishes, it generally rings true, and is worth quoting from in some length:

> I am lucky by ordinary standards to be writing this now. I have come thro' the most harassing experience of my life ... I thank 'God' with my whole heart that the trial is over and I have been given this wonderful opportunity. I don't feel bitter. The Law on the whole has been humane, and not really destructive, as it so easily could have been. I just made a false start, and I've had an all too rare chance to make a fresh one. I'm humbly grateful for it.
>
> I think it might be as well to record one or two of the happenings at the trial, as a reminder if I am ever tempted to stray again.

He goes on to describe being driven to the Assizes on the morning of 25 May, where he was met by his father, solicitor and counsel, and of how at 11am he and the other men on trial were shown into the dock. There they faced the judge, the mayoress, the Lord-Lieutenant and Lady Lord-Lieutenant of the county and other officials, all gathered for the occasion.

> Proceedings dragged on interminably the whole day. With the adjournment for lunch, I fully expected to go out to a hotel to get some lunch. For the first time in days I was really hungry ... Contrary to my expectations, we were all taken to the cells below, locked up in threes in cells that were so tiny you could hardly stand let alone sit down. We were given a tin mug of tea and an outsize sausage roll

> apiece. As soon as I saw the roll I felt the waves of nausea passing thro' me. I spent the rest of the time chain smoking.

When the trial finished late in the evening, the judge announced that he would not pass sentence until the following morning, 'due to the enormity of the case and people involved'. The men were taken below, handcuffed to one another and led to a waiting coach that took them to a large prison 50 kilometres away:

> On entering the very grim prison surrounded by high walls ... we were taken into the reception centre ... As it was fairly late and we had had no substantial meal all day we were given a Prison Tea. This consisted of a loaf cut in two, smeared with marge and a thin slice of some positively revolting looking fatty ham inside. This was accompanied by a Quart mug of evil smelling and needless to say evil tasting liquid that if one was pressed to give a name for it, would presumably be cocoa ... Several of my companions (who it would seem now I recall the incident were very knowledgeable of prison matters) urged me to try and eat and drink as much as I could get down me for it would be all I got till the next morning ... We were taken individually to an office to have our particulars taken down. I later found out we were called lodgers. We were then issued with two blankets (moth eaten), a rug, a single sheet, a towel, also a book to provide us with some reading material during the night could we not sleep. ...
>
> Having been led thro' a maze of corridors, en route encountering no less than four locked doors that were opened and shut with great alacrity, we arrived at the main building that was to be our home for the night. My first impressions were that it reminded me of a Zoo, only instead of cages being in a row, they were in tiers as well ... I was then locked in my cell. The cell was approximately 14' × 6', and was furnished with a double 8' bunk in one corner with two straw palliasses on, a table and chair of scrubbed wood, a washstand with all accoutrements necessary for one's toilet, and of all things a mirror hung on the wall with a bit of wire. Then trying to take stock of myself I decided the most practical thing to do would be make the bed and get into it ... I undressed, standing only in my underpants. I swilled myself in cold water and dried myself as best I could with one of my several hankies.

> After careful thought I decided to get into bed and wrap the sheet which was clean around me and hope for the best ... I took a sleeping tablet of which I had a limited number earlier secreted away in the lining of my uniform. The last I remember that night was of saying my prayers and asking God to bestow His Blessing on my family and friends who were surely in need of comfort as much as I was.

Nixon goes on to recount the events of the following morning, when, after a meagre prison breakfast, he and the other men were again handcuffed together and driven back to Wells by coach:

> The journey was one amid a rather enforced joviality. Everyone of us I think was terrified of what we might receive later in the morning ... All too soon we arrived at the Assizes. After a wait, we were once more led into the dock to receive our sentences. I have never been so nervous or apprehensive in all my life. I could hardly walk into the Box let alone stand to attention whilst receiving my sentence in true Military fashion. Matters were not helped by the fact that out of the 15 people in the Dock I was one of the last two to know my fate. I was verging on a state of collapse by this time. I don't think it surprising, what with 4 year, 3 yr, 2 yr and 1 year prison sentences flying about. When I heard I was to be Bound over to keep the peace for two years on condition I resided for 12 months in a mental home I could have wept with relief ... Those 30 minutes in the Box whilst each of us received our sentence were something that will stay indelibly stamped on my mind for as long as I live.
>
> At last I walked out of the Box – a comparatively free man. I can't recall feeling or thinking anything except that Mummy would be so relieved ... Then with the arrival of my solicitor I was yet to undergo another terrific shock. One of the men convicted was dead. I was utterly stupefied – I just couldn't believe it – yet subconsciously I knew that this would happen. For only a few moments previously I had been down to the cells to collect my belongings. As I did so I saw the man drop to the floor and start writhing in a convulsive fit. At first I thought he had fainted. Then slowly it dawned on me he had taken poison. I knew him very well, Smith I shall call him for obvious reasons, was the head of a world wide organisation of research

> chemists. He would have access to such poisons. I suggested this to the Doctor, or whoever it was that was attending him. I thought that as the Doctors had got to him as soon as he fell, he would be alright. I did not really think he would die. I was incapable of saying or even feeling anything. I was too glad to be free myself. The shock of the whole business didn't set in until later after I had arrived back at the hospital.

In a later journal entry, dated 16 June, Nixon wrote:

> Anyway the whole business has been salutary. I see now that quite apart from rightness or wrongness of the matter the risk just isn't worth it. A fellow gets picked up, and immediately spills the beans to the Police. Even bank robbery's safer ...

Although Nixon made no note of the name of the hospital, it was very probably Musgrove Park Hospital in Taunton. Dr R. Sessions-Hodge, who had been present at the trial in May, was in charge of its Neuro-Psychiatric Department, where among his patients were homosexual men found guilty of gross indecency. In some cases treatment included hormone therapy, such as the invasive oestrogen treatment to which Alan Turing had been subjected. Life at the hospital appears to have been relatively civilised, compared to that in prison. Although Nixon was not allowed outside the hospital grounds without an escort, he did have some creature comforts, including a small room of his own and a daily routine in which patients were allowed to watch television together until 9pm. He was set to work at first in the hospital gardens, then for a time in the laundry, followed by a spell of almost two months as waiter in the staff canteen, which was useful experience for his St Ives job at Pat's Kitchen. For the final six months before his eventual release in August 1955, Nixon managed to secure work as assistant to the catering officer, and after a time took control of menus and diets for sick patients.

While in the early pages of his journal Nixon had written of his continuing ambition to pursue an acting career, his final stage appearances proved to be those with the Taunton Thespians. The psychological bruising and embarrassment of his arrest, trial and confinement, along with the potential for gossip within theatre circles and deleterious media attention, were surely derailing factors. Changing course, Nixon now decided to concentrate on writing. Encouraged by Richard Blake Brown, in St Ives he tried his hand at some short stories, with the aim of submitting them to magazines in the hope that they might be published. In the months before his arrival in Cornwall he had written what he described as his auto-biography, *Tapestry of Innocence*, for which he devised the pen name 'Howard Maelstrom' and in which the central character is Corin Mellish. Contained, like his journal, within a foolscap notebook, Nixon's handwritten manuscript – it appears to be a lightly amended initial draft – tells of his life from childhood onwards.[9] Treading an unsteady line between autobiog-raphy and melodramatic fiction, it is shot through with occasional scenes of physical intimacy between its protagonist – 'young, naturally promiscuous' – and his mostly older male conquests. At its worst implausible and daft, the text's most convincing pages are those covering Nixon's arrest, trial and confinement, for they draw heavily on his journal entries, often copied out near verbatim.

Aside from one or two references to a psychiatrist – with whom it seems he refused to engage seriously – there is surprisingly little in Nixon's journal to indicate the type of treatment he received while in hospital. In *Tapestry of Innocence* he writes:

> This treatment which Corin talked so glibly of was really non-existent. He had indeed been asked if he would submit to Hormone treatment, but had refused as had Geoffrey [Williamson] & Stuart [surname unknown] refused ... He felt that if he wasn't able to cure himself by himself he wouldn't allow anyone else to do it. In any case he had heard from other people that Hormone [treatment] didn't do any good it only made you sexless for a period.

In his journal Nixon wrote of his own attempts at analysis:

> I have resumed my studies of Psychology – in particular the Eastern side ... and have on my knowledge attempted an [*sic*] self-analysis ... For the book, my diagnosis was this; Psychopathic personality, sexually abnormal, hysteric, an Oedipus complex with Mother fixation – in

> fact my dependence – a sort of 'Mother fixation' – is half the trouble (I believe that at last I have discovered the cause). My diagnosis seems fairly sound according to a très distingué bon ami of mine.

One is left wondering which texts, Eastern or otherwise, Nixon had been studying, and just how serious he was in this self-analysis. For such an over-the-top diagnosis was in fact typical of many professional psychiatric analyses of homosexuals at the time; simplistically Freudian, the clichéd notion of mother fixation was one that queer men were to be hobbled with for decades after.[10]

In 'The Gay Metropolis', the eighth and final chapter of *Tapestry of Innocence*, Corin, having been released from hospital, spends some time at the family home in Chester. And then, 'armed with letters of introduction', he sets out for London, where he is to stay at the house of a school friend in Hampstead. There the narrative ends.

One concludes that Nixon saw *Tapestry of Innocence*, in part at least, as a plea for understanding and justice, in a not dissimilar vein to *Against the Law*, Peter Wildeblood's famous 1955 account of the Montagu case. In stark contrast to the experienced journalist Wildeblood, however, he lacked professional writing skills. And in comparison with the factually honest *Against the Law*, reprinted within weeks of its first publication, much of *Tapestry of Innocence* appears to bear a highly selective, often tenuous relationship to actual events, as its author indulged in his ingrained impulse to romanticise.

A letter from his landlord in Chiswick makes plain the high hopes Nixon expressed for *Tapestry of Innocence*. Dated 9 February 1958, the letter serves an ultimatum, in which Nixon is told that if he cannot make payments before the end of the month towards the £110 he owes in rent, laundry and telephone bills, and including what appears a personal loan of £40, he will give him notice:

> I do not wish to be harsh but these terms must stand whether your book is published or not. I have allowed you a month's notice in case you want to leave, so as to give you time to make arrangements, but I hope you can provide the money.
>
> I wish you the best with the book, don't stop work even if it is a success as the sale won't last for ever.

The book was not published, so did not become the *succès de scandale* its author had naively imagined. There is in fact nothing on record to indicate that Nixon approached a publisher; there are occasional notes of instruction for a typist in the handwritten manuscript book, and a typescript is known to exist, but that is all. There is, though, a synopsis by Brown, which reads:

> This is a story that is concerned with the actual adventures of an innocent and charming boy who, whether for good or evil, seems destined to encounter just those very people whose emotional impact on his life, as the story shows so vividly, could scarcely be ignored.
>
> Almost this book would seem to divide itself into a series of TABLEAUX which, far from being static, marks the inescapable development of a young life and a young mind uncannily attuned to shrewder reactions than are common to the average growing boy in any age.[11]

*

Over many years Nixon cultivated not only a series of older gay men but also, regardless of his sexuality, several well-heeled older women. Of all these people, the highly unconventional Richard Blake Brown was the most important, for more than anyone else in Nixon's life he proved a profound and lasting influence, as mentor, benefactor and most especially as a role model: Nixon described him as the 'guiding force of my life'.[12] Thirty-three years Nixon's senior, Brown was a distinguished-looking man and a dandy, with a penchant for vividly coloured attire: sweaters in violet or magenta, gloves and scarves in canary yellow, worn with loud check jackets. The second of three sons, he was born to wealthy American parents in Boston, Massachusetts, on 2 January 1902. Later that same year, following his entrepreneurial father's invention of the power signalling system for the London Underground, the family moved to England.[13] Brown was educated at two public schools: Tonbridge School in Kent, and Berkhamsted School in Hertfordshire. At Tonbridge he became great friends with his classmate Rupert Croft-Cooke (1903–1979), who like him was to become a writer. Along with Brown's younger brother Lincoln, they would dress up as monks and bishops in home-made vestments and enact ecclesiastical ceremonies of Brown's devising.[14] Such make-believe antics formed an early rehearsal in a life in which artifice and fantasy often prevailed, in what Croft-Cooke later described as the 'radiant private world' that his friend created for himself.[15]

From school Brown went on to take a degree in English and History at Magdalene College, Cambridge. There he struck up a close and enduring friendship with the future fashion designer and royal dressmaker Norman Hartnell, a camp enjoyment of rarefied esoterica forming a common bond between them. Both took female roles in Cambridge Footlights revues – Brown in particular was remembered for his excellent female impersonations – and, as Hartnell's biographer Michael Pick has written, 'Their lifelong correspondence reveals the undying undergraduate enthusiasms of both for Ouida, King Ludwig of Bavaria, the Empress Elisabeth of Austria, Wagner, Daisy, Princess of Pless, Mrs Patrick Campbell and Edwardian society.'[16]

Upon graduating in 1923, Brown, undecided on a choice of career, was torn between church and theatre. He initially plumped for the latter, joining the Old Vic Company in London as a student actor for a season of Shakespeare plays, but then, concluding that the Church was his true calling, went on to study theology at Oxford. Subsequently ordained into the Church of England in 1926, in December that year he became a curate in the Parish of St Mary's, Portsea, in Hampshire. There he became thoroughly unhappy and during his first summer, after his father had written urging him to pull himself together, Brown sent him 'a full, painful and awful confession ... Telling him EVERYTHING about myself: it was a terrible task, a humiliating ordeal.'[17]

Harold Brown, while remaining highly supportive, was deeply concerned at the news of his son's homosexuality and counselled him to get married, recommending a young friend of the family. Richard refused. He left Portsea in September 1928.

By the spring of 1935 Brown had moved to live close to Croft-Cooke in the remote Cotswold village of Salperton. The move followed a weekend visit to his friend, after which he decided to rent a local cottage, where he then lived for over two years. Within an autobiographical volume published 30 years later, Croft-Cooke devoted a chapter to Brown, an honest and affectionate account of his friend's personality and habits, in which he wrote of his life both before and after his time in the village. He recounted how Brown moved to the Cotswolds with the intention to write novels, following a period as curate-in-charge of a parish near Tunbridge Wells, Kent, where to the consternation of his bishop and vicar he had resigned his orders. He described how Brown had decorated his Salperton cottage in a colour palette not unlike that of his attire, with sitting room walls painted buttercup yellow combined with pillar-box red woodwork, and bedroom walls of blancmange pink. On bookshelves coated in turquoise lacquer he housed volumes by his favourite authors, among them those to whom he remained devoted long after they had fallen out of fashion, such as William Le Queux, Robert Hugh Benson and especially Ouida. There were also queer writers, including Baron Corvo, John Addington Symonds, Carl Van Vechten and Ronald Firbank, whose rococo novels are perhaps closest to Brown's own stylised confections.

Brown's idiosyncrasies were apparent from a young age, and in his adult life many considered him merely an eccentric. To reduce him to the caricature that such a label might suggest would, though, underestimate his complexity and ultimate depth of experience. What is more, as Croft-Cooke noted of him:

> His were not affectations, which are for the public eye, his attitudes were entirely to please himself. He had outgrown adolescence and the wish to impress others and when he wore unusual clothes in intolerable colours it was for his own amusement.
>
> ...
>
> It was quite futile to judge Richard by normal standards of conduct since for him they did not exist. He had to be accepted or not – nothing was gained by criticism.[18]

In 1938 Brown published *Mr Prune on Cotswold*, a fictionalised travelogue in which, over the course of many summer days, the eponymous Sebastian Prune journeys around the Cotswolds, travelling mainly by bicycle and stopping over at inns and small hotels. The narrative recounts Prune's passage through the countryside, his visits to towns and villages, and opinions of their architecture (there is much on the merits and demerits of church buildings). He writes, too, of his encounters with various folk: landed gentry, know-all eccentrics and working-class lads. Written in the third person, the book is in a curious English tradition that combines acute observation, whimsy and a love of artifice with the arcane; it bears relation to the work of other queer writers such as Denton Welch and E F Benson, both of whom Brown greatly admired. In one episode Prune stops at Salperton, where the author himself makes an unnamed appearance, in a description that seems knowingly to combine ironic self-knowledge, parody and celebration of his undoubted individualism. Arrested by the strains of an Edvard Grieg piano concerto heard through a cottage's open door, Prune stops to listen. Soon there appears through the door a young man, clad in white shirt and shorts: 'He had fair wavy hair and his knees and legs were covered with a positive down of champagne-coloured hirsuteness.'[19]

This blond vision – a premonition of Nixon – is soon followed by the pianist himself:

> a tall, animated personage in bottle-green corduroy shorts and a salmon-pink jersey ... 'Come and have a glass of sherry with us,' he cried, not waiting for an answer but dashing back into the cottage to get this refreshment ... The host now returned with sherry and glasses, and waiving the formality of all further introductions, he poured out generous libations, handed them round, and proposed that they all drank to *Colour*![20]

There follows a tour of the cottage, its dining room walls painted a 'blinding yellow' with woodwork 'a violent shade of pillar-box scarlet' and bookcase shelves turquoise blue. And so forth. It is all as Croft-Cooke described. The book contains 16 black-and-white photographs, all but one taken by Harold Brown, who it appears had accompanied his son on a driving tour of places featured in its narrative.

By the time Nixon first encountered him in 1957, Brown had published 12 novels, with that year a thirteenth entitled *Yet Trouble Came*; he dedicated his fourteenth and final novel, *Bright Glades* (1959), to Nixon. Along with these were eight volumes of autobiography, only one of which found a publisher (*Apology of a Young*

Ex-Parson, Duckworth, 1932). He also kept up a correspondence with a wide circle of friends and acquaintances, writing on fittingly idiosyncratic stationery; his notepaper often bore the die-stamped legend 'L.W. DROWNED JUNE 13 1886', in homage to the dramatic death at the age of 40 of his greatest idol, Ludwig of Bavaria, about whom he wrote an unpublished biography.[21] There was also a series of foolscap journals that he kept locked away in a case, which was itself then locked inside another. Written in his large, highly legible handwriting, they served not only as journals but also as travelogues and scrapbooks, with newspaper cuttings and printed ephemera pasted in. He often adorned his pages with photographs of nude or shirtless young men, swimwear models from the Vince Man's Shop catalogue, and pop stars and actors such as Adam Faith and Tab Hunter. Together the journals constitute a fascinating personal and social document of a queer twentieth-century life. Their diverse written content includes passages of fantastical flights of the imagination and, it must be said, displays of an unpleasantly misogynistic attitude.

While Brown had some private income, and might have continued to use it in support of a full-time writing career, ultimately he was driven by his religious faith. Therefore, following his time at Salperton he resumed his Church orders. His next 15 years or so were peripatetic, ministering variously in Cumbria, Derbyshire, Devon, Hampshire and Berkshire; his most sustained period was as a Royal Naval Volunteer Reserve chaplain (1941–47). At the start of the Second World War, perhaps seeing it as advantageous to his career, he had married the daughter of a bishop, but they soon separated, and divorced when the war ended.[22]

It was only when Brown became chaplain of Bristol Prison in 1952 that he seemed to find his true vocation, and he remained in post until the year of his death. His friend Mervyn Stockwood (latterly the Bishop of Southwark) had suggested the role to him, rightly considering him to have the requisite skills for a job that was by its very nature far removed from the sequestered, private world in which he had spent much of his earlier life. At Bristol he provided religious and moral support and guidance to often desperate prisoners, including those condemned to death.[23]

In 1969 Nixon made a written summary of his life thus far. Within it he recounted how, on the eve of his 22nd birthday in July 1957, he had first met Brown at a dinner at The Ritz in London. Nixon's then boyfriend Peter had asked if he might invite Brown along:

> It is easy to recall that first meeting with the distinguished & handsome Richard (though I thought at the time rather loudly dressed in a vivid bookmaker style black & white large check suit & salmon pink pullover underneath with an especially vivid tie of magenta & white broad stripes) – so far removed was he of my preconceived ideas of what he would be like. Though Peter had told me he was not a conventional type of cleric – I was still hardly prepared for this apparition – but so courteous & gentlemanly.

Brown was clearly entranced by his new acquaintance, an attraction that seems to have been mutual, each of the new-found soulmates finding an idealised version of himself in the other. In the weeks following their first meeting their friendship escalated, and was to prove lifelong. Brown began to address Nixon as 'Broth' or 'Brothy', a pet name derived from his 1933 novel *A Broth of a Boy*: Nixon reciprocated by using the same pet name for his friend. Brown soon became guide, counsel and teacher, introducing the young man to aspects of culture that formed part of his own passionate interests. In October they were at the Royal Opera House in Covent Garden for *Die Walküre* (1856), Nixon's first Wagner opera. They then holidayed in France, staying in Paris (where they bought neckties at Dior) and visiting Versailles and Chartres. There are shades in all of this of Rodewald's infatuated largesse towards Milne.

On Christmas Eve 1957, Brown noted in his journal that Broth had telephoned him the night before to say that he had fallen in love with someone, news that appears to have been greeted with gladness and understanding. Then in February, Brown wrote that Nixon was in Amsterdam with yet another man: his 'newest friend', a 52-year-old who had taken Nixon for a holiday following the suicide of his father on 17 January. Born in Belfast in 1912, John Capper Nixon was a retired military man who had served during the Second World War with the Royal Ulster Rifles, to which he was promoted Captain in 1947. He and his wife Maureen had divorced while Julian was in his teens (she was now living in Canada, where her second son had emigrated some time before), and he was now living with his second wife in Surrey. Of his father's death, Nixon later wrote: 'Apparently beset by ill health & God knows what else – though certainly not financial trouble – he went into his study one morning after breakfast & shot himself through the head.'[24] Nixon, who had been estranged from his father after running away from and being expelled from school, attended the funeral in London.

Nixon's employment at Pat's Kitchen ended with the close of the tourist season in September. That autumn he left St Ives, but he returned in the following spring, living again at Trewyn, where he helped Milne to run the house. Earlier that year Denys and Jess Val Baker had moved with their six children to St Christopher's, a house on Porthmeor Road that backed directly onto the beach. It had a 20-metre-long basement room that at one end opened onto the Porthmeor sands, only about half a metre above high-tide level. The couple's existence was often impecunious, and with a view to generating more income Jess had the idea to open part of this room as a beach café. To make it viable she would need someone to help manage it, while she concentrated on commercial pottery production, which she did in a ground-floor room at the front of the house, her wheel positioned in the window looking onto the street. With the idea of her new enterprise in mind, Jess wrote to Nixon. Her letter is undated but is likely to have been written early in 1959, before he had returned to St Ives:

> Dear Julian,
>
> I am thinking of turning my long room or part of it into a café for the summer. I can't manage it on my own as of course I have the pottery as well but I wondered if you would be interested in coming in with me – as a partner? It's all completely in the air at the moment dependent on whether I can get someone like yourself to help me and also on having a small amount of capital ... I won't enlarge any more until I get your response, cos you might say BALLS as you have other plans. Anyway maybe I'll see you soon, and in any case treat this in confidence. Could you reply to Trewyn as Denys is simply not interested in business and I don't want to discuss my little plans until they are crystallized.

Subsequently, an agreement having been reached between Jess Val Baker and Nixon, 'St Christopher's Beach Café' was planned to open in mid-May.[25] In preparation, Nixon set about decorating the basement room, draping fishing nets along its walls and installing furniture that he painted bright red, along with a counter with red and white stripes along its edge. Nixon was typically lavish in ordering stock but seems to have been effective in selling at least some of it, and one imagines him floating around the long room, charming and disarming holidaymakers as he took their orders. However, as Denys Val Baker later noted, by the end of the tourist season the café had only made about £150 in profit, and, following 'a real humdinger of an argument' with Jess, Nixon had walked out.[26] Jane Val Baker, then 11 years old, recalls how:

> Julian ordered masses of stuff, trying to take it up a level – but it was actually a beach café, and there weren't the customers, you know, not back in the 1950s. People wanted to come up off the beach and get their ice creams or their cakes. They didn't want all this beautiful stuff. Because he thought it was bigger than it was.

The café continued to open for three more summer seasons, each with a different manager, none of them delivering a worthwhile profit.

*

Alan Lowndes first met his wife Valerie while both were on holiday in France during the summer of 1959, she having travelled there from her native Sheffield. Following a brief courtship they married in October, then honeymooned for a week in Paris, from where Lowndes contacted Milne, asking him to find a flat or house for them to rent in St Ives. He had persuaded Valerie of the charms of the place, and she had agreed to move to live there with him. Of her first encounter with the town, she said years later, 'I was entranced with it, and still am. It's a place you really fall in love with, isn't it?' Their first day there was a hectic one:

> We travelled on that dreadful overnight train from London. I wasn't used to it then. John was giving a party that night. I remember it because I was exhausted. I was wearing my travel-stained clothes. You know, we'd landed in the morning; we'd looked at a flat, and moved into a flat. I *must* have got changed. But I was feeling shabby and worn out. I'd had no sleep the night before on that train. And I met all these people. There was Brian Wall, Willy [Wilhelmina] Barns-Graham, Boots [Mary] Redgrave, Bill Redgrave, Anthony Benjamin. Of course I didn't know any of them.[27]

Valerie recalls how she and Alan had met his friends the poet 'Sydney' (WS) Graham and his partner and fellow poet Nessie Dunsmuir in the pub, and how the couple had announced to them: '"There's a party at John Milne's, let's go." And it was quite a select party – Francis Bacon was there. I think it was probably given in his honour; I don't know. So somebody phoned John up and somehow wangled an invitation for Alan and me. I was quite bewildered by it all.'

Nixon wrote rather pretentiously to Brown about Bacon's arrival at Trewyn in a letter postmarked 27 September 1959: 'We have a new guest arrived to stay for a few days – Francis Bacon a very well known modern painter & one whose works I have admired for a long time. He has come down & is to take a flat here for the winter so that he can paint.'

Tony Shiels remembers Bacon's presence in St Ives and how he first stayed with Milne before finding a local flat to rent:

> Francis Bacon stayed at his house, with his boyfriend Ron [Belton], before renting a place by the harbour. Ron was a friendly, London, black leather lad ... he often wore a black leather biker's jacket ... He [Bacon] would sometimes drink in the Sloop [Inn] and seemed to enjoy the often ridiculous St Ives 'art colony' banter. I remember him trading barbed wisecracks with Peter Lanyon, on a couple of occasions, in the Sloop (although Peter preferred to drink in the Golden Lion and was only rarely to be seen in the Sloop).[28]

Whereas Nixon was able to deliver his own brand of spectacle to St Ives, Bacon brought with him the more sophisticated cachet of metropolitan queerness. He was a controversial figure whose artistic reputation had gained pace during the course of the decade. In 1954 his work had been shown at the Venice Biennale along with that of Ben Nicholson and Lucian Freud, and his first retrospective took place at London's Institute of Contemporary Arts in the following year. Bacon was now at a pivotal stage in his career, having signed a ten-year contract with the Marlborough Gallery in London little less than a year before. The gallery had lured Bacon away from the Hanover Gallery – to the intense chagrin of Erica Brausen, who, with a sole exception, had given him a show every year from 1949 onwards. (Incidentally, Brausen's gallery was financed by the immensely wealthy Arthur Jeffress, a queer friend of Brown's.) Bacon's first show with Marlborough was scheduled for March and April 1960, and he had decamped to Cornwall with the intention of finding somewhere quiet where he could focus on making the requisite work.

Bacon had not made arrangements to rent a studio space in St Ives prior to his departure from London, so he was fortunate when William Redgrave suggested he sublet No. 3 Porthmeor Studios from himself and Peter Lanyon. A large space, with windows looking directly onto the beach below, Bacon agreed to rent it for six months for the sum of £38, which he paid in advance. Other occupants of the studios during Bacon's time were Wilhelmina Barns-Graham at No. 1, Lucy Walsh at No. 2, Terry Frost at No. 4 and Trevor Bell at No. 8. There was also Patrick Heron at studio No. 5. Given Bacon's expressed loathing for abstract painting, one might assume that the two would not get on, but in fact Bacon and Belton spent a convivial Christmas Day with the Heron family at Eagle's Nest, their home at Zennor.[29]

Bacon was 50 that October, his working-class lover Belton 30 years younger. Famously, the artist enjoyed sessions of masochistic sex, during which he was whipped or beaten by his lovers. This had been true during his relationship with Peter Lacy, one of the great loves of his life, and it applied also with Belton, who was happy to give him a thrashing. Known to sleep with both men and women, Belton had also been an occasional boyfriend of the writer and broadcaster Dan Farson, a friend of Bacon's and a fellow Soho habitué. Handsome, and by several accounts very well-endowed,[30] Belton was also 'very sweet and charming in his rough-and-ready way, not boring', according to the antique dealer and aesthete Christopher Gibbs, who knew him around and about in Soho. At the same time, Gibbs was aware of Belton's 'latent violence' and how it was unleashed under the influence of alcohol. And that violence certainly surfaced in St Ives, where, after an argument with locals outside the Sloop Inn, Belton had punched Bacon in the face, dislodging a tooth.[31]

Although Nixon left St Ives not long after Bacon and Belton's arrival, Milne kept him abreast of developments in his missives from Trewyn. One such, dated 15 December, included this report:

> Ronnie has been misbehaving himself and creating disturbances in the pubs. He is really getting out of hand. He was even going to tear Francis apart last night and went around the streets (after midnight) shouting for him. Francis slept at Boots' and Ron tried to get at him even there. Boots threatened the police so – at 5am he eventually went home. Not a word of this to anyone by the way! On your honour! Poor Francis. I think he desperately wants to be rid of him – but how? It is impossible. We were right when we forecast trouble before the winter was out.

There are 13 extant paintings made by Bacon while in St Ives; some are likely to have been started there and finished on his return to London.[32] Among those made in St Ives is a portrait of Belton, painted, according to the artist's friend Lucian Freud, from life.[33] At 48.25 by 45.75 centimetres, *Head of a Man* (1959) is a relatively small, even intimate painting, cut down from a larger canvas. Appropriately, given its subject, the portrait combines tenderness with brutality, as the artist rearranged Belton's face in a kind of reversal of the violence his boyfriend often meted out to him. Another of Bacon's subjects was Boots – they had become good friends during the months in St Ives – and he made two portraits of her soon after he went back to London. Both entitled *Head of Woman* (both 1960), they share with the Belton portrait – and indeed other paintings from the same time – a particular use of viridian, deployed as a backdrop and in combination with the butchered flesh tones of the figures themselves. Claustrophobic in its intensity, the green is the antithesis of that one might associate with a 'St Ives' palette.

From St Ives, Bacon wrote to his friend the artist Denis Wirth-Miller (1915–2010), who lived in Essex with his partner and fellow friend of Bacon, the artist Richard Chopping (1917–2008). The following two letters are quoted here in full, retaining Bacon's idiosyncratic spelling and grammar.[34]

Segall House
The Wharf
St Ives
Cornwall

Monday 16th [November 1959]

Dearest Dennis
I often think of you and wonder how things are – it is terribly isolated here I have only finished 3 pictures so far but I hope they are a bit better but I could never live down here and am longing just to finish the work and leave. I often feel so lonely and unhappy. If Dennis dear you go to the Colony [the Colony Room Club in Soho] – would you try and find out from Leonard where Peter [Lacy] has gone if it is back to Mallorca or not and any news of him you can get – often I feel so distressed about him I do not know what to do. He wrote me such terribly unhappy letters and wanted to see me and then suddenly he wrote the letter I sent to Paul – I long to be free of Ron – I really wish he would get a job – I am in the most ghastly financial state I feel sure I shall never get straight – I do hope the work is going well. This is a stronghold of really dreary abstract stuff and they are all fanatical about it I can't tell you how bad it all is – do let me know if Frank's show is good if you see it [Frank Auerbach's show at Beaux Arts, London]. If you ever felt like coming down you know I would love to see you both if you have a car it is the most wonderful country around this part. When you have time I would love to hear your news
Fondest love to you both
Francis

> 21/12/59
> My dear Dennis
> Thank you so much for your letter – I will write to Erica [Brausen] I do not in the least want any book to be done. I have really learnt my lesson this time never to move from a large town I can't wait to leave this dump – I doubt I shall ever get the pictures done for the show – Fischer [Harry Fischer of Marlborough Fine Art] could not come down thank god as he had to go to Germany but is coming now on 15th of January. I hope some miracle will happen that I can do the work. I am very upset to hear Peter hawked that awful picture I did for him of his home in Barbados all round London I made it look as awful as I could so that he would like it – he said he would never try to sell it but there you are I think this has been quite the worst year of my life I just long to get back to London – I know the show will be a disaster even if I do get it done. Do write to me when you can I love to hear from you
> My fondest love and best wishes to you both –
> Love
> Francis

By early January, Bacon had had enough and returned to London, leaving Belton to tidy up the Porthmeor studio. Over the course of a few days, Belton burned works that the artist had rejected; others were transported to London. As William Redgrave wrote in his journal, the studio was left in a total mess: 'Francis used anything for mixing paint dishes bowls pans chairs and all four of the small tables caked with paint still wet.'[35]

Belton later returned to St Ives, as is plain from the following extract from a letter Milne wrote to Nixon in September 1960:

> Ronnie Belton has returned (perhaps I told you) – with a rather camp young man from town – name of Tom Chumley. In the Western [Hotel] last night – a local man thinking to embarrass them (what a hope) – said 'what lovely hair you have – give me a kiss dearie.' Tom, put his head down and gave him a long and passionate kiss (in a full public house) – which produced a face like the rising sun. To the man he said, 'If you weren't such an old queen – we'd ask you to join us for

dinner.' These sophisticated London ladies! They also went to the palais on Saturday and danced together!

Bacon also made return journeys to St Ives, for despite his declared reservations about the place he had made several friends there. It is unlikely that he stayed at Trewyn after that first visit in 1959; his preference was for hotels. He did, though, revisit the house on at least one occasion, signing the guest book, both for himself and on behalf of his boyfriend George Dyer, on 1 April 1965.[36]

*

Back for a time in London, Nixon was engaged to be married, and introduced his betrothed to Milne while he too was in the capital early in 1961. From St Ives, Milne wrote to Nixon on 18 January: 'It was so refreshing to see you (but *so* briefly) in London. You looked younger than ever and very well indeed. I was a little dumbfounded by your fiancé [*sic*] – and not at all sure what I should say or not say. Are you *really* getting married. Even now – I can scarcely believe it.'

Milne went on to ask what Brown thought of the situation; there is nothing in Brown's diary to suggest that he did, or indeed that he was aware of it. In fact, the engagement was to prove short-lived, as Mary, the woman in question – a widow with children – died, as is clear from a letter of sympathy Rodewald sent to Nixon on 23 March, in which he wrote that he was 'extremely sorry to hear that the episode of your engagement had such a cruelly tragic denouement' and that 'I hope that things will work out all right for her poor younger son, through your efforts on his behalf.'

The exact circumstances of Nixon's relationship with Mary have not surfaced, nor is there any verifiable information about the cause of her death. Soon afterwards, in April, Nixon sailed from Liverpool aboard the *Empress of Canada*, a cruise liner bound for Montreal, having gained employment as the ship's librarian. He spent the next few years working on cruise ships, with holding addresses for mail in Belfast, New York and Bermuda.

4 The Playground

All life, once lived, is fiction.[1]
—Norman Levine

During the periods when Nixon was away from St Ives, he and Milne corresponded frequently. Nixon's letters to Milne seem not to have survived – he may not have kept them – but Nixon retained Milne's letters, which are now held in a private collection. There are a great many of them, and read in their entirety they reveal much about the nature of the friendship between the two men. Evident throughout is a shared love of camp humour and gossip, subversive expressions of queer solidarity. And while the tone of many of Milne's letters is light-hearted, there are sometimes references to more serious matters as he entrusts his friend with details of his intimate thoughts and experiences. The earliest is dated 3 October 1958, only six months after the two had first met; here Milne addresses Nixon as 'Dearest daughter' and signs off with 'Yours, mama'. Not all of Milne's missives are dated, but quite often one is able to ascertain when a letter was written from certain of its contents or, where the envelope was retained, from a postmark. Although the last dated letter is from 3 September 1965, the correspondence continued for some time beyond then: for example, there is a letter from Tangier, which Milne first visited in 1967. In it he writes of meeting the actress Tallulah Bankhead in the louche Dean's Bar, a place of serious drinking frequented by a largely queer clientele that included Francis Bacon (whose lover Peter Lacy had at one time been resident pianist) and the socialite Hon. David Herbert (1908–1995), referred to by the writer Ian Fleming as 'the Queen Mum' of Tangier.[2] The majority of Milne's letters were penned at Trewyn, and they provide many insights into life in St Ives during the years of the correspondence. He reports on visitors to the house, local events and intrigue, with frequent asides about Hepworth, Boots Redgrave, Rodewald and others, along with many of the town's artists. Milne also wrote during or soon after forays to London, where he visited galleries and engaged in the social round, seeing friends and going to gay bars and clubs such as the Gigolo in Chelsea and the A & B in Soho.

One is struck by the many allusions to both his and Nixon's conquests and affairs in Milne's letters, which leave no doubts about their sexuality. Given the times in which they were written, letters such as these were potentially explosive, for, as Nixon was more aware than most, if intercepted or confiscated they could then be used as evidence in criminal proceedings. Most communication between gay men during this period was necessarily covert in nature. Conversations in public spaces sometimes utilised coded vocabulary, such as that of Polari, which draws on Romani and other languages as well as rhyming slang and back slang (words pronounced as though spelled backwards, for example *riah* for hair). Discretion was also often applied in written correspondence, with gay men sometimes using female forms of address or a single initial in order to conceal identity; envelopes bearing names and addresses could be destroyed by the recipients. One might add that many of Milne's letters are addressed to 'Julian' and signed 'John', the camp 'Julypoos' making occasional guest appearances.

Homosexuality remained a matter of contentious public and political debate in the 1960s, in the years both leading up to and well beyond the Sexual Offences Act, which received royal assent on 27 July 1967.[3] Only weeks before, on 7 June, BBC television screened 'Consenting Adults 1: The Men', a *Man Alive* documentary, in which a number of gay men, one retaining anonymity by keeping his back to the camera, spoke openly of their sexuality and experiences. An accompanying documentary, 'Consenting Adults 2: The Women', in which several lesbians were interviewed, was screened a week later. Filmed in black and white, the documentaries are notably even-handed and anti-sensationalist; they are records of love in a dark age, albeit one in which there were glimmers of light. Changes in public perceptions of homosexuality proved slow, however. Only two years before these broadcasts, an opinion poll found that 93 per cent of those questioned considered homosexuality a form of illness requiring medical treatment, a notion that persisted.[4] There was also an entrenched homophobia, much of it stoked by prejudicial newspaper journalism. Richard Blake Brown often glued cuttings from newspaper reports related to homosexuality into his journals. Among them are a couple from February 1962 concerning the murders of two men, both strangled in their London homes. They make for appalling reading, not only because of the gruesome nature of the crimes themselves but also the deeply hostile attitudes and dehumanising language of the reports. One, by Jack Miller from the 25 February edition of the scandal sheet *News of the World*, began: 'These are the twilight murders ... Two men, if you can call Norman Rickard and Alan Vigar men, lived in the twilight world of the homosexual and they died in the garrotter's noose.'

Reports vary on attitudes to homosexuality in St Ives during the years Milne lived there, although they were undoubtedly influenced in some quarters by press coverage such as this. Homophobia and sexism were by no means absent from the British art world, in which a blokey, sometimes misogynistic element often held sway. Asked about knowledge of Milne's sexuality among the St Ives art community, Brian Wall, who had arrived in the town in 1954, reflects: 'He fitted in: he was gay, but you know, so many people in the art world are – though at the time there was still major prejudice against gay people, in the 1950s. But he was completely accepted. It never struck me in any kind of way to think that he might be discriminated against because he was gay.'

While Jane Val Baker's recollections echo those of Wall, she speaks also of more widely held local attitudes:

> It was very weird, really: it wasn't until I got to London that I realised that a homosexual was not ordinary, or a lesbian. Being brought up in St Ives, it was quite normal, it really was. It was such an extraordinary little place. People's sexuality was 100 per cent accepted by everybody, even the fishermen ... So John and Julian, in my knowledge, were never harassed ... I never heard any talk. I never felt they were ostracised in any way whatsoever.

Yet such tolerance cannot have applied to the entire population of St Ives during the 1950s and 1960s, and one questions how deeply this liberality ran. For while they formed a familiar part of the local populace, the artists themselves – regardless of their sexuality – were viewed warily by some residents, as bohemian types of questionable moral character. Such feelings came against a backdrop of strict Methodism, in which churchgoing fishermen and their families looked for God's protection against the loss of life at sea. Trewyn, hardly visible behind its high perimeter walls, was additionally suspect once its reputation as a bastion of homosexuality had taken hold. Notwithstanding the recollections of Wall and Jane Val Baker, Milne's sexuality did set him at a remove. For instance, as Reg Singh remembers of staying with Milne for a time in the late 1950s: 'After I'd been staying there for a week or two, I took a girlfriend home, and when she realised I was staying [at Trewyn] I didn't see her for a few days, because it was so infamous, the place, she just thought I was gay.'

Many of Milne's visitors and guests were gay men who lived outside Cornwall. Among the most regular were close friends such as the actor Richard Wattis (1912–1975), who travelled down from his London home, and Stanley Sellers, an architect from Birmingham. From Manchester came Rodewald and his partner Victor Sayer. There were also the brothers Peter and Ronnie Lande, both gay and from a wealthy Manchester Jewish family. Peter worked in the family textiles business, Ronnie as a doctor in London, where he lived with his partner Walther, who often accompanied him to Trewyn. Like Rodewald, Sayer and Milne, the Lande brothers included Neville Rawlinson in their social circle. Other gay visitors included Milne's friend from his student days David Field, who worked as a textile designer, and Tony Warren, who, following the success of *Coronation Street*, became a public figure: one imagines him fascinated by Hepworth, given his penchant for strong northern women. London-based photographer Peter Kinnear was another of Milne's close gay circle, first met through Ronnie Lande, who introduced him to a number of St Ives artists. Kinnear went on to photograph much of Hepworth's and Milne's work.

Trewyn was not the only place where gay men socialised in and around St Ives. For even in remote Penwith, although some doubtless remained isolated and lonely, others were able to acquaint themselves with fellow homosexuals; it was a question of knowing where to look. Michael Hunt first moved to St Ives in 1961 while in his mid-twenties. Looking back, he describes what was then a thriving gay element in the town: 'At one time St Ives was really, really gay. The back bar of the Sloop was a gay bar. Lelant Beach was a paradise. It had the reputation as being a gay place. We used to have tea dances on Lelant Beach. There were orgies [on Lelant Beach]. The cottages were all gay. It was certainly gay when I came down here.'

There was also a lesbian contingent in St Ives, and what has been described as 'a very active lesbian pottery scene', of which the ceramicist Janet Leach (1918–1997) was a key figure.[5] She set up the New Craftsman Gallery on Fore Street in 1965, having first taken over a previous business, The Craftsmens Shop, run by her husband Bernard's eldest son David and local furnituremaker Robin Nance. Boots Redgrave – also known to have had lesbian relationships – was her business partner. The renamed business had a very different stock from the old one, which advertised its wares as 'baskets, toys and craftwork'. The New Craftsman Gallery stocked ceramics by Lucie Rie and Hans Coper, Scandinavian glass and tableware, and kitchenware by Le Creuset and Spong & Co. There were also paintings by St Ives artists, including Patrick Heron and Bryan Wynter. Michael Hunt worked at the shop for decades. When Janet died in 1997, she bequeathed the Leach Pottery to Boots, who then ran it until her own death five years later.

As Jane Val Baker indicated, there are no suggestions that Milne was ever subjected to any kind of direct and serious homophobic abuse in the town, nor evidence that the gay men who congregated at his house were victimised. There is, however, mention of a local queer-bashing case in a letter Milne sent to Nixon in New York, dated 25 June 1962:

> Big drama in St Ives over this case of two teds beating up an Australian Queen ... the idiotic Aussie, admitted in court last week, that he is *homosexual*! Fool – the one thing one should always deny. Now the case takes on an entirely new aspect. It has been transferred to Winchester – of *all* places! Glad I'm not involved in any way, tho', I do know one of the Teds verrry [*sic*] well.[6]

The case was reported on 1 June, the leading front-page story of the *St Ives Times and Echo* under the heading 'Injured Man in Flat: Two Charged'. A longer, more detailed report followed three weeks later. What Milne described as a 'beating up' was in fact a severe assault. As the newspaper described, the 42-year-old victim, who worked in a London hotel and was holidaying in St Ives, had been hospitalised. Suffering with a badly bruised and lacerated face and head, he awaited a preliminary report on a suspected fractured skull. The perpetrators, aged 19 and 27, were both labourers who lived locally and had been invited back to the older man's flat after drinking with him in a bar in the town. Much alcohol had been consumed in the hours before the attack took place. Charged jointly with causing grievous bodily harm and malicious wounding, the older of the two also facing a theft charge, they were both placed in custody before their trial at Winchester Assizes in July; the outcome of the judicial decision has not been traced.

*

Another long-term inhabitant of Trewyn was Milne's lifelong close friend from his Salford days, Katherine Dowd. For many years she had her own room at the house. The Val Bakers knew Dowd, and Denys wrote of her in one of his many volumes of autobiography. Describing her as an Irish girl from Manchester, he went on to recount that:

> [Her] life had become curiously split down the middle – by day she was a school-teacher at the local secondary school, by night she wandered through the sophisticated world of the art colony. A slim, slight, almost elf-like creature, a paradoxical mixture of Celtic emotionalism and Manchester hard logic, Katherine touched some spring of protectiveness in both Jess and me. She came from a working-class family and had fought her way up by merit and intellectual hard work. There was every reason why she should have achieved great things, yet somehow, almost perversely it often seemed, she had continued to drift. It was very much the same with her love life: she was vivacious and attractive and drew to her many interesting men, yet always she appeared to choose the most utterly wrong and hopeless ones.[7]

And so it was. Milne was always loyal to Dowd, but she began to drink heavily and could be trying at times.

The American ceramicist Byron Temple (1933–2002) also stayed at Trewyn for a substantial period. Born to a working-class family, he was raised on a rural farm in Indiana. He began to study ceramics and, like many of his generation, read Bernard Leach's hugely influential *A Potter's Book*, first published in 1940. In 1953 he moved to New York City, where he became a student at the Brooklyn Museum School under the potter Ka Kwong Hui. While stationed in Germany in 1955 during his army draft, Temple gained access to the camp's craft workshop and began to make pots and learn about glaze recipes. And it was when he was in Europe with the army that he first visited the Leach Pottery, founded by Bernard Leach (1887–1979) and the Japanese potter Shōji Hamada (1894–1978) in 1920. He conversed with nobody at the pottery, but had simply felt compelled to make the journey, a sort of pilgrimage. Later, awarded a scholarship to study at the Haystack School of Mountain Crafts in Maine, Temple met the Leach potter Kenneth Quick (1931–1963), who in 1959 had temporarily joined the school's teaching faculty. In the following year, Temple contacted Bernard Leach when he and Janet, who was born in Texas, were touring America. Following an interview at Ann Arbor during which Temple showed the couple a range of his pots, they offered him a position at the Leach Pottery.[8] Keen both to work and to learn, Temple's initial agreement with the Leaches was that he would remain with them for two years, a plan that served his future ambition to set up as a potter in his own right. He arrived in St Ives in September 1960 and, after a month of lodging elsewhere, moved to Trewyn, where he then lived for the next 18 months or so, during which time he and Milne developed a lasting friendship.

Shortly before leaving for England, Temple had fallen in love with another man, referred to in his diary as 'T'. Here are three extracts from his diary, the first from an entry dated 27 October 1960:

> Milwaukee started a separation I'm not certain I'll stand under for 3 years with B.L.[9] The station in Milw. was drowsily busy on a Fallish Sunday afternoon – mostly sailors returning from Sat. night binges. T and I sat on the hard benches – difficult in knowing what should

be said – the deep look into his eyes, the clean, sharp cut of his face, all are here today, as last week on a stroll to St Ives Western station, one track, the summer people departed – one glance and T is in Madison. The raising of my hand from my seat to T on the platform as we slowly pulled out of the station. Each time I find my hands in the same position I suddenly halt mental mechanics – all goes to Milwaukee. Mail has come to close the gap of distance and time but yet I question my being at the pottery. I've dreamed, planned and saved to come here. Ideals to solidify, these first 5 weeks are so rich I cannot yet separate. One cannot have the cake and eat it also – so I can not have my work with B.L. and receive love and give love as I've so longed to do – T came at a time following my decision and acceptance at St Ives – impossible to turn back – only time will tell of the outcome. Possibly T and I will sit down to read this together some years hence – love of love drives me on and I will achieve my goal here – not the end of a struggle but the start of the greater.

18 November 1960

Mail today from home ... No word for 3 weeks from T – my brain twisting at all times to reassure myself the relationship can hold – with growth on both sides a longing and fulfilment of my life to date.

27 November 1960

The house is empty except for myself as John Milne is in London – mainly for the exhibition of new Henry Moore sculpture.

... Mental pain – something very new for me – many banged knees and cut fingers – but inside me now is my interpretation of mental anguish – again what standards. The loss of someone near, a visual display, a real sense of lost friend – where to draw the line?

My pots grow each hour and I seem to just be beginning to utilize my mental abilities or at least able to 'touch' them. The problems and tensions of the Leach Pottery are only pin head size when I weight them along side my ideals and my standards. My pots look now more relaxed and with a 'probability' of speaking than the 1928–33 pots of B.L.'s ... Learned recently that he (B.L.) feels for *his* own pots only the past 5 years' work has *begun* to approach his standard. I do have hope in my overwhelming desire to contribute to my fellow man. The love

> of clay will drive me on and the love of T makes living all important in this Byron Temple world.[10]

Although in later years Temple identified as gay, during his stay in England he had relationships with women, one of them a fellow worker at the Leach Pottery, and in October 1961 he and Katherine Dowd were married in Penzance. Their union was short-lived, the reason behind it difficult to ascertain. Had Temple wanted to stay in Britain, it might have been a way to achieve permanent residence or right to remain, but that is doubtful as by the following year he had returned to America alone. In the month of his marriage to Katherine he had written to Bernard Leach, then visiting Japan, telling him that he was leaving the pottery in spite of their verbal agreement that he would stay for two years, and that he knew that in doing so he was letting Leach down, and was grateful for having been 'part of the crew'.[11] The 'problems and tensions' at the pottery – referred to in his diary – related to certain personalities there, and, finding them impossible to work with, Temple decided to leave. Katherine subsequently lived and worked abroad for many years, teaching English in Africa and in Italy, where she had a long love affair.

*

The grey skies and shorter days of the winter months often exacerbated Milne's sense of isolation. Being alone in the house intensified his insecurities, and for company – and it seems Milne longed for company – he would place advertisements, such as this one from 17 October 1962, in the personal column of *The Times*:

> CORNWALL – Young bachelor offers gentleman share of seaside house, winter months, exchange light duties and slight expenses. – Write Box P.1404, *The Times*, E.C.4.

One wonders what motives lay behind these advertisements. Was it that he simply wanted the company of other queer men, so that his own sexuality presented no issues? Advertisements such as his were coded for interpretation by gay men – 'young bachelor' the key phrase here – a fact of which Milne was entirely cognisant. He certainly kept an eye open for such things; in another of his letters to Nixon (undated), he included: 'I have noticed that the Times P.C. has been quite "lively" recently. Did you see the bachelor who wanted to take a young male comp – to Paris, Geneva, Monte Carlo, Rome, Brindesi and Athens (*and* Corfu) – ?'

While St Ives could feel especially isolated during winter, it was also a time of parties, which proliferated during the out-of-season months when the town was emptied of tourists. Parties often began with people meeting at the Sloop Inn overlooking the harbour, from where they progressed to other venues. One such was the Val Bakers' house, St Christopher's, where, as Tony Shiels describes, Jess proved an 'enthusiastic party hostess'.[12] Trewyn was also very much on the circuit, the scene of many parties. Of them Michael Hunt states intriguingly: 'I couldn't possibly tell you about the parties there, because they were scandalous.'[13] Reg Singh also attended a couple of the parties at the house: 'Were they wild? Not that wild. There were men trying to seduce me, you know', he recalls with much laughter.

The artist, musician and writer Jonathon Xavier Coudrille was born in 1945 on the Lizard Peninsula. Growing up, he never visited Trewyn, but knew of its reputation:

> I lived with my parents and my father warned me to stay 'well away', as he was strongly homophobic and deeply puritanical – strange for someone in both the visual arts and theatre who painted nudes.
>
> I could only observe that the visitors to Trewyn had very covetable motor cars, excellent clothes and included many recognisable faces; certainly Richard Wattis was in frequent evidence. My mother observed that John Milne looked somewhat like Francis Bacon, and that his friends 'always looked a lot cleaner than the other artists'.
>
> The parties; Hedonistic? Contextually, VERY wild parties went on then throughout the arts community, and few marriages survived long. Certainly John Milne's parties were enviably noisy and protracted, and on occasion it was reported that there was violence or accidents involving actual physical injury; there was a certain antipathy in the climate of the times between the Artists and the Town, and

> people love to exaggerate. Obviously alcohol was involved, but I don't recall any talk of illegal substances.[14]

Coudrille may in fact be thinking here not solely of the parties at Trewyn but of those at Hanter Chy, the downstairs flat where Heather Jameson lived with her partner Eddie Craze, a volatile Cornishman who owned a garage on Downalong. And it was at Hanter Chy that the rather more raucous parties took place. Dark-haired and voluptuous, Heather enjoyed the sensual pleasures of food, drink and sex. She is remembered fondly as a generous woman whose hospitality extended to putting on big Sunday lunches for assorted friends. She and Milne were close friends and, as Brian Wall recollects:

> There was a whole social scene around John and the people who lived downstairs ... a big social scene: John, Heather and Eddie Craze. He was a local boy. So they had a social scene. I was a very minor part of that ... Occasionally after drinking at the Sloop or somewhere everybody would go back to Heather's, and then John would come down perhaps with his friend. And sometimes we'd go upstairs ... there was a great deal of drinking going on, and stuff like that.

Nancy Patterson (b.1936) arrived in St Ives in March 1959, living first close to the centre on the Stennack, then for a couple of months with Patrick and Delia Heron at Eagle's Nest. Soon afterwards she met Anthony Benjamin – she was to become his second wife following his separation from the weaver Stella Benjamin – and the couple moved to live at the former stable building at the back of Trewyn. She too remembers the frequent parties, both at the house and the flat: scenes of drunkenness, with loud noise, and occasional fights when things turned nasty.

Patterson recalls that Heather Jameson had a collection of work by friends among the St Ives artists:

> I think that Heather became a collector, more because she liked the artists and wanted to support them, than wanting to actually own a lot of art. But her home downstairs ... was a perfect place for the art to be seen at best advantage: plain white walls, grey slate floors, minimal

> furniture... it could have been a gallery, but it was used more as an artists' club. Heather and Eddie were very generous (possibly too generous) and great party hosts ... the drink flowed very freely and the slate floor was often awash with the overflow. She had a couple of Ant's [Anthony Benjamin's] paintings (probably in trade for rent?), also a couple of Brian Wall's early wooden constructions (very Nicholson/Mondrian-ish) as well as a larger welded metal piece and several Bob Law paintings, which were ahead of their time but now well regarded ... There was local art on all available walls as well as sculpture.[15]

The Canadian writer Norman Levine (1923–2005) based a number of works of fiction on life in St Ives, his characters lightly veiled representations of his friends and acquaintances in the town. A native of Ottawa, Levine had succumbed to St Ives on his first visit during the summer of 1949, having sailed from Canada to England that June. As he later described, 'My first reaction – I hadn't seen anything like this. The colours of the sea, the sky, the clouds, the far shore fields. Godrevy Lighthouse in the bay (I found out this was Virginia Woolf's *Lighthouse* even though she placed it in Scotland).'[16]

Levine had travelled to England to study on a postgraduate fellowship for ex-servicemen, commencing that September at King's College, London. Afterwards he decided to remain in England and, following his marriage early in 1952, decamped with his wife Margaret to St Ives, where they were to have three daughters. He was to live and work in the town for over 40 years. Levine became close friends with Peter Lanyon and wrote of how when leaving the Golden Lion pub together one Saturday afternoon in September 1959 they bumped into Francis Bacon, accompanied by a young man; this would have been Ronnie Belton. From this first impromptu encounter, Levine and Bacon formed an enduring friendship. They would sometimes meet in London, and Bacon would telephone in advance of travelling to St Ives to ask Levine to secure a hotel room for him. His visits, two or three times each year, continued until Margaret Levine's death in 1978.[17] The writer based a character on Bacon in *From a Seaside Town*, a novel published in 1970, in which St Ives – the town of the title – is renamed 'Carnbray'. When telling his friend that he wished to write about him in its pages, Bacon responded by saying, 'Make me the way I am. Make me a queer', to which Levine replied that he fully intended to do so.[18] The book is narrated by 'Joseph Grand', a Canadian travel writer stranded with his wife and children in a remote seaside town. Bacon appears as 'Charles Crater', a name surely derived from that of the painter Charles Breaker, who lived at Newlyn with his partner and fellow artist Eric Hiller, both of whom Levine would have known. His lightly fictionalised depiction of Bacon, clearly based on personal knowledge, constitutes a fascinating portrait of the man. It includes the following vignette of the artist in St Ives:

> When he comes down to Carnbray it is to get away from London and the kind of life he leads. But for us his presence is a high point in our lives. People I don't see all year round will phone up to ask if Charles is down. He will take Emily and me out to a good restaurant. Then go by himself for a ride on a bus across the moors. Or have tea in a crowded cheap café with lots of people about.[19]

Levine based a number of his fictional characters on artist friends: another example is the figure of 'Henry', based on Terry Frost, in the story *Soap Opera*.[20] He also wrote factual accounts of artists and their work, including an affectionate anecdotal piece for a posthumous show of Alan Lowndes's paintings at the Penwith Galleries in 1979.[21]

Nine years before the appearance of *From a Seaside Town*, Levine had published *One Way Ticket*, a volume of short stories, all but one of which had been written between 1956 and 1960 (the exception being 'A Sabbath Walk', from 1950, based on the St Ives primitive painter Alfred Wallis). The first and longest story – in fact a novella of over 60 pages – dates from 1960, and although no place name is given, it is very obviously set in St Ives. Entitled 'The Playground', it is narrated by 'Bill Stringer' (Levine again), who, in setting out his *mise en scène*, describes the town's harbour front, stone piers and beaches, all eminently recognisable to those who know the place. Adapting the rather detached, somewhat cynical tone common to much of his work, Levine summons forth the boredom and inertia of seaside towns, the 'determined gaiety' of tourists, and the meat and drink of continual gossip upon which the town's inhabitants thrive. He writes too of social change: of how, for instance, locals were manoeuvred to live in council housing on the outskirts so that those more prosperous could take over the centre. His cast are those he encountered at the summer parties of 1959, many of them easily identifiable. Denys and Jess Val Baker are 'Julius and Bernice November'; their house on Porthmeor Road, with its large bare room opening directly onto the beach, re-christened 'Atlantic Waves' (although in Levine's telling it opens not onto Porthmeor but the smaller Porthgwidden Beach). At the centre of the story is 'Driftwood Heights' (Trewyn), deemed 'the best place for parties'. Milne, 'a pleasant shy young man of 27', appears in the guise of 'Garry Diamond', Nixon as 'Red Cutler' and Rodewald as 'Sir Edward Lolli'. There is also 'Rosalie Grass', who combines characteristics of both Katherine Dowd and Heather Jameson. An entertaining and gossipy tale, 'The Playground' provides an insight into the social scene it describes from the point of view of an insider with a keen observational eye. It is marked by a sardonic humour that one appreciates all the more when aware of the characters upon whom it is based. The passage of most interest for the purposes of the present narrative describes Bill's first encounter with Garry, Red and Rosalie on the beach:

> 'You know who you remind me of?' Red Cutler said.
>
> 'I've been mistaken for a lot of people,' I said.
>
> 'Joan Fontaine.'
>
> I thought it very funny.
>
> I saw them again a couple of days later on the front.
>
> A frigate had come in the Bay for a courtesy call. It was in the local paper that the Navy would be guests of the town for the weekend ... Garry and Red were promenading along the front with everyone else. Red was wearing a black silk cape that was crimson on the inside. They said they had prepared a meal back at Driftwood Heights and they were going to pick up some sailors and bring them back. They were as excited as any child with the thought of adventure.[22]

As word spread following publication, 'The Playground' became something of a local sensation, the story's contents embellished in the retelling, often by those who had not in fact seen a copy of the book.

There was much talk among its thinly disguised protagonists of grounds for libel. Of those Levine depicts, 'Julius November' is the author of 'numerous joke books' and the town's worst gossip; he also has a wooden leg, suggesting that Levine based the character not solely on Denys Val Baker but also on Norman Stocker, who indeed had a wooden leg. Stocker, who worked for Hepworth on her large sculptures, was gay, and close to – although not necessarily intimate with – the potter Kenneth Quick, himself gay. While the figure of 'Rosalie Grass' suggests a woman free with her sexual favours, it is the character based on Nixon that comes across worst of all, so much so that one concludes Levine felt a strong animus towards him. He is easily identified as 'Red Cutler': 'a plump bouncy boy of twenty-five ... Gossip had it that he lived in a fantasy world. That he lied. And helped himself to other people's change when nobody was around.' There are other references that serve to identify Nixon, among them his 'rich, nervous voice', his tangerine bathing trunks, pink and blue cashmere knitwear, and a letter he addresses to 'Ludwig Jones'.[23]

It was at least a year after the book's publication before Nixon was alerted to his characterisation in Levine's story. Yet to read it himself, he wrote from Bermuda to his solicitor in Birkenhead, informing him that he had heard there might be grounds for libel. Overdrawn at the bank – to which Brown and Rodewald were both acting as his guarantors – he probably imagined successful litigation leading to a substantial payout. Then, having received from Ronnie Lande a copy of Levine's book, Nixon's solicitor wrote to him on 20 February 1963, enclosing copies of 'the offending pages' and asking him to explain how exactly he could be identified within them, stipulating that unless he was substantially identifiable there would be no cause of action. In a long and detailed reply, Nixon enumerated the various ways in which he, Milne, Katherine Dowd, Rodewald and Trewyn were recognisable in Levine's narrative and, in referring to the scene on the beach, wrote:

> Of the occasion he mentions – true the Navy were paying a courtesy call to St Ives – in connection with the local St Ives Arts Festival weeks in June. We were actually on our way to the ships which were open to the public – & indeed it was our intention to invite a number of the

> sailors & *officers* back to the house – for we had organised a party & they would swell the numbers.[24]

Nixon goes on to make a comprehensive itemisation of the ways in which he could be identified in Levine's portrayal. He mentions also that he understands that Milne did not come off so badly in Levine's characterisation, and that, not wishing to court bad publicity, he has therefore decided against pursuing legal action. There followed another letter from Nixon's solicitor on 15 May, in which he stated that, having read Levine's story, and in the light of what he had himself outlined in his letter, he agreed there was a prima facie cause of action, and that he had now written to the publisher, printer and to Levine himself to that effect and was awaiting their replies. He wrote once more on 27 June, informing him that the solicitor acting for Levine and his publisher repudiated liability, and asking Nixon for his instructions.

Writing to Nixon on 12 June, in a corroboration of what Nixon had told his solicitor, Milne reported:

> Rubenstein Nash Ltd, whom I saw in London last week, advised me *not* to start proceedings against Norman Levine. They said that if it were to go to court, unless I was prepared for it to be in all the newspapers – I would find it too embarrassing and it may be too late to withdraw once I'd started the ball rolling. What have *you* done about it[?] After the Duchess of Argyll *and* Mr Profumo, I'd hate to create a third scandal around poor little me – even for few hundred pounds.

At the point at which Milne wrote his letter, the Profumo scandal was playing out in public. John Profumo, Secretary of State for War and husband of actress Valerie Hobson, resigned from the government on 5 June 1963 after admitting an affair with Christine Keeler, something he had previously denied in a parliamentary statement that March. The so-called 'Profumo affair' was one of a series of sex scandals involving prominent figures, including the Duchess of Argyll, and generated huge publicity.

Nixon did not in the end pursue libel action. His decision was surely based – in part, at least – on an awareness of the potential for a lonely and exposed place in the spotlight, in which his 1954 trial and hospitalisation might be revisited, both in the courtroom and the newspapers. And so there the matter ended. No clear evidence of litigation by others has surfaced, and Levine's book was published in a second, unaltered edition later that same year of 1963.

Eddie Craze was a generous host, and some of those who attended parties at Hanter Chy took advantage of his innate kindness. Denys Val Baker wrote of him as 'tortured – even schizophrenic', of how he seemed torn between his Cornish background and the bohemian world of artists and their hangers-on with whom he found himself involved, and of how his plight became exacerbated by financial worries.[25] In 'The Playground', Levine includes what appears a straightforward account of Craze's suicide. Giving him the name 'Starkie', he recounts how, after partying followed by arguments on New Year's Eve, he had disappeared and was found dead in his garage on the first morning of 1960. Milne wrote to tell Nixon the news, ten days or so after the event:

> A very tragic thing occurred on New Years Eve – when, after dinner at Truro – Eddie got into one of his neurotic states – had a tremendous row, and then left us in the middle of the row – miles from St Ives.
>
> We did not know what happened to him after that but – it was discovered the next morning that he had committed suicide by gassing himself. The funeral is tomorrow at 2.30.
>
> I will write more when I have time but I thought that you ought to know. Heather is desperately upset so please don't ring her – she can't speak on the phone – Love John.

In his story Levine wrote, too, of the suicide's aftermath:

> There is always a little excitement after a death, especially a violent one. And for the next few days people talked and discussed Starkie. Some said it was his financial position, that he couldn't keep up Rosalie's 'salon' and the manor house. Others said he really wanted to be a painter; that he was becoming homosexual; that he realized how corrupt he had become. Others said he wasn't intelligent enough to become corrupt. And in the Back streets Cornish parents used

> Starkie's death as a warning to their restless children to 'keep away from them artists'.[26]

Boots's husband Bill Redgrave recorded the fallout in his journal, in an account indicative of an ominous, long-standing resentment threaded with homophobia:

> Peter Lanyon in the Sloop last night talking only to me but with artists listening said 'Feeling is running pretty high. You should listen to those people up in the town – I dare not go in to the Golden Lion. The locals having been dropped by Eddie who made new friends among the artists ... are in an ugly mood. They've got it in for them and one of the first places they think of is Trewin [*sic*] and those queers. They hate all the goings on – the parties which always annoy the neighbours.'[27]

Upon reading this account, one wonders if Craze's death had been the catalyst for Levine's decision to write 'The Playground'. It certainly acted as a marker for many, including some artists and their families. As Nancy Patterson recounts, 'When Eddie Craze committed suicide that was very much the end of the "fun" for me, and I wanted to leave; and by coincidence Anthony [Benjamin] won an Italian government scholarship to study in Italy ... and so we left together in October 1960.'[28]

Notwithstanding local resentment, after Heather had undergone a period of mourning, hedonism was resumed at Hanter Chy. Michael Hunt recounts how the parties 'began on Saturday night and ended on Tuesday'. And there are plentiful anecdotes, some surely apocryphal, not all of which emanate from those who were in attendance.

*

In a dispatch to Nixon dated 1 December 1960, Milne reported:

> Barbara has scored a local victory. For some time now, she has been complaining about the dreadful noises of the Palais de Danse, and the disturbances of people leaving there, late at night with motor bikes

> and cars. Today's *St Ives Times* (*and* the other *Times*) – announced her solution – 'Miss Hepworth *purchases* the Palais de Danse'. Perhaps you read of it. That's one way of getting quietude. All it needs now is for someone to buy ST IVES and keep out all those noisy tourists!

Hepworth's purchase of the former cinema and dance hall not only reduced local noise but also enabled her to work on significant large-scale commissions, such as her *Winged Figure* (1961–62) for the John Lewis department store building in central London, and *Single Form* (1961–64), her memorial to Dag Hammarskjöld for the United Nations headquarters in New York.

Only months before Hepworth's acquisition of the Palais de Danse, Milne had described recent antics at the venue in a letter to Nixon. Although undated, it was probably written in late August or early September. The event was a party given by the Penwith Society:

> It was an 'artist's hop', and filled with tourists – agog to see what went on. We gave them their fill of spectacle. The Trewyn contingent arrived – (not to say *fell*) – into the hall about half way through the dance – which, until then, had been comparatively quiet – with great aplomb! I escorted 'Maria', a German 'artist' who is living at Heather's. I wore white trousers, she – black leather ones. I remember nothing of what happened but I was told – later – that we created a sensation. Fortunately, Barbara left before we arrived so she did not witness our drunken debacle. After the dance (at 1am-ish), we continued the party at Heather's – until well into the night – or rather, the morning. I finished up being put to bed by a young farmer – (who spent what was left of the night with me) ...
>
> Your policeman sounds divine but *do* be careful. – remember all the stories one hears of police confidence tricks etc.

The 'young farmer' appears again in a letter of 12 September 1960: 'I have a new friend. A farmer on holiday, from Kettering (wherever that is) and he comes up to see me most evenings ... Cosmo plans a visit, early in October, and my girl friend from Canada.'

The 'girl friend from Canada' was a writer named Isabel Batcheller, here making a first appearance in Milne's letters. Born in Thunder Bay in north-west Ontario, Isabel had lived in England for a time as early as 1948, initially in Cheltenham. She and Milne may have met when she arrived in St Ives in 1956 to visit Hepworth, about whom she was to write an article for the quarterly magazine *Canadian Arts*. Commissioned to coincide with forthcoming exhibitions of Hepworth's work in Toronto and Montreal, 'Barbara Hepworth, Sculptor' was published in that year's winter edition.[29] Subsequently, around 1957, Isabel moved to live in St Ives, renting a small house on the harbour. As a single woman from North America she became a figure of local interest and intrigue, and it was shortly after her arrival that she received an invitation to come to dinner at Trewyn. Ten years older than Milne, she was to become besotted with him. How long she spent living in St Ives is uncertain, but it appears that by 1960 she was again domiciled in Canada, from where over the years she made a series of visits to St Ives, staying each time at Trewyn. She had spent a number of weeks there during that autumn and winter of 1960, as outlined in the following extracts from Milne's letters to Nixon:

> 12 November
> The house is beginning to quieten down now that most of my visitors have left. It's not lonely really, because Isabel is still here and Byron permanently around too and, of course, the Jameson gang below ... Jess and Denys had another party last Saturday. To me, it was the usual performance, but Isabel was quite surprised at the abandoned way people carried on. There were no real fights but Sydney Graham was knocked down by a local boy. Heather's John ~~(yours) (mine)~~ (ours) – got frightfully drunk and made a pass (several) at Isabel. I was rather bored because I have had to lay off drinking much for the past three weeks owing to a mild attack of jaundice.

> 1 December 1960
> Isabel left this evening after a champagne Christmas dinner. She is a very sweet person and I have so much enjoyed having her here these past weeks. She is a mature person and a good, steadying influence, in this chaotic and unbalancing community. Byron too is [a] reliable and steady sort of person to have in the house. He looks after everything very well and he is very considerate.

Isabel had a son, Guy Milne, who lives in Ottawa. Born in Vancouver, he was two years old when his mother and Milne married at the registry office in Penzance on 4 May 1967. He believes that the marriage was entered into for his benefit, to legitimise him by providing him with a surname. By prior mutual consent, Isabel and Milne were later divorced, with a decree nisi issued on 22 February 1973. They remained in regular communication for the rest of Milne's life. Isabel did not remarry and continued to be known as Isabel Milne.[30]

*

In was in St Ives that Nixon first met Milne's friend Stanley Sellers (1933–2013), with whom he formed a relationship that proved one of the most genuinely important in his life. Eighteen months or so his senior, Sellers was born in Birmingham, where he studied at the city's school of architecture. The majority of his professional career was spent with two Birmingham-based architectural practices, at which he worked on many major projects; one of these, the Mander Centre in Wolverhampton, incorporated – at Sellers's initiative – Hepworth's bronze *Rock Form (Porthcurno)*, installed in 1968. A cultured man with a love of art and classical music, Sellers became good friends with Hepworth and several other St Ives artists. He amassed a large collection of ceramics, including pots by Bernard Leach and Lucie Rie, which he bequeathed to the Birmingham Museum and Art Gallery. He also became a respected potter in his own right. His life partner, from around 1969, was Richard Butt, a BBC Radio 3 producer who was for many years conductor of the Birmingham Bach Choir.

Sellers's intimate relationship with Nixon appears to have lasted several years but was irreparably damaged when Nixon, back in St Ives between cruise liner voyages in the autumn of 1964, began an affair with a solicitor who had many connections with the local artistic community. A divorcé in his early fifties, Tom became the latest in a string of older men to become infatuated with him. The typewritten letters he sent to Nixon, often two or three pages long, were written at first obsessively, on consecutive days. They show a man both besotted and in turmoil about his emotions and sexuality. Many are addressed to Nixon at his stopover addresses in New York and Bermuda. Read in their entirety, they document an enthralment gradually turning to cynical disillusion as the manipulative and underhand aspects of Nixon's character sunk in. The first, dated 18 November 1964, was written soon after Nixon had again set sail:

> Julian, dearest boy,
>
> It was very sweet of you to dash off the short note before sailing. I too enjoyed our time together almost beyond measure ...
>
> Dear Julian, and I feel that you are very dear, there is a whole world of difference between us. You *seem* to be happy floating in your balloon amongst pink clouds. I could float for part of the time – as indeed I have done since I met you – but I would drag your balloon down into the dark realistic clouds of such tedious and mundane matters as living within one's income. The pink clouds would be gone and the pretty balloon would become a tattered rag.
>
> Believe me, I type this with a lump in my throat and tears in my eyes: this is true. It has been sheer delight to know you for these few days and I want to see you whenever you come to England on leave. You have done a great deal for me in this short time and I shall never forget this: I was flat and finished when we met but now I feel that I am alive again. I only wish and hope that you are able to feel and say that I have done something, however little, for you.
>
> Ever most affectionately,
>
> Tom

Notwithstanding the ambiguity in Tom's note, their affair did in fact continue, and by February 1965, his *Empress of Canada* days now over, Nixon was back in St Ives, where Tom provided him with some kind of paid employment. He had got himself into great difficulty with gambling debts while working on the cruise liner, both off- and onboard ship; and then ran up various debts in St Ives, including some while living for a time at Tom's apartment. It is clear that by July the situation had become altogether too heated for Nixon to contend with, for in a letter to Richard Blake Brown, written at Trewyn, he reported that he was about to leave and would be staying 'more or less indefinitely' with Reg Moon at Henley-in-Arden in Warwickshire. Soon after his departure he threatened Tom with blackmail, implying he would send some of his intimate letters to the Law Society, a threat that appears not to have been carried out. Over the 11-month duration of his correspondence, Tom's endearments ceased and were replaced by increasingly damning assessments of Nixon's character, describing him, among other things, as a common cheat and congenital liar. Tom was no pushover, and Nixon had taken on more than he could handle.

Tom's final letter to Nixon – written after a gap of more than four years – dates from April 1970 and begins: 'My dear Julian, Thank you for your letter which I much appreciate.' It concludes:

> You are energetic, enthusiastic, intelligent and excellent company and you could lead a grand life if, without prejudicing those qualities, you could still a little that demon which is your greatest enemy and which drives you relentlessly from one place and situation to another.
>
> The very best of luck,
>
> Tom

By now Tom had lessened his ties with St Ives and was working in a managerial capacity for a charity elsewhere. He and his former wife had become reconciled, and were later remarried.

5 Le Quartier St Ives

> St Ives in the 1960s remained a good place for lost souls to look, learn and live in poverty. The extraordinary light and the neolithic landscape between St Ives and Zennor made up for a lot.[1]
>
> —Tanya Harrod

The photographer Ida Kar (1908–1974) was a rather exotic presence in London during the 1950s and 1960s. Born to Armenian parents in Russia, she met her future husband Victor Musgrave (1919–1984) while living in Cairo during the Second World War, when he was stationed in Egypt with the Royal Air Force. They married in 1944 and later moved to London, where Musgrave – a writer and promoter of avant-garde art – established Gallery One in 1953. There he exhibited the work of European artists including Yves Klein, as well as India- and Pakistan-born artists such as F N Souza and Anwar Jalal Shemza, and gave the English painter Bridget Riley her first show. Having established her London studio, Kar went on to produce documentary and portrait photography, achieving particular renown for the latter. She was highly prolific, travelling widely in order to photograph her subjects on their home ground. They were drawn largely from the arts and included Georges Braque, T S Eliot, Alberto Giacometti, Le Corbusier, Jean-Paul Sartre and Dmitri Shostakovich.

Kar had begun to work regularly for the *Tatler and Bystander* magazine in 1958, and they commissioned her to travel to St Ives in June 1961 to make a series of photographs of its artists, subsequently published as a picture story over four pages of the July issue under the title 'Le Quartier St Ives'.[2] The text accompanying the article began: 'It's a long way from the Left Bank and the local inns don't keep bistro hours, but so many artists have moved their homes and studios to the neighbourhood that this Cornish fishing town can fairly be called Le quartier St Ives.' The artists featured included both Milne and Hepworth, along with Denis Mitchell, Peter Lanyon, Terry Frost, Michael Heard, Patrick Heron, Alan Lowndes, Tony Shiels and an Australian potter 'who prefers to call himself just Buster', who was then working with Bernard Leach's eldest son David in Devon and in town on a visit. There was also Monica Wynter, wife of the artist Bryan Wynter, who was in hospital during Kar's visit. Monica was photographed with their baby son.

In the published set of black-and-white photographs, Hepworth, the sole female artist represented, is shown in her garden with her bronze sculpture *Curved Form (Trevalgan)* (1956). The accompanying caption describes her as 'easily the district's most famous resident'. Milne, meanwhile, is shown embracing his aforementioned *The Kiss* (1957), in Portland stone, and is described as 'a painter as well as a sculptor'. The article goes on to note: 'At 30 Milne has exhibited in many countries and carried out several specially commissioned works. He runs a guest house in St Ives during the summer – "to keep myself working here for the rest of the year".'

Kar took many photographs of Milne during her visit to Trewyn, the majority in square-format black and white (there also exists a single colour transparency). There is a sequence shot in the garden, and several in which Milne reclines or sits on the wall of his upstairs balcony. There are also a couple for which Kar used the balcony as her vantage point, focusing her camera on Milne as he stands in the garden below, town and harbour visible in the distance. Throughout, Milne appears a picture of sun-bronzed health. He wears cotton trousers, sandals and a short-sleeved shirt, or – as in the published photograph – is shirtless. In several he smiles or smirks as he flirts with the camera. There is also a portrait taken inside the house, in which he is seated on the floor, a white coffee cup and saucer beside him and behind him a bookcase on which are displayed two of his sculptures: the bronze relief with wires *Les Baux* (1959), and an unidentified piece in Nigerian guarea that resembles, and may be an earlier version of, *Totemic Form* (1963). There is also a large abstract canvas – very likely by Milne's friend Anthony Benjamin – propped against the wall on top of the bookcase. The *Tatler and Bystander*'s description of Milne as 'a painter as well as a sculptor' is erroneous, as there are no known paintings by him. There are, though, many drawings, including some quite large in scale, and these works on paper were probably considered paintings when it came to writing the article caption.

'Le Quartier St Ives' presents a rather idealised view of the town as a place where artists are integrated into the life of a thriving community, as people's neighbours and fellow workers. While both Terry Frost and Michael Heard are seen in their studios, Alan Lowndes is photographed alongside local fisherman Bill Ninnis on Smeaton's Pier, and Tony Shiels walks towards the camera accompanied by his wife and two children among the bustle of Fore Street shoppers. The article serves as a reminder that the town's artists were drawn there from all points of the compass. Of those featured, Peter Lanyon, as a native of St Ives, is an exception. Denis Mitchell, resident since 1930, had grown up in Swansea; while Frost, originally from Leicester, moved to live there soon after the war on the recommendation of the painter Adrian Heath, befriended when both were prisoners of war. Shiels, born in Salford, had grown up in St Anne's, near Blackpool; Heron was originally from Leeds. There was also among the artistic community a notable diversity in terms of class. Lanyon, photographed in the garden at Little Parc Owles, the large house he shared with his wife Sheila (née St John Browne) and their six children at Carbis Bay, was certainly middle class, as too were Bryan Wynter and Patrick Heron; the latter is shown with his wife Delia and their two daughters standing on a rocky outcrop in the grounds of Eagle's Nest. There were, though, also many working-class artists in St Ives in the 1950s and 1960s: Milne was one of them, as was fellow sculptor Brian Wall. Born in 1931 in Paddington, then a poor district of London, Wall arrived in St Ives in the summer of 1954; at the time he was working as a painter but within two years was concentrating exclusively on sculpture, at first in painted wood, then welded steel. Like many other artists moving to the town, on arrival he needed to earn money to cover basic living costs and so worked for a time at the Tregenna Castle Hotel. He quite soon got to know other artists, including Denis Mitchell, whose studio in the centre of town was a meeting place for various artist friends. It was Mitchell who recommended him to Hepworth in 1956, when she needed an assistant with experience in working with

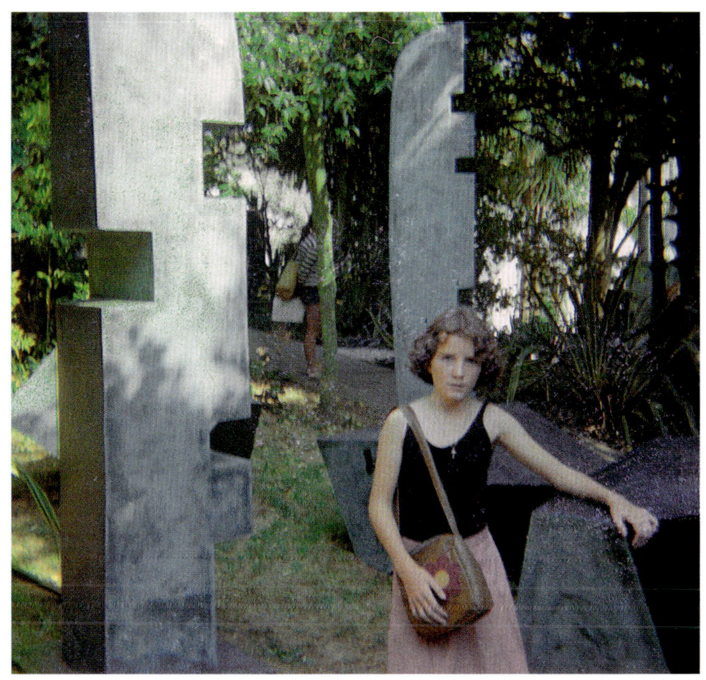

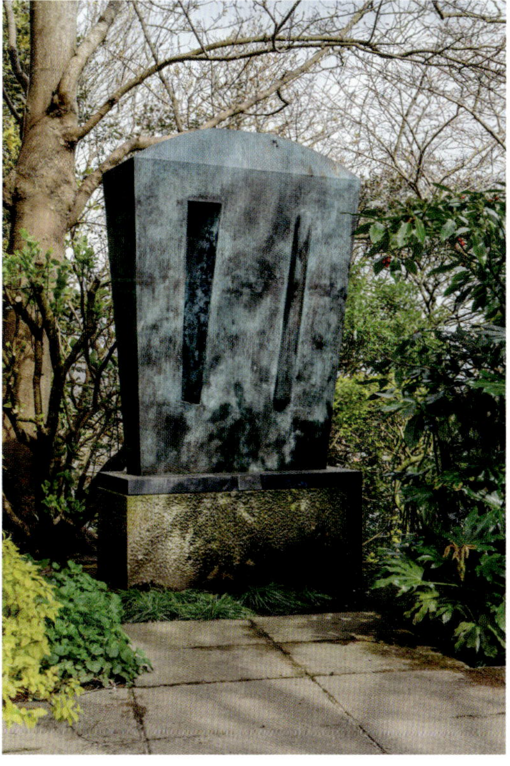

above: Lydia Massey at the Barbara Hepworth Museum, 16 August 1976

left: John Milne, *Megalith II* (1974), Trewyn Gardens, St Ives

above: John Milne, *Seated Figure*, 1949, terracotta

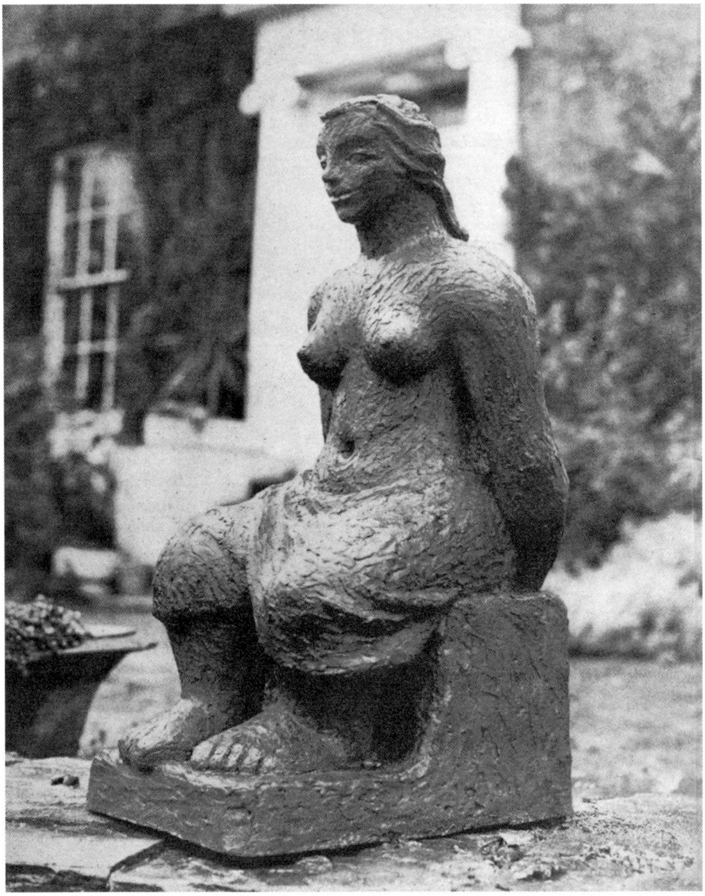

right: John Milne, *Minerva*, 1952, pre-cast stone, approx. 65 × 65 cm

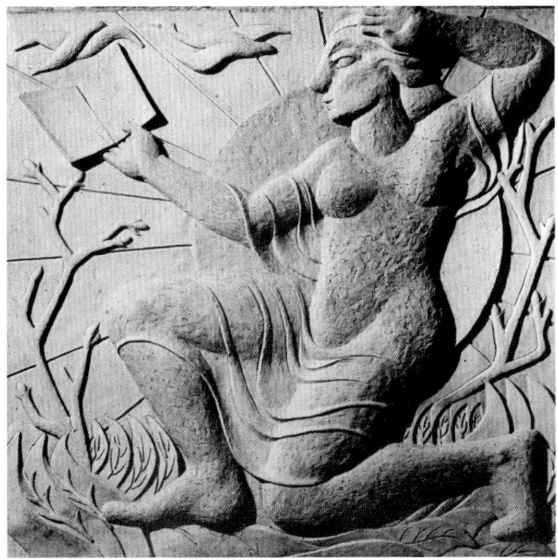

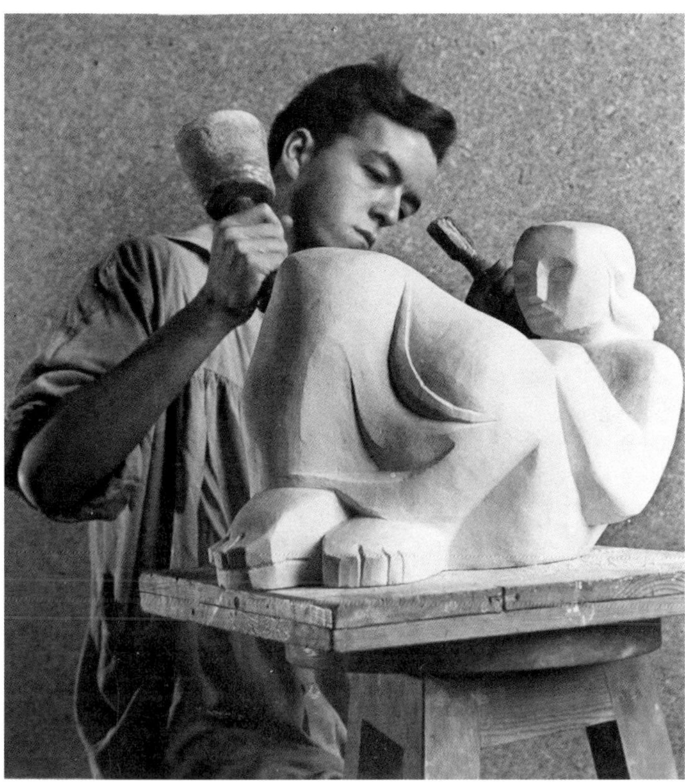

above: John Milne with *Reclining Figure*, 1948, carved plaster

below: Student Rag Week, 1951: John Milne, Reg Moon, Benny Sirota and two unidentified female students

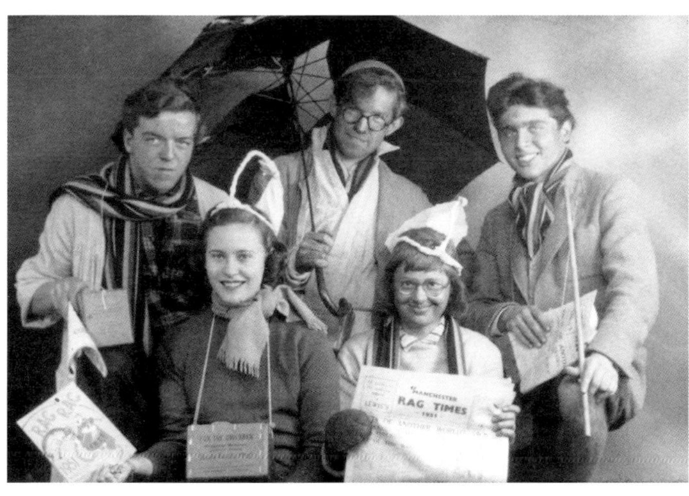

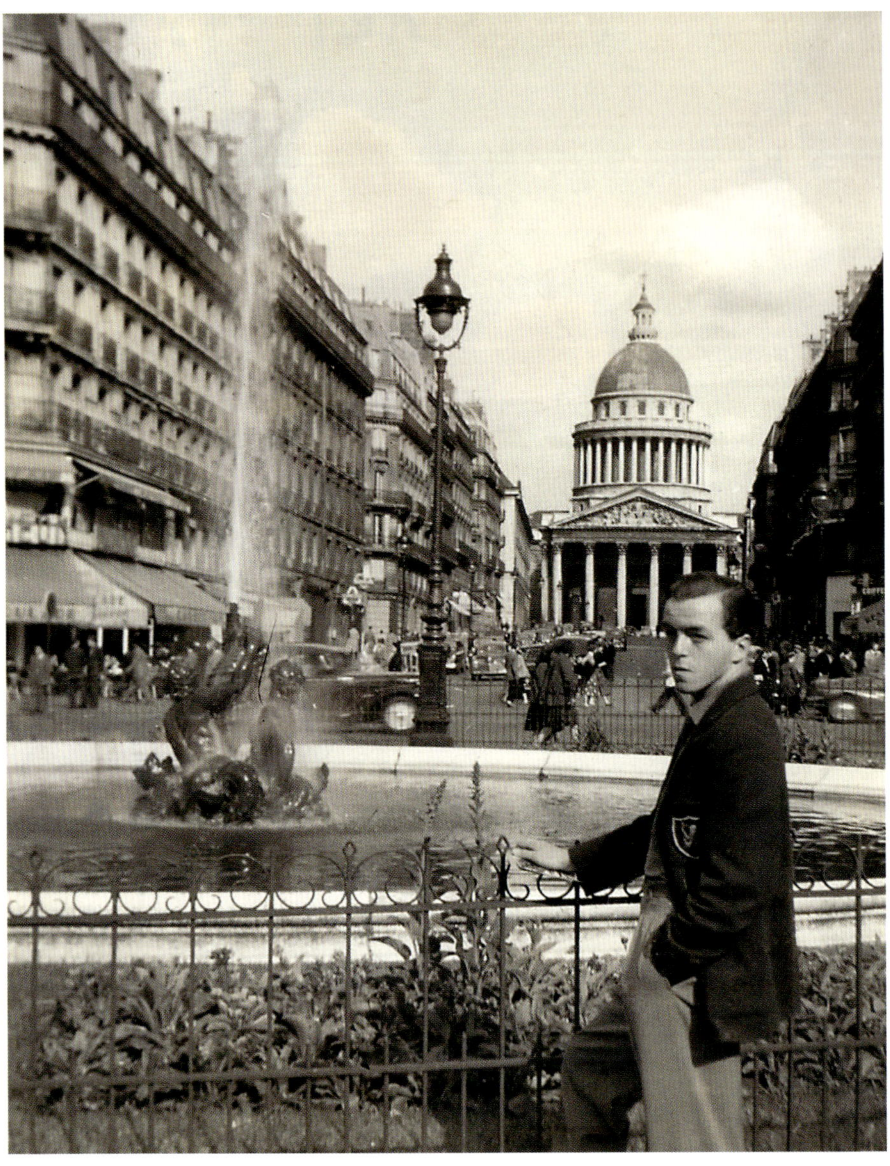

John Milne, Paris, 1952

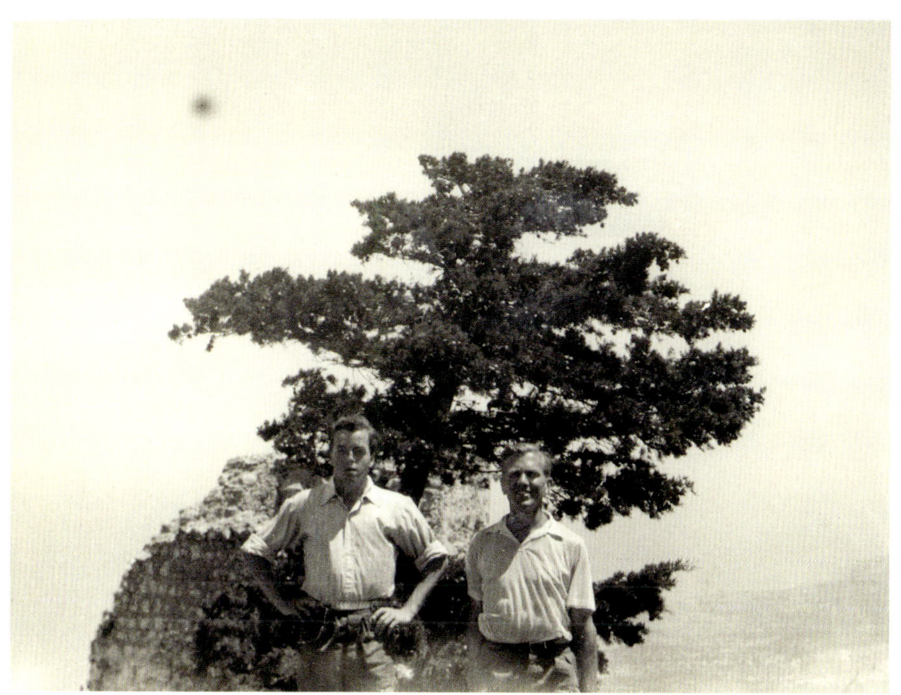

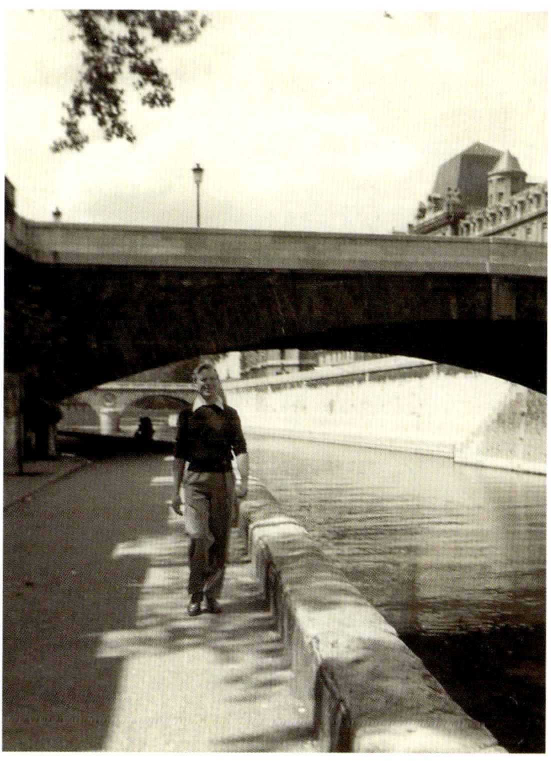

above: John Milne and Cosmo Rodewald, Greece, summer 1952

left: Cosmo Rodewald, Paris, 1952

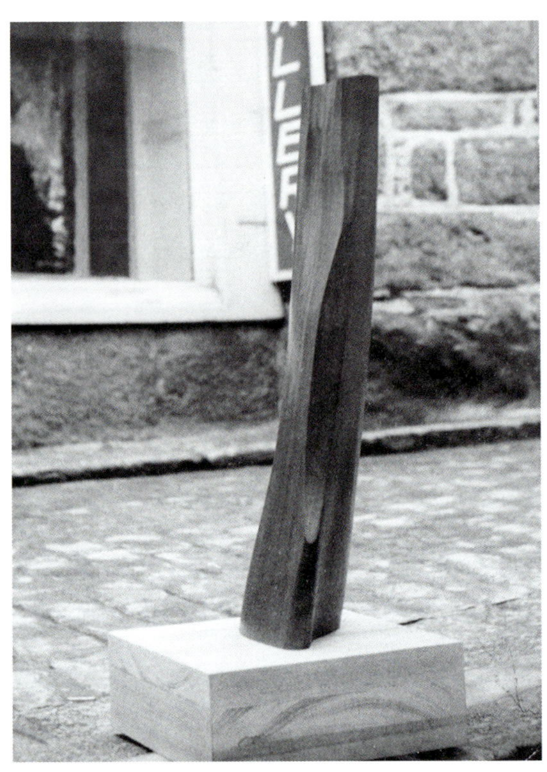

John Milne, *Vertical Form*, 1958, Nigerian guarea, H: 92 cm

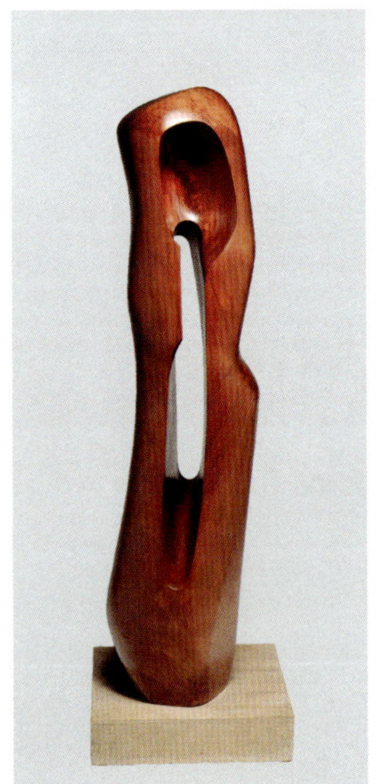

Barbara Hepworth, *Figure (Churinga)*, 1952, Spanish mahogany, 133.4 × 40.6 × 39.4 cm

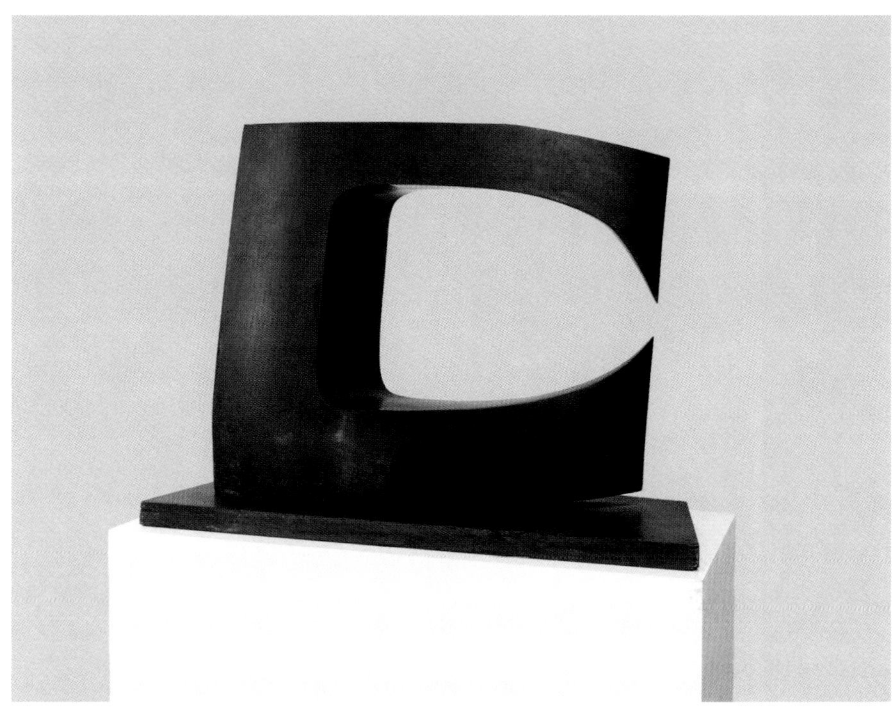

John Milne, *Gnathos*, 1967, patinated bronze, H: 64 cm, W: 86.4 cm

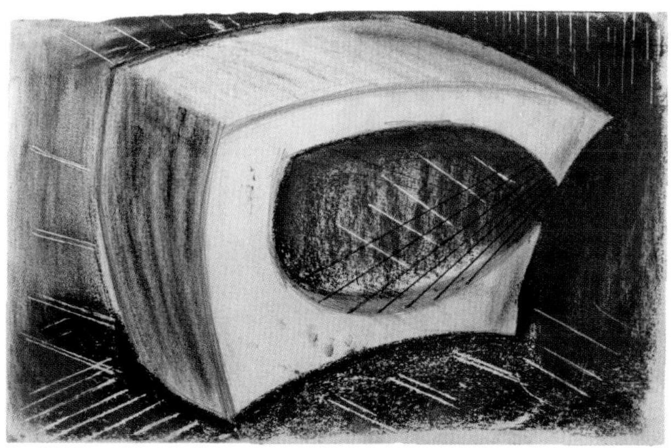

John Milne, drawing for *Gnathos*, 1957, charcoal and pastel on paper, 22 × 34 cm

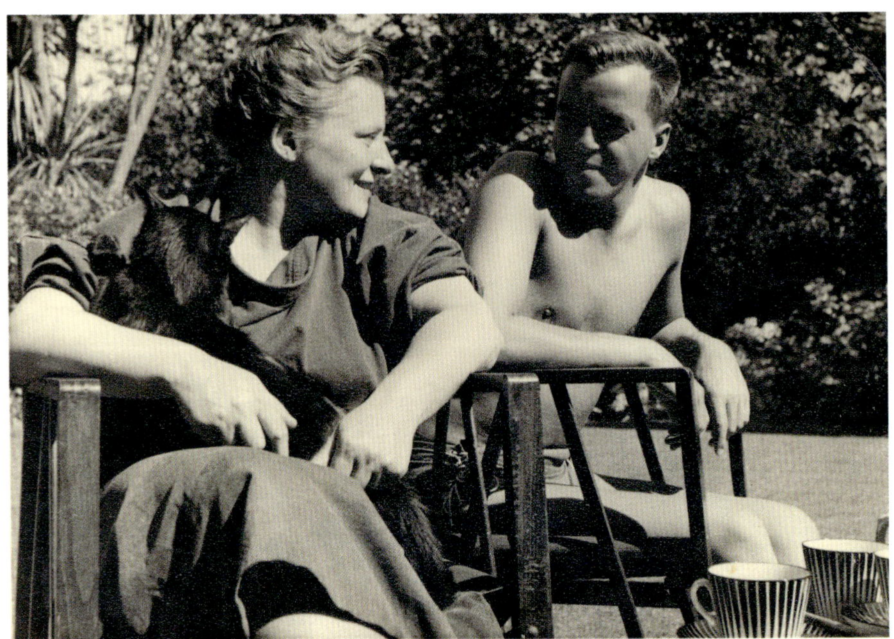

above: John Milne and Boots Redgrave, *c.*1956

right: Alan Lowndes, *Portrait of John Milne*, 1956, oil on canvas laid onto board, 75.6 × 50.8 cm

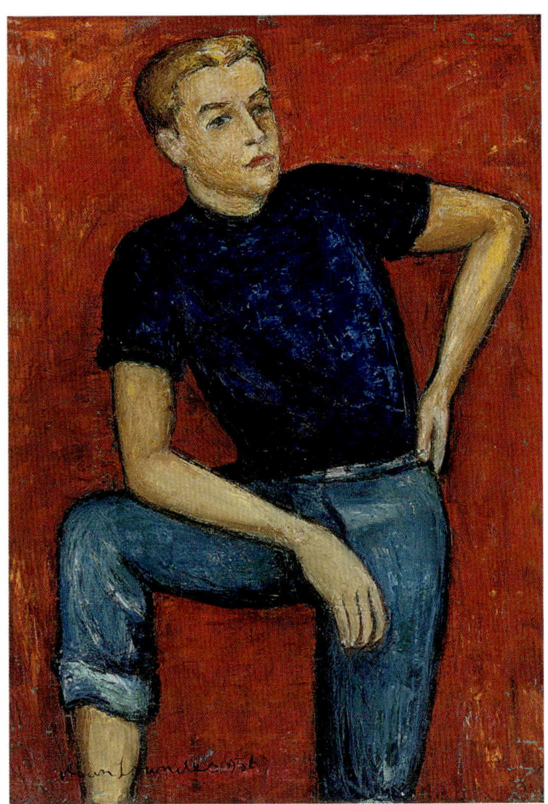

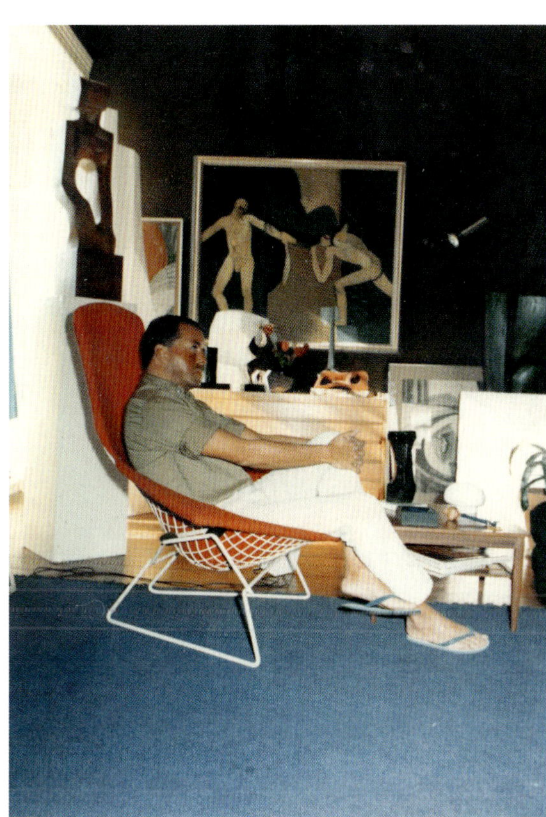

John Milne at Trewyn, 1971. The sculpture on the plinth behind Milne is his *Torso* (1955), walnut; the large painting is Keith Vaughan's *Two Figures in Sequence (5th Assembly)* (1957–58)

The sitting room at Trewyn, *c.*1960, with Anthony Benjamin's painting *Trink* (1960) and John Milne's *Gatos* (1960)

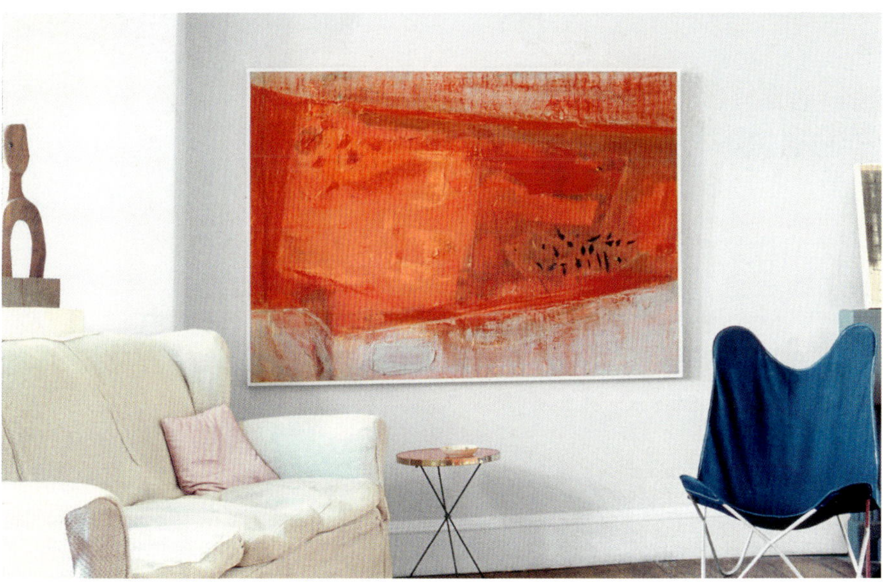

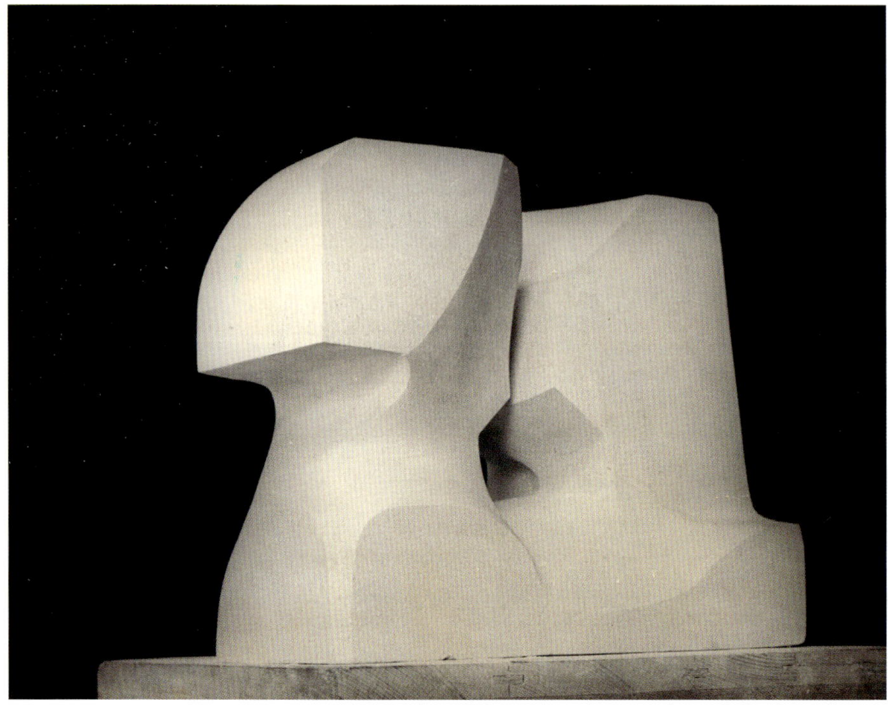

John Milne, *The Kiss*, 1957, Portland stone, L: 61 cm

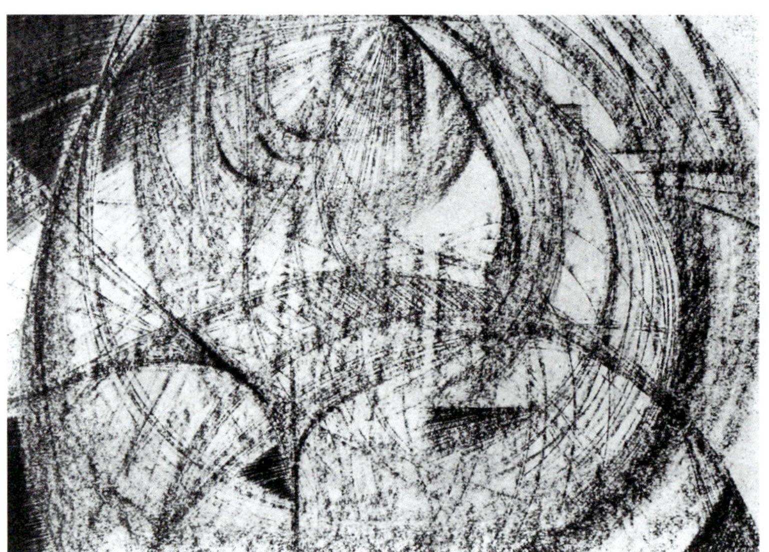

John Milne, *Drawing for Käthe Schuftan*, 1958, Conté crayon, 55.8 × 76.4 cm

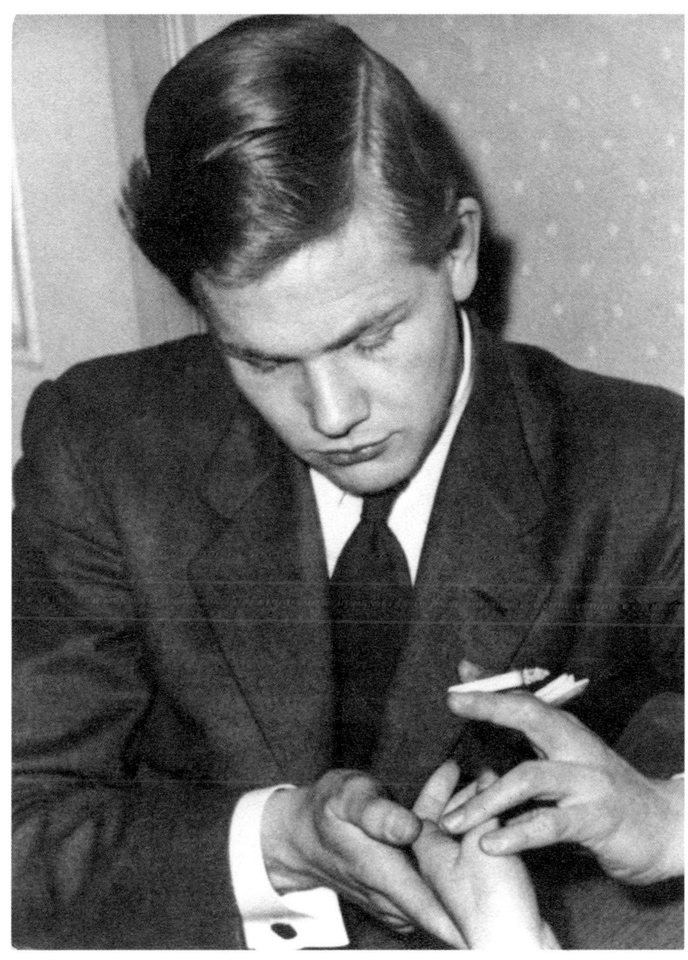

Julian Nixon, Dublin, 1956, photographed at a reception for the Ballet de France, led by Ludmilla Tcherina (whose hand Nixon holds) and Milorad Miskovitch

Studio portrait of Richard Blake Brown by Lenare. The photograph is inscribed: 'For Julian with every possible good wish, from Richard, 1957'

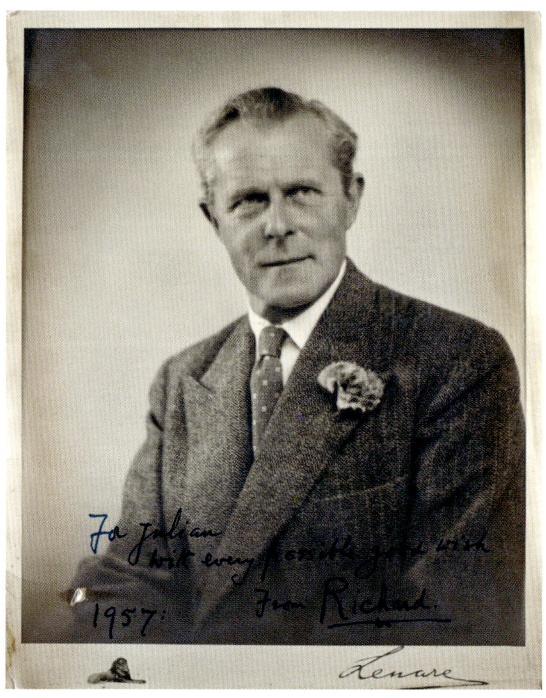

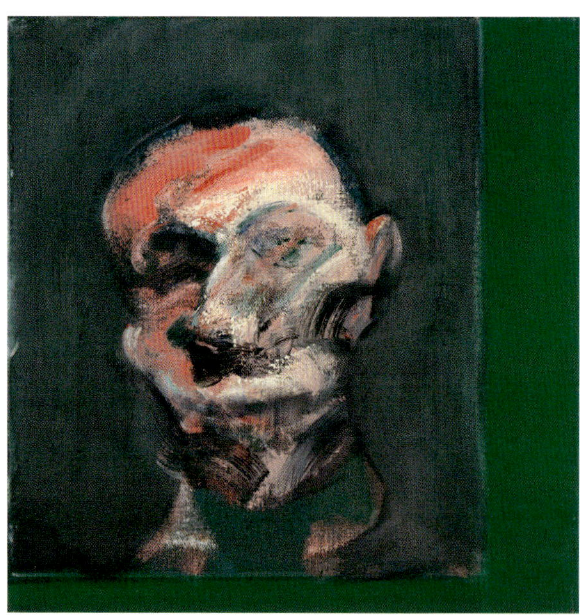

Francis Bacon, *Head of a Man*, 1959, oil on canvas, 48.25 × 45.75 cm

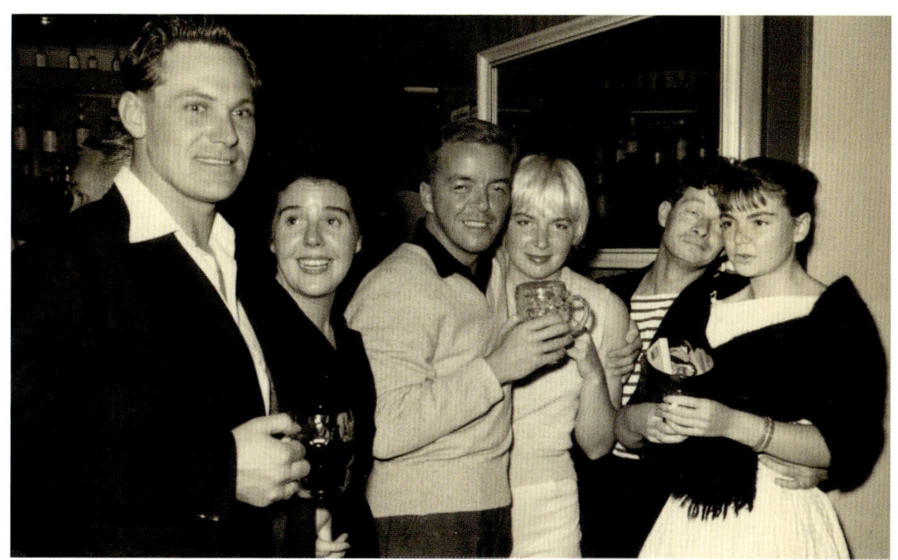

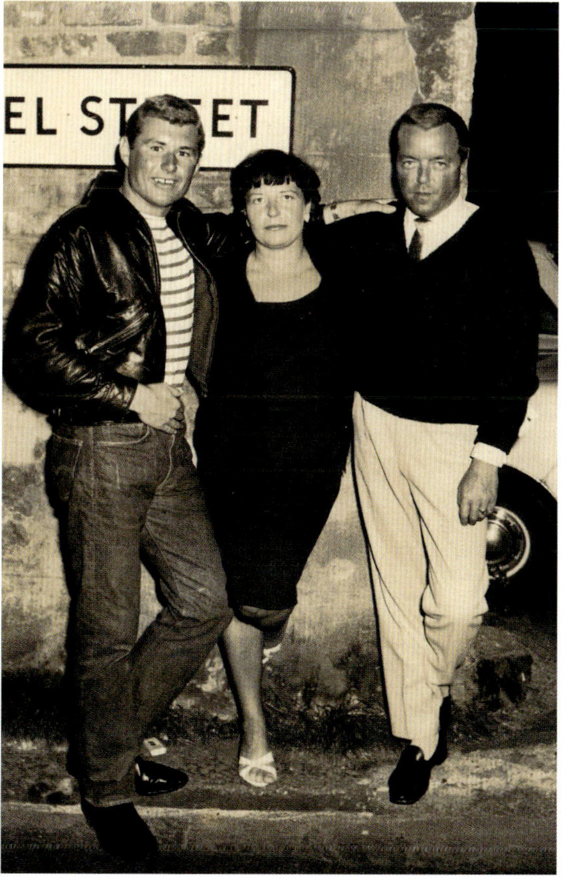

above: The Union Inn, St Ives, date unknown. Left to right: unidentified man and woman; John Milne; a woman thought to be Katherine Dowd; Alan and Valerie Lowndes

left: John Milne (right) with Heather Jameson and a man thought to be Johnny Brooks; he and his partner Toops ran a restaurant in Penzance and were great friends of Milne

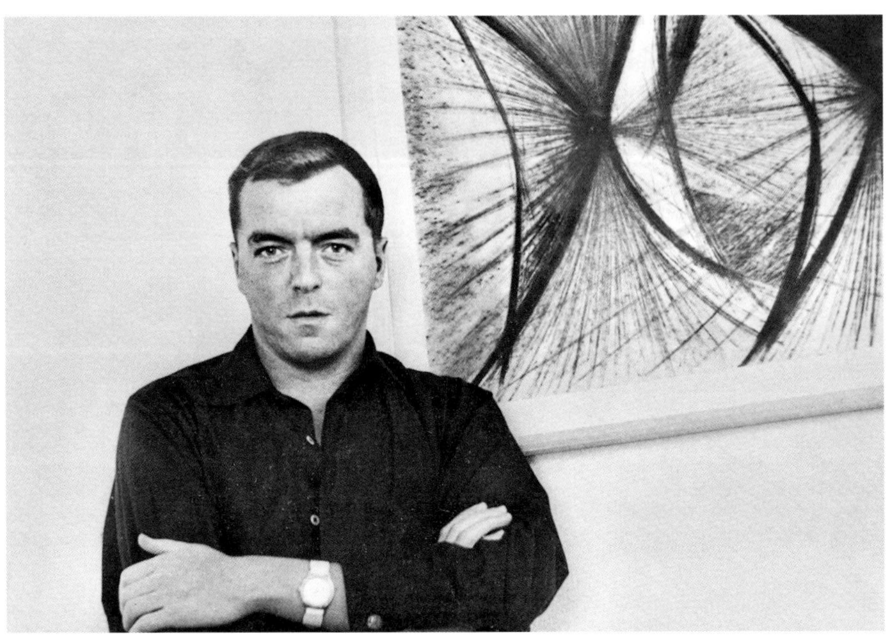

John Milne with one of his drawings
at the Penwith Gallery, St Ives, *c.*1963

'John had a distinctive way of dressing that was both casual and smart. During the day in St Ives his daily attire would be washed-out cords, faded, good quality (usually light), with a nice casual cotton shirt, sometimes short-sleeved or rolled up to just below the elbow – these tended to be small checked (blue and white to match his eyes) or red and white, sometimes other colours but discreet and tasteful. He always wore a good leather belt. He more than often wore these with flip-flops or, on cool days, nice leather or suede loafers without socks. Most of his clothes came from Aquascutum, Austin Reed, Liberty's, with cashmere jumpers from The Scotch House or Harrods. He always looked tasteful, casual and unassuming. He wore an expensive white leather watch strap at all times.'

—Christine Farrington, 2020

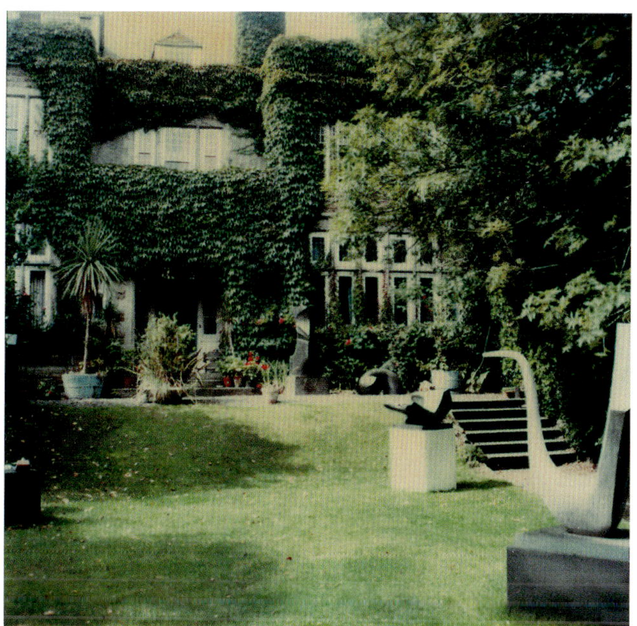

Polaroid of Trewyn, *c.*1975. The sculpture on the right is Milne's *Leda* (1968), cold cast aluminium

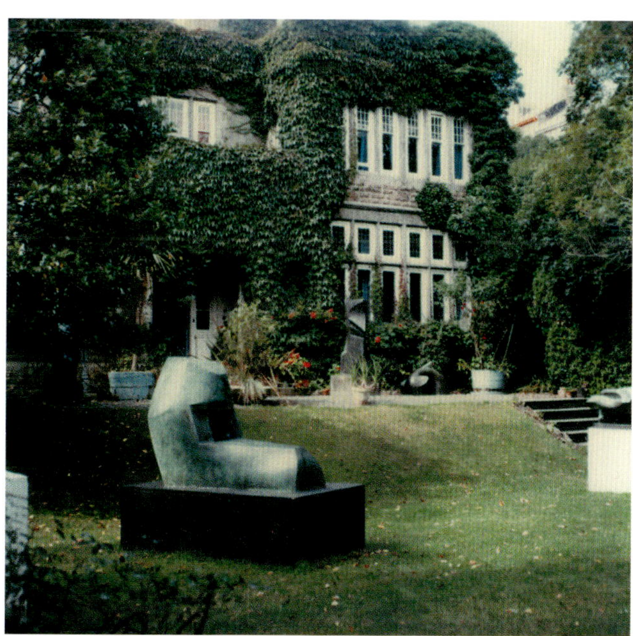

Polaroid of Trewyn, *c.*1975. The sculpture in the foreground is *Propylaea II* (1974), cold cast bronze

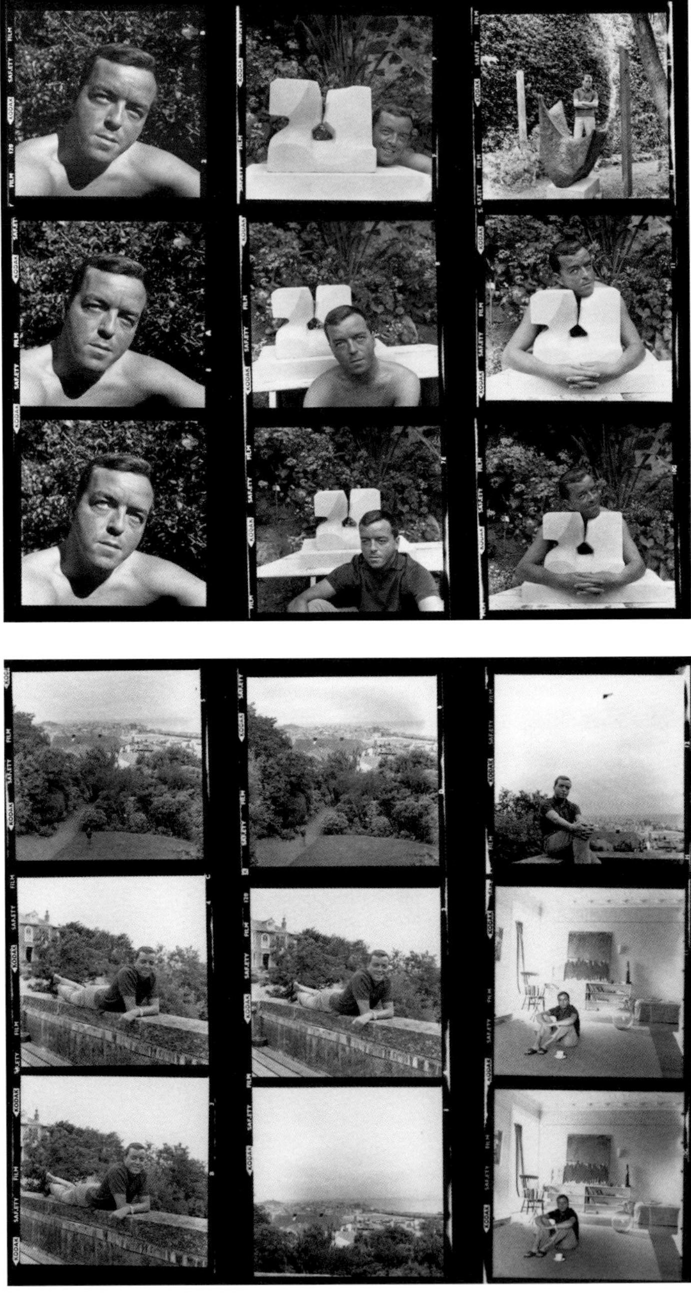

Ida Kar, contact sheets of photographs of John Milne at Trewyn, 1961

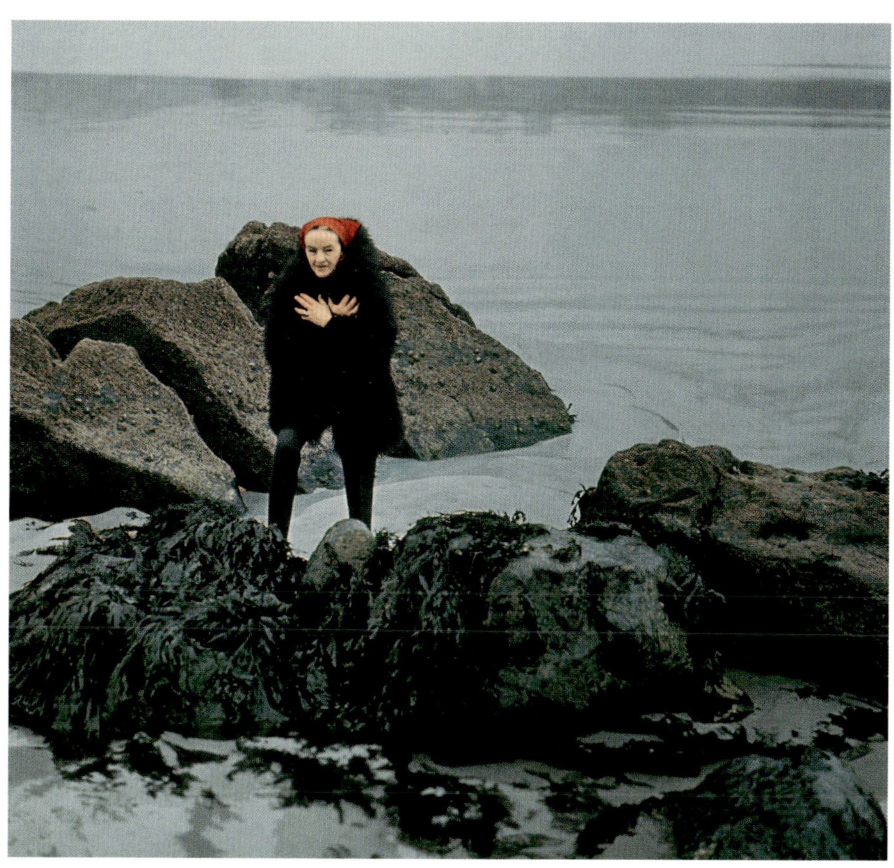

Barbara Hepworth photographed by
Snowdon on Porthmeor Beach, St Ives,
February 1964

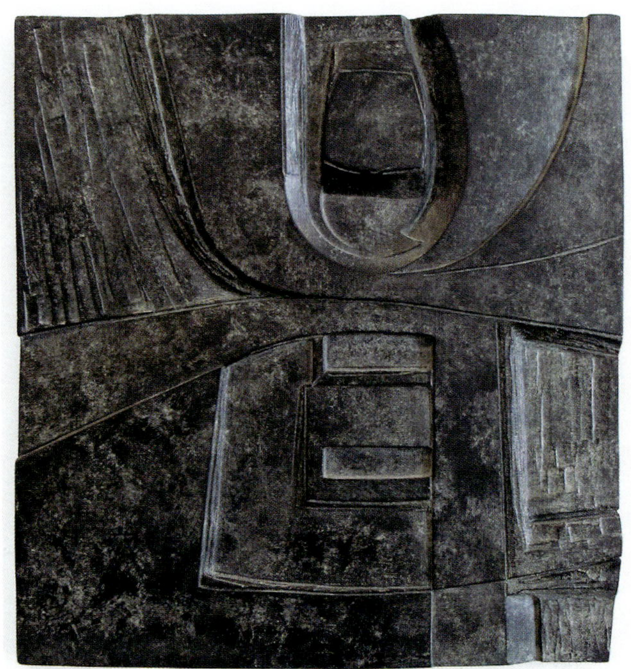

John Milne, *Delphi*, 1965,
bronze relief, 31.8 × 29.2 cm

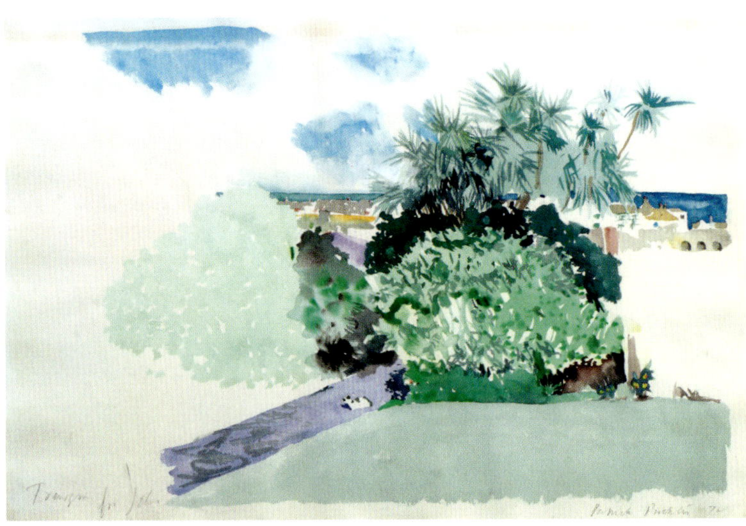

Patrick Procktor, *Trewyn*, 1972,
watercolour, 35.4 × 50.8 cm

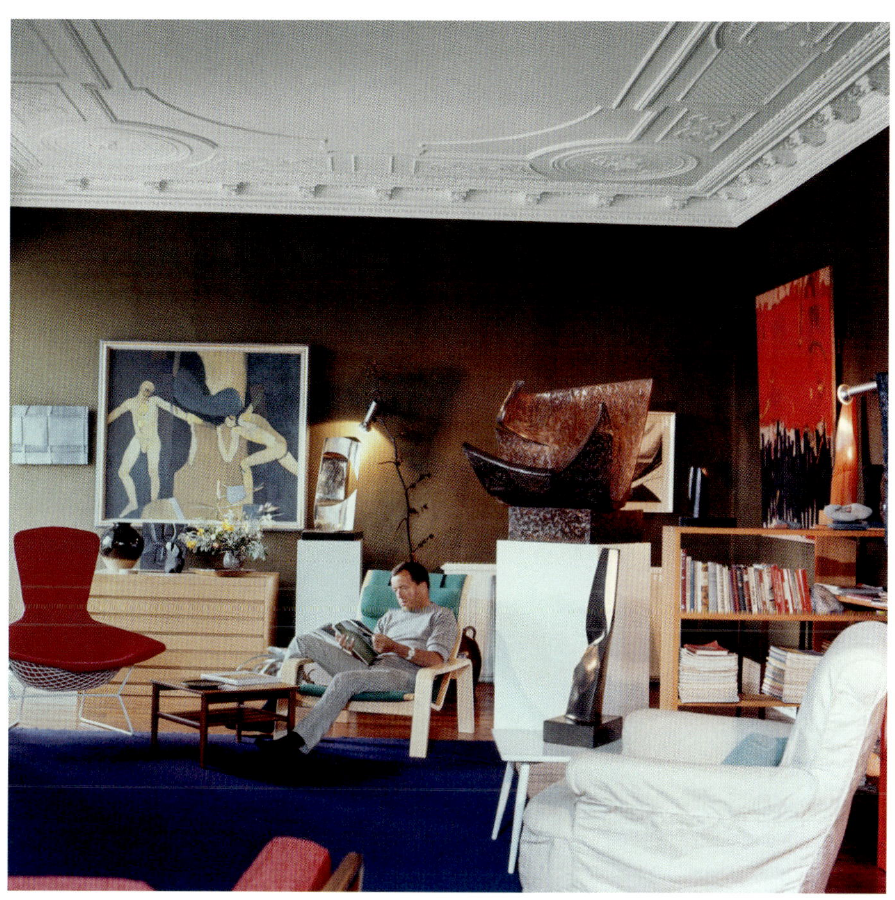

John Milne at Trewyn, *c.*1972.
On the white plinth to Milne's left is his *Anakalypsis* (1968), cold cast bronze; in front of it is *Poseidon II* (1971), cold cast aluminium

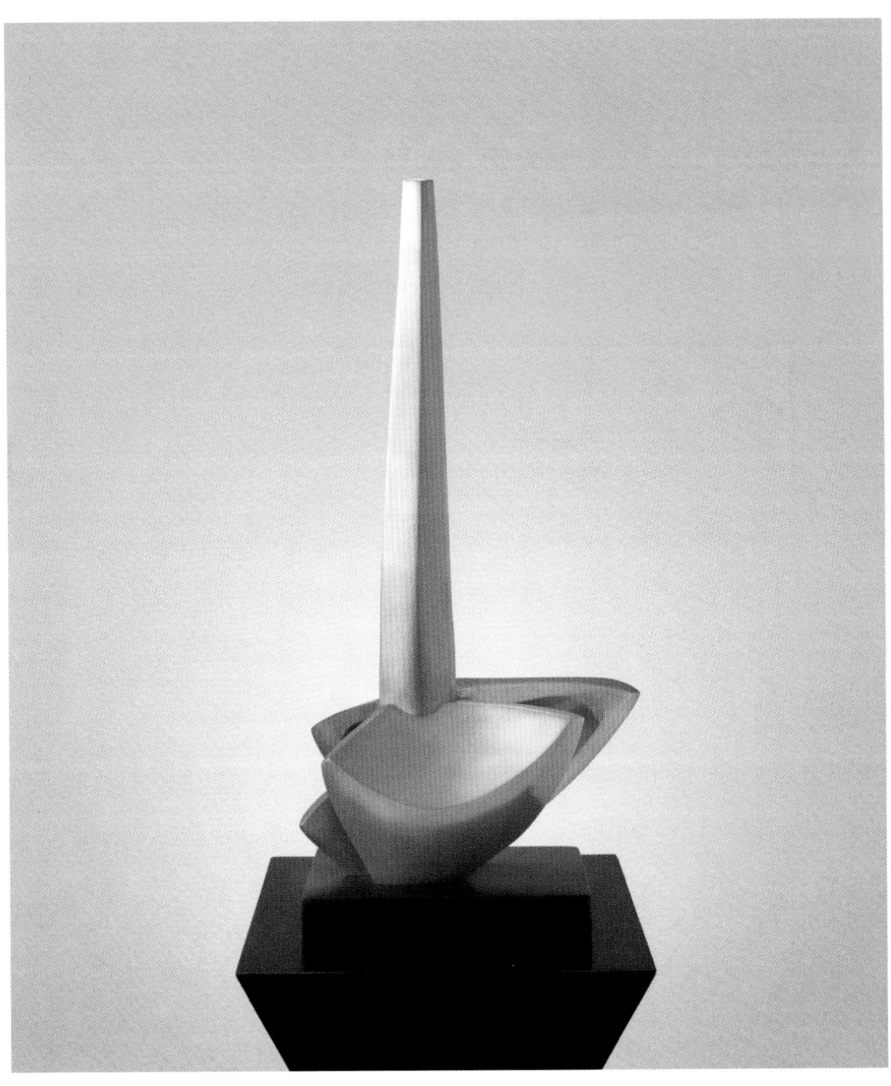

John Milne, *Project*, 1969,
cold cast aluminium, H: 53 cm

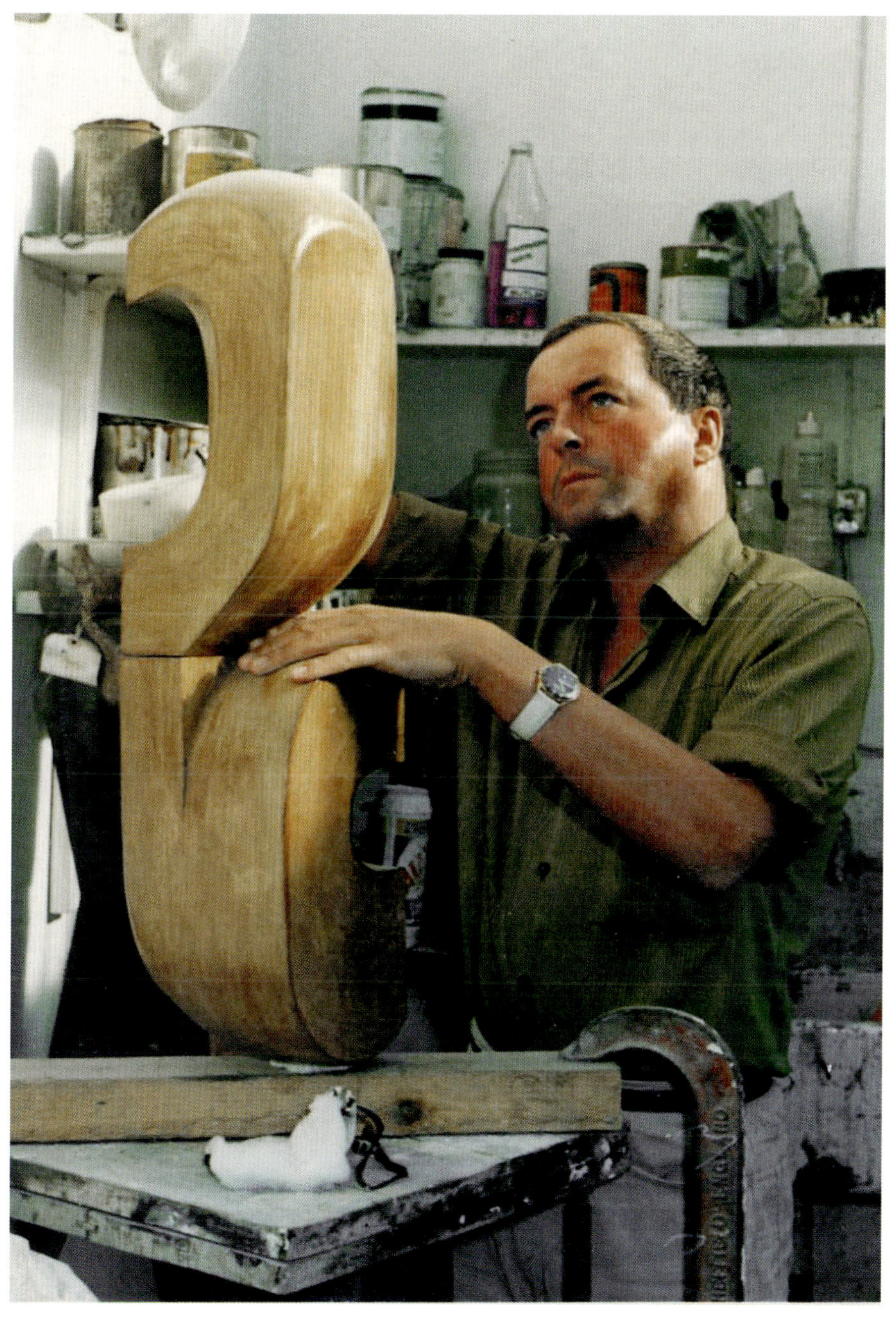

John Milne working on *Oracle*, Trewyn, 1971

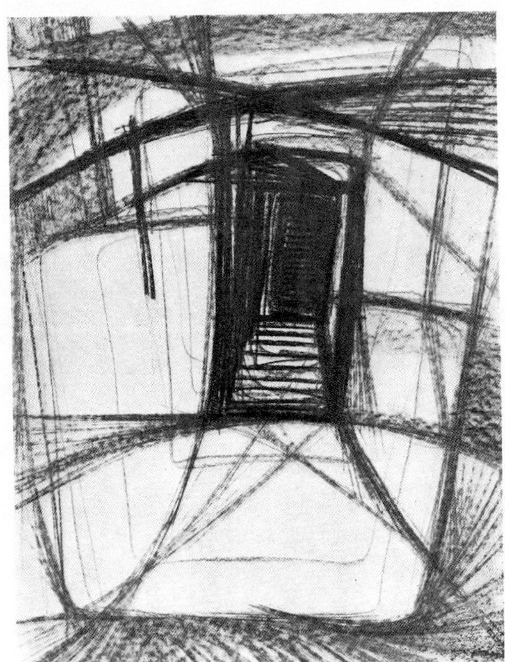

John Milne, *Les Baux*, 1957, charcoal, 66 × 50.8 cm

John Milne, *Les Baux*, 1959, bronze relief with wires, 55.8 × 46.9 cm

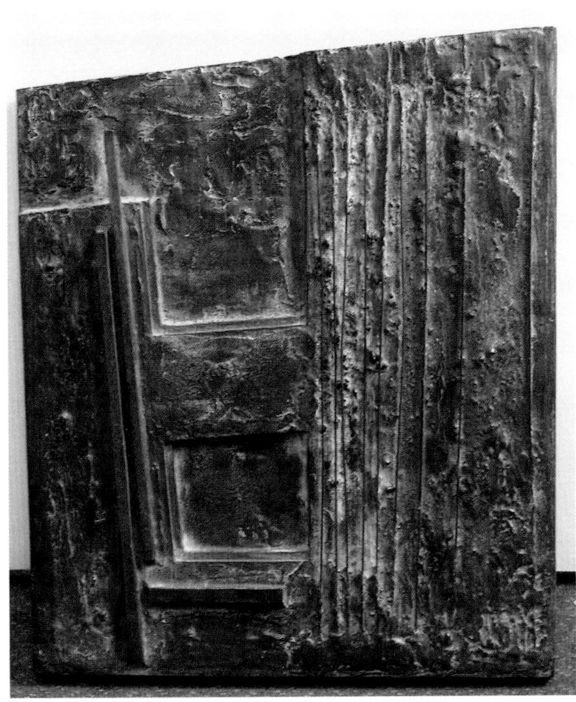

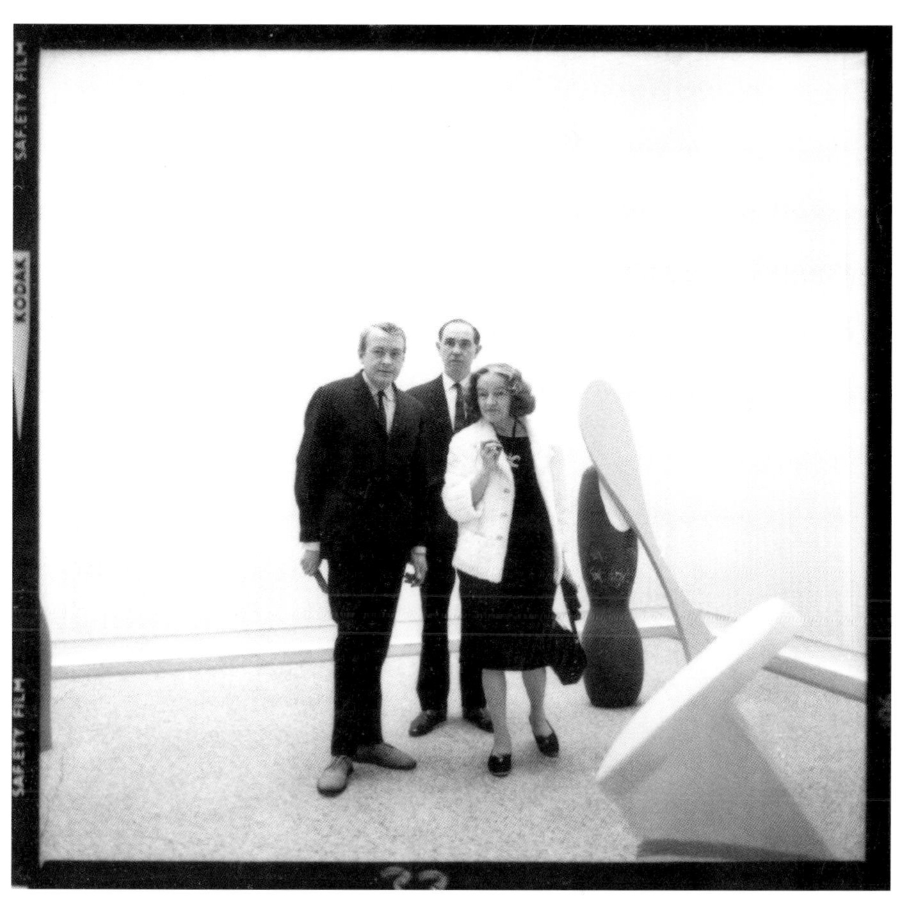

Bryan Robertson (left) with Barbara Hepworth and an unidentified man, Whitechapel Art Gallery, London, 1965. The sculpture is by Phillip King

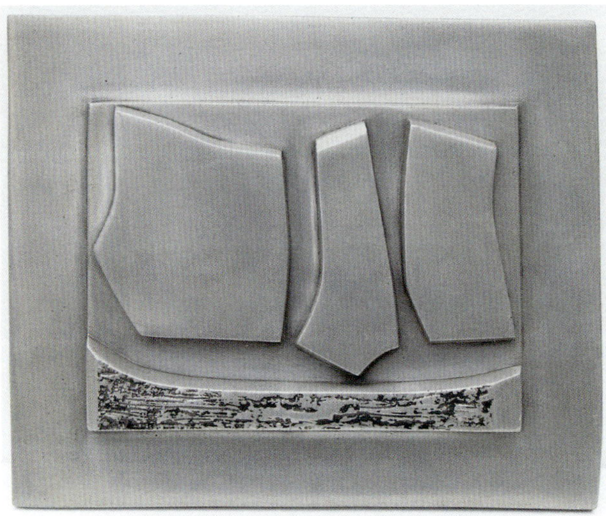

John Milne, *Storm Lifting*, 1968,
cold cast aluminium relief, 27.9 × 33 cm

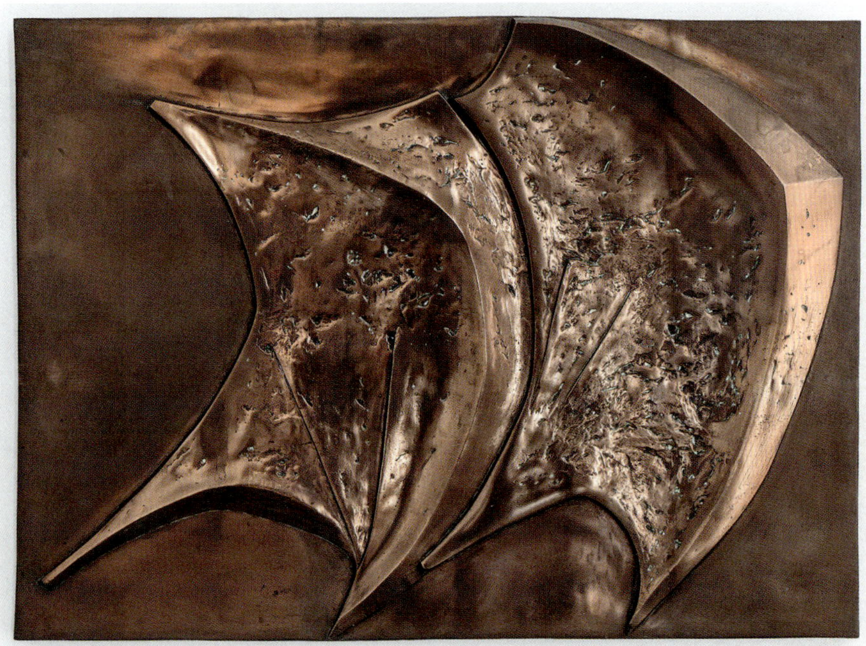

John Milne, *Wave*, 1967, cold cast bronze
relief, 74 × 99 cm

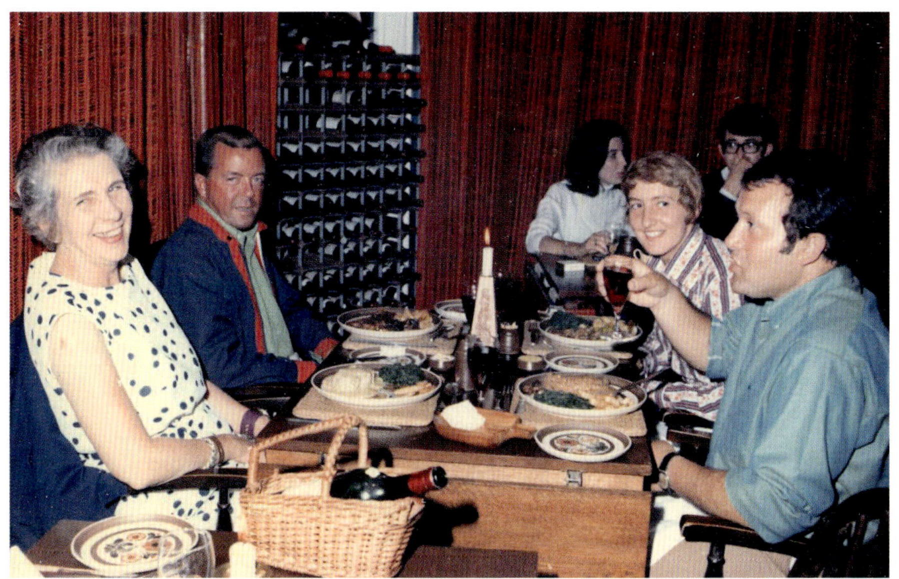

The Outrigger restaurant, St Ives, *c.*1969.
Left to right: Marjorie Parr, John Milne,
Christine Farrington, Ivaldo Ferrari

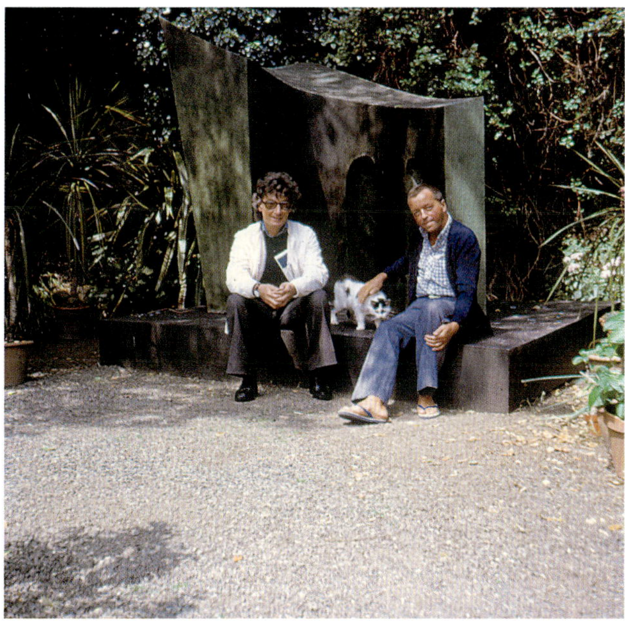

Brian Smith and John Milne, Trewyn, *c.*1974. The sculpture is Milne's *Persepolis II* (1973), cold cast bronze

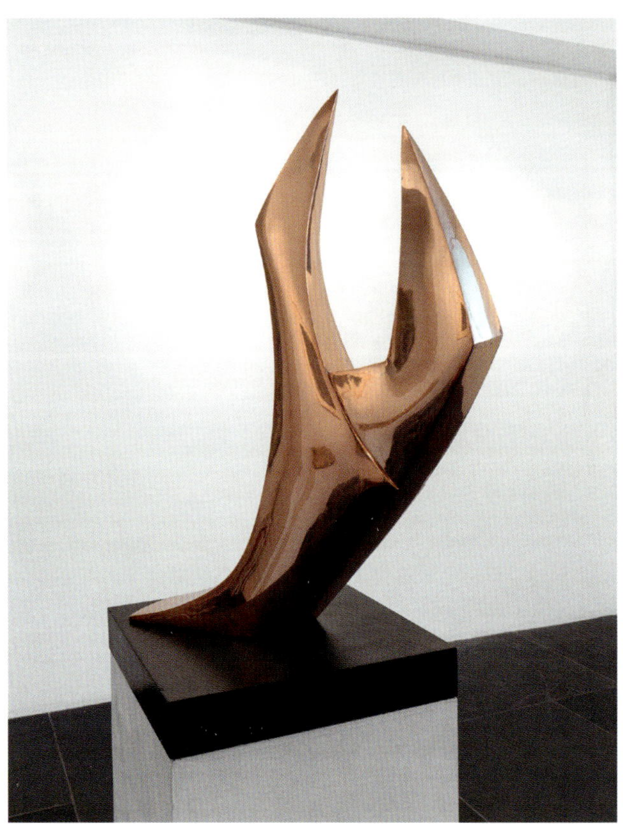

John Milne, *Credo*, 1974,
polished bronze, H: 94 cm

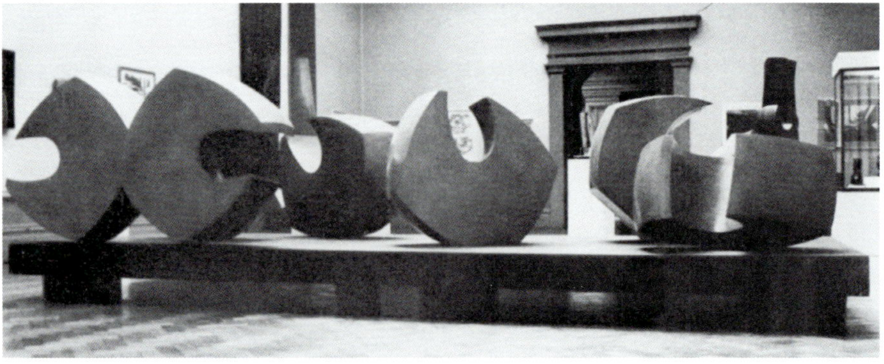

John Milne, *Variations*, 1971,
cold cast aluminium, L: 472.5 cm

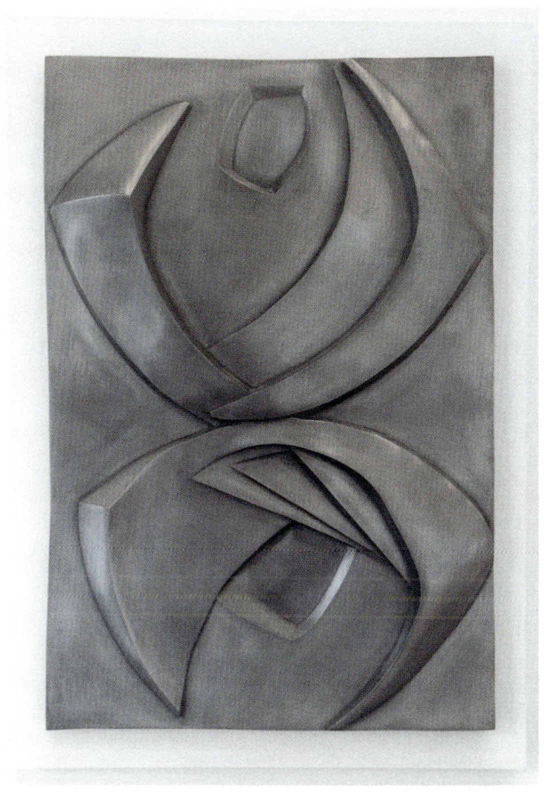

John Milne, *Icarus*, 1967,
cold cast aluminium relief,
75 × 50 cm

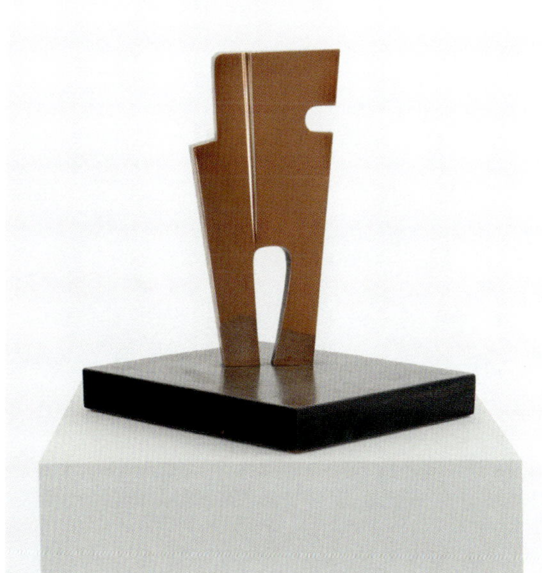

John Milne, *Persian Monolith*, 1972,
polished bronze, H: 23 cm

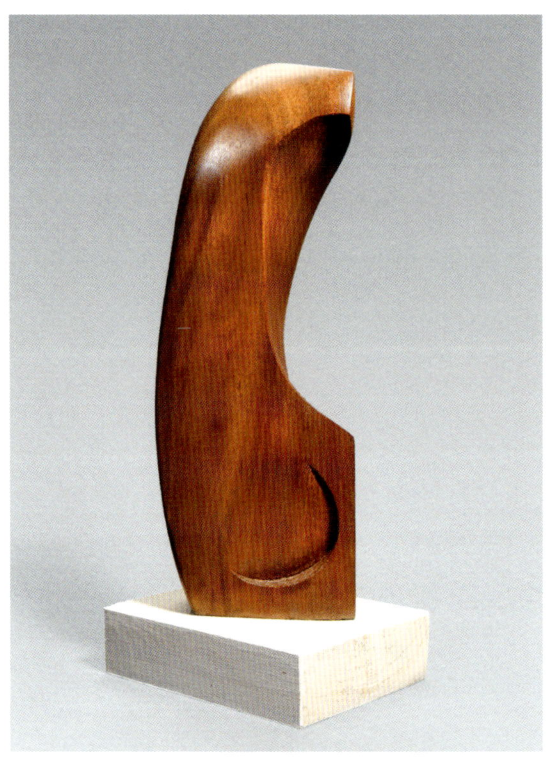

John Milne, *Vertical Form*, 1977, Nigerian guarea, H: 48 cm

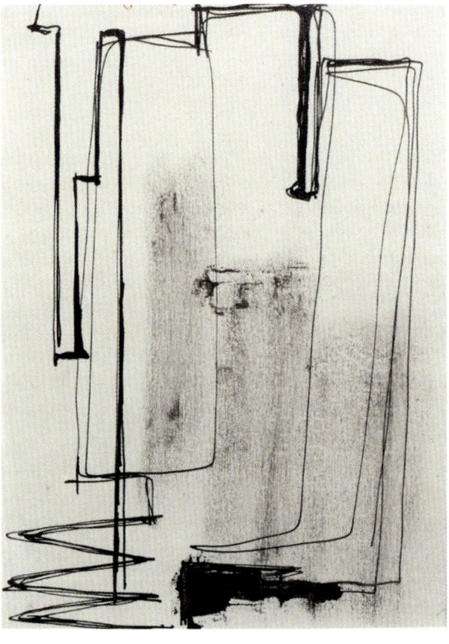

John Milne, untitled ink drawing, undated, 17 × 13 cm

John Milne, *Syrinx*, 1976, patinated and polished bronze, H: 41 cm

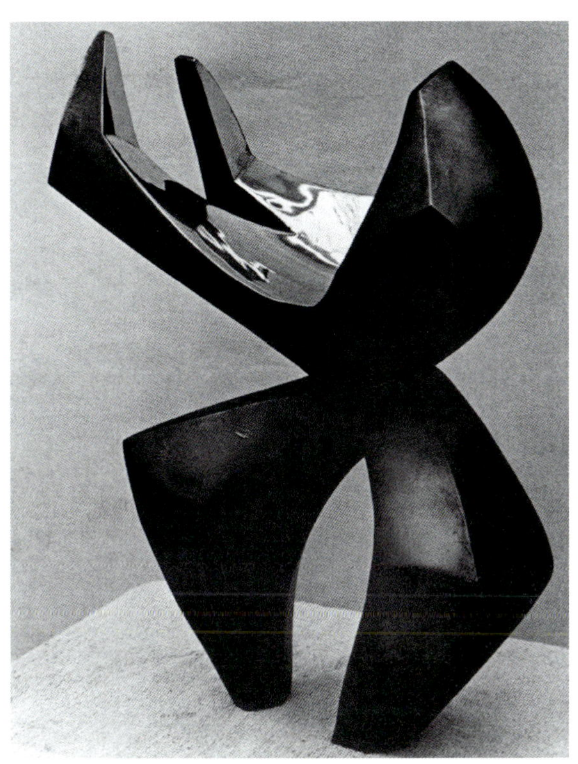

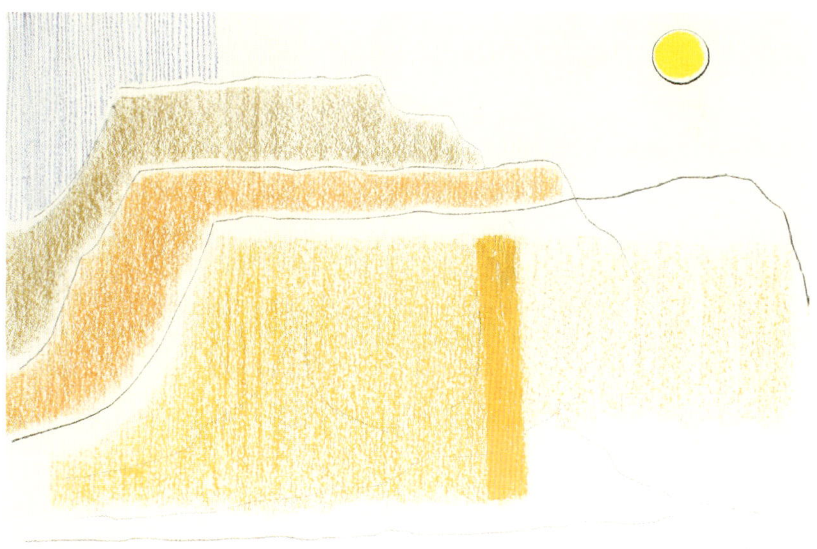

John Milne, *Abstract Landscape*, 1974, pastel and charcoal on paper, 41 × 58 cm. The drawing is based on Milne's memories of the Atlas mountains

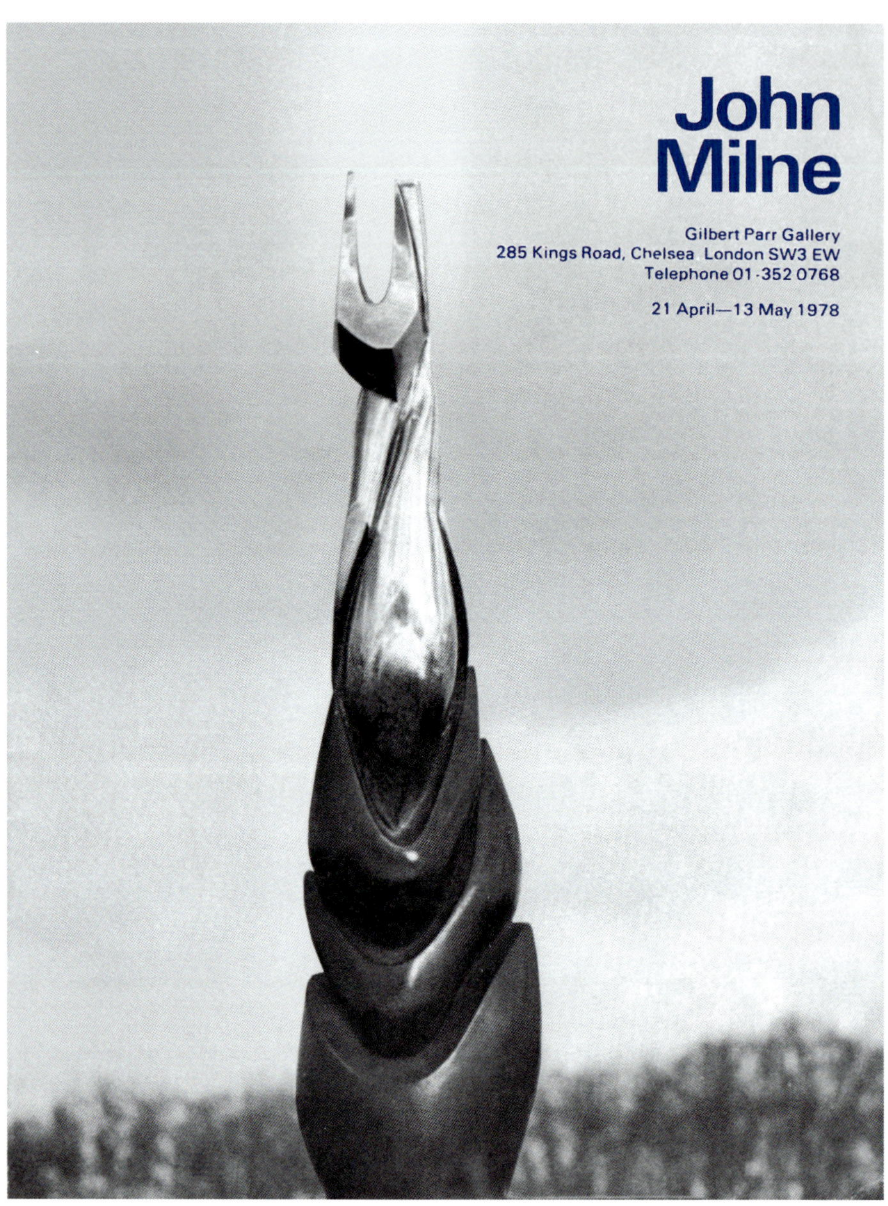

Catalogue for Milne's show at Gilbert Parr Gallery, London, 1978. Illustrated on the cover is *Birdsong*, 1975, polished and patinated bronze, H: 60 cm

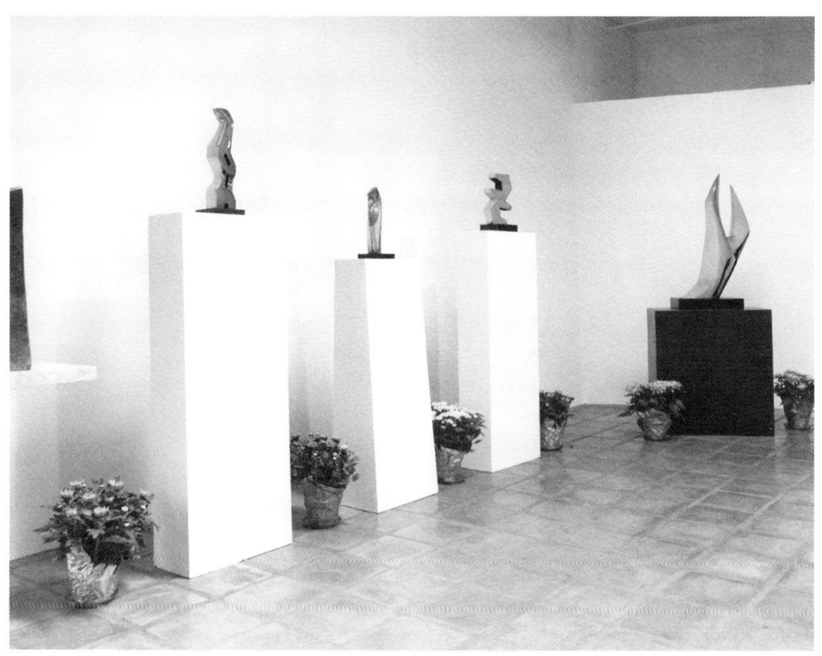

A Retrospective Exhibition of Sculpture and Drawings of the Late John Milne, Gallery Rose, Los Angeles, October 1978

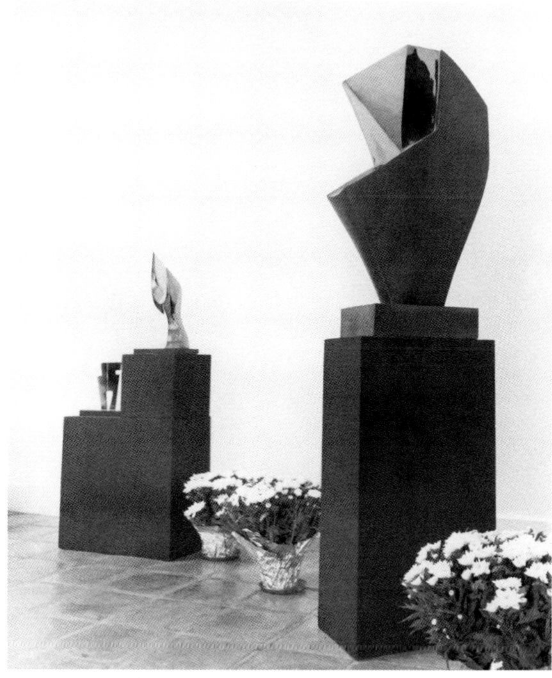

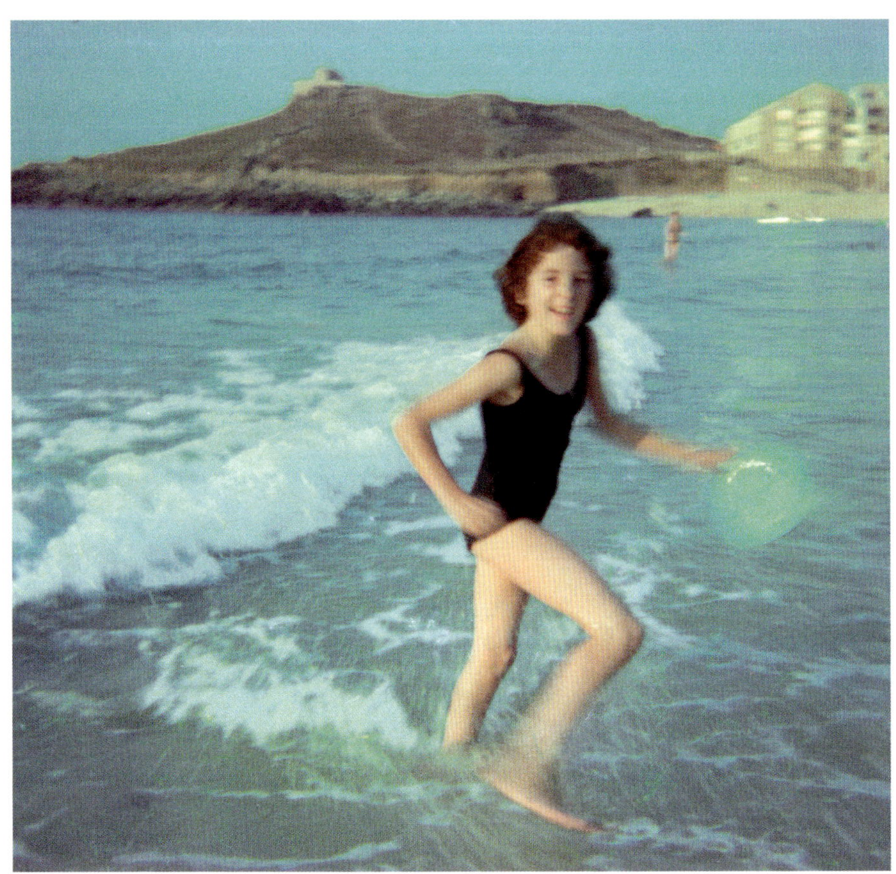

Lydia Massey, Porthmeor beach,
St Ives, August 1976

metal; she then employed him for two or three days each week. In discussing the theme of class in St Ives at that time, Wall relates:

> You could have a great time, there were a lot of really working-class people there at that time: Trevor Bell, Alan Lowndes, Anthony Benjamin, on and on – everybody was. Barbara wasn't that far away from being working class ... I think she changed her voice. Because her mother was very Yorkshire – she once said to me: 'You know, lad, you should be doing a real job.' She had a real Yorkshire accent. Barbara was terrified of her.

Wall concurs with the idea that working-class artists would have been unlikely to congregate in such numbers elsewhere, certainly not in London:

> It could only happen in a place like that; it was so small. The class differences weren't allowed ... of course you had people like Patrick Heron, and Ben [Nicholson], and Roger Hilton. The working-class thing – that *made* St Ives in that era of the late 1950s.

The lure of St Ives was manifold. While its standing as a centre for progressive art was naturally a central factor, as an essentially working-class town the costs of living were far lower than in the conurbations to which artists might otherwise have gravitated. There were also the physical attractions of St Ives: not only its topographical beauty but, as Wall indicated, its human scale, which ensured that it was easy to meet and socialise with fellow artists, both in their studios and, more often, in pubs. This is not to suggest that life there presented an easy option, for many artists struggled, some existing in poverty for long stretches of time. It was possible, however, to forge beneficial connections, both within the art community itself and with the aforementioned national and international art world figures, many of whom stayed at Trewyn.

It was not only artists who were attracted to the town. Long established as a place of pilgrimage for those drawn to alternative lifestyles, in the late 1950s Cornwall, and St Ives in particular, became a destination for beatniks and dropouts on what later became known as the hippie trail. Representatives of the counterculture, they were politically left wing and often allied with the Campaign for Nuclear Disarmament (CND). From a broad range of social backgrounds, many were students, a good proportion of them art students. Their key texts were by the American Beat writer Jack Kerouac and Colin Wilson's existentialist study of social alienation *The Outsider* (1956); Wilson had himself moved to Cornwall in the late 1950s. The beatniks hitched rides down to Cornwall, where they made money by washing up in hotels and cafés, or from busking. They slept in tents, outbuildings, spare rooms or on the beach; Milne found a group of them squatting in his greenhouse, where they remained for several days.[3] The younger local populace often found them deeply attractive: 'Beatniks were political, they were intellectual, they were sexy, they were cool. We all aspired to beatnik chic ... that was the style of the day.'[4]

The town elders and moral guardians had an entirely different view of the beatniks, however, for they soon became classified as a social nuisance, in their day as subversive a threat to moral standards as were the punks of the late 1970s. Young men with beards or long hair were refused service in the local pubs. Folk singer Ralph McTell was among the musicians drawn to St Ives: 'To be honest when we first arrived, you can understand why they were so suspicious of us beatniks. Cornwall was a very naïve and uncorrupted place. It was gentler and more relaxed: a mixture of the parochial and mystical. It was like another country.'[5]

*

As the *Tatler* had put it in 1961, Hepworth was easily the district's most famous resident, an enduring status that continues to this day. Born the first of four children in 1903, she had set her heart on becoming a sculptor while still at school. Her parents, Herbert and Gertrude, always treated their son and three daughters equally, Herbert insistent that they should all be given the same educational opportunities. A civil engineer, he had worked his way up from a lowly position to become county surveyor of the West Riding of Yorkshire, a job that gave him his own car, which was rare in the early years of the twentieth century. Although Herbert and Gertrude Hepworth were not cultured people and had little or no understanding or appreciation of art, they did nothing to impede their eldest daughter's youthful ambition. John Skeaping wrote of meeting them for the first time in Yorkshire in the summer of 1925, soon after he and Hepworth had married while in Florence that May: 'I found her father pompous and her mother stupid. I had never expected Barbara to have come from this very middle-class background.'[6]

Skeaping had clearly assumed that his talented wife's parents would be rather more sophisticated than the petit bourgeois couple he described. (One also notes his perception of class distinctions, at variance to that of Brian Wall in his impression of Gertrude Hepworth.) His dismissive reaction was probably based on comparisons with his own family, for his father was a painter, as was an aunt, and the family history had its share of colourful characters. But where Hepworth could be seen to be her father's daughter was in her drive and tenacity, and as she later wrote in fond tribute to both of her parents, 'Their lavish love and their necessary stern frugality were the basis of my training.'[7]

The American writer Édouard Roditi stayed at Trewyn in the summer of 1958. He was in town to interview Hepworth for his *Dialogues on Art* (1960), a book composed of a dozen chapters, each based on a conversation with an individual artist.[8] In a preamble to his published dialogue with Hepworth, which was accompanied by a photograph of her by Michel Ramon, Roditi described what amounted to a self-invented character shielded by a protective carapace:

> The artist's appearance, her gestures, her manner of speech, even her style of dress, suggested unusual poise and efficiency. Without being merely pretty, her features are beautifully modelled, as if her mind had sculpted her body from within. One cannot help feeling that she is exactly as she would like to be. Yet there is nothing odd about her, no histrionic Bohemianism, no flim-flam-flummery of facile protest. One would not be surprised to discover that such a handsome, pleasant and obviously intelligent woman is a brilliant physician or a successful politician rather than an artist. Yet she speaks of her art with a rare awareness of dedication, in a tone of authority and also of humility.

In becoming 'exactly as she would like to be', Hepworth had evolved a persona and mode of presentation in which the eradication of her Yorkshire accent was fundamental, for, as Wall perceived, she had refashioned her speaking voice so that its modulation bore a purity in keeping with the surfaces of her sculpture. She cultivated her own defences, reserve and distance, and was necessarily ruthless in how she elected to expend her time and energies. Like all artists she was a product of her time, navigating life and career within the circumstances in which she found herself. As a woman, Hepworth had of necessity to adopt particular strategies for survival. In an interview for *The Times* in 2015, Wall spoke of how high the odds were stacked against her in her career as a sculptor, and of how the male establishment marginalised her:

> I was a young man, so she wouldn't confide in me, but she was never happy with the status quo. She was part of a struggle, a real struggle that continues to this day. As a woman, what chance did you have at that time? It isn't as if she was painting lovely pictures and putting them in the local shop. She was on the international platform with these guys.[9]

Wall goes on to describe how, although the couple had separated in 1950, Ben Nicholson would call to see Hepworth from time to time while he was still living in St Ives, and how she, valuing his judgement, could be greatly distressed when he issued an unkind word. Talking about Nicholson in his 2015 interview, Wall commented: 'I think he was jealous ... I think he knew she was better than he was, because of the games he played. He could be very, very nasty. But she was the better artist.'[10]

Wall has also stressed that while Hepworth could sometimes be stern, she was also a supportive employer and an important role model: 'For the first time I learned what it was to be a professional artist ... I realised how hard I was going to have to work if I was going to make anything. It happened at a time when it was necessary for me to be told or shown how difficult the problem is and how hard you have to work at it.'[11] For all that she could appear formidable and austere, there are many indications of Hepworth's generosity of spirit and of her genuine capacity for friendship and indeed humour. As Sophie Bowness has written, she had a 'profound sense of identification with St Ives ... and repeatedly declared her need to belong to a community and to play a part in its development'.[12]

What is more, while intensely focused on her work, her international world view extended beyond the boundaries of career. Following the Second World War she had become an avowed pacifist and was a member of the Peace Union. Long committed to left-wing politics, she joined the Labour Party at the time of the Suez Crisis and campaigned against the death penalty and apartheid. She was also actively involved with the CND, of which she was a sponsor. Her political beliefs can in fact be seen as a natural extension of her inherently utopian project as a modern artist.

*

On 24 February 1964, Milne wrote to Julian Nixon:

> Tony A.J. was down last week to photograph Barbara. Very informal – he even had a coffee at the espresso bar on the front so I expect they will put up a 'By Appointment' sign for the season! Barbara is off to the US soon for the unveiling of the Hammerskold [*sic*] memorial outside the UN building, her biggest commission to date.

Antony Armstrong-Jones – also known as Lord Snowdon, husband of Princess Margaret – was in St Ives to photograph Hepworth for *Private View*, an ambitious large-format book. Subtitled *The Lively World of British Art* and published in 1965, it is now acknowledged as a seminal record of the period. Throughout its 300 pages are portrait and documentary photographs by Snowdon along with reproductions of artists' work, and texts by Bryan Robertson and John Russell.
The volume documents not only artists but also art historians, critics, dealers, London art colleges and heads of cultural organisations such as the British Council and Arts Council. Hepworth features on four consecutive pages; on two of them there is a group of black-and-white photographs in which she is shown with assistants at Pollard's in London, finalising work on the large bronze *Single Form* (1964),

the aforementioned memorial to her friend Dag Hammarskjöld. The photographs Snowdon took of Hepworth in St Ives are in colour and include a wonderfully theatrical portrait of the 61-year-old artist standing in the pale February light among seaweed-strewn rocks and shallow tidewater on Porthmeor Beach. In a scarlet headscarf and matching lipstick, she wears close-fitting trews and a dramatic knee-length hooded coat of Tibetan wool, both in existential black. She leans forwards a little, bending her right knee slightly to steady herself against a rock. Arms folded and hands crossed, lips pursed and eyes hooded, she looks intently at the camera like a kind of seafaring sorceress, inscrutable and benign.[13] Accompanying the photographs is a text by Robertson that begins with a reference to Herman Melville's novel *Moby-Dick* (1851):

> At home, and at work, Barbara Hepworth is rather like an extremely amiable Captain Ahab, forever in search of a particularly alluring White Whale – in her case, the next sculpture. An energetic, supremely disciplined north countrywoman with an extremely passionate and sensual idea of beauty and, for that matter, of life, she has brought up four children, lost one, married twice, survived – like [Henry] Moore – the rigours of long early years without money or recognition, and established a perfect working environment in the warm air and bright light of the south-west Cornish peninsula, at St Ives. Here she has studios and a tropical garden for working out of doors which might well content Picasso himself.[14]

Hepworth was among several St Ives artists featured in *Private View*. Others included Patrick Heron, seen in a group of four sequential photographs as he painted his canvas *Four in Deep Cadmium* (1964) in the Porthmeor studio he had inherited from Ben Nicholson. The latter, now living in Switzerland, was represented in the book by two works of his own choice and without a photographic portrait, as was his wish. There were also two monochrome shots of Roger Hilton: one in which he appears as though a blurry dancer balancing on one foot and the second in close-up, swigging from a half bottle of Bell's whisky. Also featured was Peter Lanyon, photographed among the ruins of tin mines at Levant, near St Just; Robertson's text makes reference to the artist's death a few months later following a gliding accident in August 1964.

By the time *Private View* was published, Hepworth and Robertson had been friends for over a decade, during which time he had made regular visits to St Ives, often staying with Milne at Trewyn. Robertson was director of the Whitechapel Art Gallery in London, a role to which he had been appointed in 1952 at the age of 27. There he developed a highly significant programme of exhibitions of both British and international contemporary artists, particularly notable for a series of shows by American painters. His links with America were forged during his initial visit in 1956, when first-hand experience of art, and discussions with painters in their studios, led him to conclude that New York had become the most important centre for advanced art. His understanding of the significance of American abstract painting led to Whitechapel shows of the work of Jackson Pollock (a memorial retrospective in 1958), Mark Rothko (1961) and Mark Tobey (1962). These were followed by Philip Guston (1963), Franz Kline, Robert Rauschenberg and Jasper Johns (all in 1964), and Lee Krasner (1965). Robertson kept up a correspondence with a number of American artists, including Robert Motherwell.

A stalwart supporter of artists, Robertson became one of Hepworth's most important postwar champions. The 1954 Whitechapel retrospective of her work, which he organised, proved instrumental in rejuvenating her career; a second show, of sculpture made between 1952 and 1962, followed at the gallery eight years later.[15] The catalogue published for this second exhibition includes an essay by Robertson, a section of which he later used in edited form in his text for *Private View*. Twenty-two years her junior, he and Hepworth developed a warm and trusting friendship in which humour played no small part, as is evident in several of his letters to her. His first, dated 30 March 1953, is a respectful, formal affair in which he addresses her as 'Dear Miss Hepworth'. Following a visit to St Ives in June of the following year, however, his tone has become altogether chattier. Writing from London, he begins 'My dear Barbara', and in what is a generally solicitous letter he clearly feels sufficiently confident of their friendship to advise her strongly against taking part in an American show, before describing the great success of her Whitechapel retrospective:

'17,040 people have seen it. Daily average over 51 days was 333 daily. 1,124 catalogues were sold – apart from a vast number of complimentary ones given away. Etc etc.'

He goes on to ask about a sculpture that one assumes she had offered to him as a gift:

> Barbara, I am obsessed, literally, with the *Standing Figure* – wood and strings. It is a monstrous thing to ask, I know, but could I have this *instead* of the large hand sculpture? I feel that we are now on sufficiently intimate and relaxed terms with each other, to say anything we like to each other; so if you are not happy about this, you must say so at once. I feel frightful asking you, but I love it so; & it would work in wonderfully with its surroundings in the flat ... it is a large and expensive carving, I know, so I feel doubly awful in asking for it ... Do look after yourself, dear Barbara, and have confidence in the future. I have it, and I sense that things are gradually coming your way, though you will find this difficult to believe at this particular moment.
>
> Much love – Bryan X
>
> P.S. I can never thank you enough for that wonderful holiday. It was marvellous. When we meet, will tell you about the trip with Peter Lanyon. If you made a move (friendly!) I'm sure he would respond.
>
> Sorry to have left those socks with you![16]

Hepworth clearly appreciated Robertson's friendship, and while reliant on his support, she was also genuinely very fond of him, as is clear in her letters to him, one of which, dated 1 May 1955, ends, 'Do come to St Ives as soon as you can. So much to talk about. With much love Barbara.'[17]

There is a letter, too, from October 1959, in which Robertson writes about *Moby-Dick*:

> Ahab – *Captain* Ahab – is the hero of the greatest American novel, Melville's 'Moby Dick', a novel of startling metaphysical implications written in the most subtle, haunting & limpid prose. *Moby Dick* was the monstrous *White Whale* that he spent his life tracking down in the

> vast reaches of the Atlantic ocean. The White Whale is perhaps Ahab's soul ... or life, or death, or absolution or many, many things.[18]

Before this, in the same letter, he writes, '[Hepworth's] Fine dotty protest over the marine-fish *metaphors* is quite funny really.'

From this one deduces a teasing disputation with Hepworth about his use of such metaphorical references in analysing her work, and that his description of her in *Private View* as 'an extremely amiable Captain Ahab' was an extension of an in-joke between them. What is certain is that Robertson – who by many accounts could be hilariously funny – felt able to rib Hepworth in this way. He probably did so as a deliberate tactic to draw her out of herself, given his awareness of what he calls in his essay for her 1962 Whitechapel show her 'innate shyness' – an interesting insight, and another factor behind her self-created carapace. Long after Hepworth's death, he described her to an interviewer as 'loving, humorous, warm and generous', while stating also that she was 'a bundle of affectations and manipulations'.[19]

Robertson formed great friendships with several other female artists, including the English painters Prunella Clough and Thelma Hulbert, to both of whom he gave Whitechapel retrospectives, in 1960 and 1962 respectively. He also mounted a show of more than a hundred of Ida Kar's photographs at the Whitechapel in 1960. The introduction in the accompanying catalogue is by their mutual friend the writer Colin MacInnes.[20]

Robertson developed a fond friendship with the American abstract painter Lee Krasner. Having mounted the first ever retrospective of paintings by her late husband Jackson Pollock at the Whitechapel in 1958, Robertson went on to publish a monograph about him two years later. There followed Krasner's own first retrospective in 1965, again at the Whitechapel. Robertson was gay, his sexuality widely known but unspoken among art world circles, and as Krasner's biographer Gail Levin has written of her, 'She cultivated gay male friends. They satisfied her interest in handsome, often younger men, and could be bright, attentive, unthreatening and loyal.'[21] Levin includes Robertson – who reliably demonstrated each of these four qualities – in the group of gay men to whom Krasner was closest.

Importantly, Robertson brought with him to St Ives a number of artist friends, who stayed as guests at Trewyn. Among them were Krasner and her fellow American abstract painter Helen Frankenthaler (1928–2011), as Milne mentioned in a letter to Nixon dated 26 May 1964:

> Bryan Robertson was down here recently with Helen Frankenthaler – You may not have heard of her but I'm sure your painter friend [identity unknown] will have. She is the wife of Robert Motherwell – and herself a well known artist. At present she is showing in Bond St – Bryan says their home in NY (they have two) – is full of fabulous Matisses – Braques, Brancusis etc. She has asked me over! But (like in the song) – 'how to get there that's the thing.'

The Bond Street gallery to which Milne refers was that of John Kasmin, where Frankenthaler had a show of her paintings in 1964. Five years later she too had a Whitechapel retrospective, for which Robertson supplied the catalogue introduction.[22]

Although his intimate relationships were primarily homosexual ones, Robertson informed certain friends that he had on several occasions slept with women. As the art historian Andrew Lambirth has written in his book about Robertson:

> What is certain is that Bryan from time to time asked women to marry him. More than one of his friends recalled his plans to marry Bridget Riley, and [the artist] John Hubbard remembered a special lunch at the Connaught when Bryan delightedly announced his intended marriage to Helen Frankenthaler [she and Motherwell were divorced in 1971]. Beatrice Monti, founder in 1955 of the Galleria dell'Ariete in Milan, one of the first European galleries to show the new American art ... recalled: 'Bryan always told me – I don't know whether it's true or not – that he had an affair with Helen Frankenthaler. He said, "It was very good because I had the reputation of being gay, so she could go out with me and nobody could believe we were lovers".'[23]

Another of those whom Robertson accompanied on a visit to St Ives was the artist Patrick Procktor (1936–2003): they stayed at Trewyn in 1961 while they were in a relationship. The two had first met when both were invited to dinner by the painter Keith Vaughan, who taught Procktor at the Slade School of Fine Art in London (1958–62) and remained his lifelong friend. Robertson believed strongly in Vaughan as an artist, giving him a substantial Whitechapel retrospective in 1962. Procktor had been to St Ives before, having spent two months there in a rented cottage in the winter of 1957, when he produced a body of work to take with him for his interview at the Slade. Of the trip to St Ives he made with Robertson, Procktor later recounted in his autobiography how the pair had paid a visit to 'Keith Vaughan's new studio on Porthmeor Beach ... which he had recently bought.'

He later describes Trewyn as 'a rather nice boarding house with bright, colourful bedrooms. It was a Victorian villa with a garden and a high wall surrounding it, high above St Ives bay – and bang next to Barbara. Bryan and I stayed there, as Keith [Vaughan] had before he'd found a studio.'[24] While Vaughan certainly visited, and very probably stayed at Trewyn, aside from this mention in Procktor's autobiography – an untrustworthy record on various counts – there are no references elsewhere that suggest Vaughan bought or indeed rented a studio in St Ives. There are, though, many drawings and paintings of Cornish subjects by the artist, the latter all made at his home studio in Hampstead. He had visited the county as a child, making a series of drawings that constituted his first ever exhibition when they were shown at his school in Sussex. Vaughan quite often travelled to St Ives from London with his friend and doctor Patrick Woodcock, and occasionally with Procktor and Robertson. His introduction to Milne most likely came from Cosmo Rodewald, whom he had first met during the Second World War when, as fellow conscientious objectors, they were both enlisted in the Pioneers Corps. They were to establish an enduring friendship. While highly intelligent and well read, the mostly self-taught Vaughan had not attended university and found himself awed and overshadowed by the scale of Rodewald's erudition, describing him as 'a talking lexicon'.[25] He was also impressed by his friend's personal connections, and through him met members of the largely queer London artistic and literary circle with whom Rodewald was acquainted via his Oxford networks. In London, Rodewald introduced him to the wealthy collector and sponsor of *Horizon* magazine Peter Watson, who in turn introduced him to the painter Graham Sutherland, whose work exerted a profound influence on Vaughan's output of the late 1940s. At Watson's London salons, Vaughan met the writers Christopher

Isherwood and Stephen Spender, both of whom subsequently purchased his work. He was also introduced to the writer John Lehmann, who published some of Vaughan's wartime drawings and writings in *Penguin New Writing*, the literary magazine of which he was editor. Introductions such as these proved vital to Vaughan's career.[26]

Born in 1912, Vaughan was aware of his homosexuality from an early age, and in adult life documented his sexual activities in some detail within the 62 volumes of his journals. His first entry was written on the eve of war in August 1939, and his last quite literally just before losing consciousness after taking a fatal overdose on 4 November 1977, in a long-premeditated suicide that followed a period of excruciating illness caused by the cancer he knew to be terminal. Taken together, the journals chronicle an overwhelming and unquenchable sexual obsession, frustration and feelings of isolation. Of the full, unexpurgated journals (carefully selected extracts were published in book form in 1966, with a second in 1989), the artist's friend Alan Ross described 'the contrast they expose between the public face and the private misery'. Certainly, those who knew Vaughan found him urbane, charming and highly cultured. But his journals, like those of many queer men of the period, were where he confided the shadow life of his sexuality.

In September 1955 Vaughan accepted an invitation from Patrick Heron to visit him at Eagle's Nest, his house overlooking the sea near Zennor. During his stay Vaughan made pencil drawings in Heron's garden, and several of cottages and tin mines in the nearby landscape. Back in his London studio these then formed the basis for paintings, such as *Zennor* (1956) and *Landscape at Zennor* (1956). There are other paintings, made after a subsequent visit to Cornwall, including *Morvah* and the striking abstract canvas *Porthmeor* (both 1961).

Heron introduced Vaughan to several artists during his 1955 visit, among them Ben Nicholson, Peter Lanyon and Paul Feiler. He also met Hepworth, whose energy astonished him. Years later he wrote of the meeting in his journal, remembering her as 'a tightly wound spring of tension. But without a trace of self-doubt, self-questioning. Everything always going forward ... Ben just the same.'[27]

Vaughan wrote to a friend shortly after the visit:

> I definitely decided I did not like communities of artists. It might be different if one admired or liked what they were doing. The countryside is also full of young artists living in little stone huts with absolutely no money and artistic wives and a sort of negative satisfaction of having escaped from something. Of course none of them paint very well.[28]

Patrick Procktor returned to stay with Milne on at least one further occasion, when in 1972 he made a watercolour of a view of the garden at Trewyn, with part of Smeaton's Pier visible in the middle distance. He inscribed it 'Trewyn for John'.

A list of some of those who stayed at Trewyn – including Robertson, Krasner, Frankenthaler and Procktor – is included in a letter Milne drafted to Beatrice Miller, editor of *Vogue* magazine, in January 1972. It is worth quoting extensively for what it tells us about the house and its visitors:[29]

> Dear Miss Miller,
>
> I am a sculptor, living and working in St Ives for the last 17 years. My home is a large old house overlooking the harbour and, when I acquired it in 1957 my intention was to run it as a guest house for painters, sculptors, and people generally connected with the arts, whilst at the same time pursuing my career in sculpture.
>
> 'Trewyn' is quite unique in that, although situated in the very heart of St Ives, it is completely secluded behind high granite walls and the gardens protected by palm trees provide an exotic oasis and peaceful retreat during the summer months when the streets are crowded with tourists and traffic. It is an old house, and its earliest artistic connection was when Whistler painted the view from the front porch overlooking St Ives Bay towards Godrevy lighthouse, which figures in Virginia Woolf's novel 'To the Lighthouse'.
>
> Among guests who have stayed with me are many well-known people. The late Sir Herbert Read (poet, and international authority on modern art), Marc [*sic*] Tobey, Francis Bacon, Helen Frankenthaler Motherwell, Lee Krasner Pollock, Patrick Proctor [*sic*], Hazel Guggenheim, [Shōji] Hamada – the most distinguished living Japanese potter – and Bryan Robertson, who was responsible for making the White-

> chapel Gallery world famous. Other regular visitors are Richard Wattis, Sir Edward Hulton, Keith Barron, Fanny Carby, Adrienne Corri and Peter Vaughan.[30]
>
> The original property is now divided into two sections which contain my house and studio and also the house and studio of my neighbour, Dame Barbara Hepworth.
>
> Some of my biographical details are in the enclosed catalogue [that of his 1971 retrospective at Plymouth City Art Gallery]. Since the Plymouth Exhibition, I have participated in several other shows, including the Westward T.V. Open Art Exhibition when I won the major sculpture prize (which was followed by several appearances on television and a documentary film about my work). I have works in many private and public collections including the Tate Gallery. In April I have another One-Man Exhibition at the Marjorie Parr Gallery in Chelsea ...
>
> Would you be interested in making an article for your magazine using this information – the history of the house, the people who have stayed here, and my work. Together with the catalogue I enclose a photograph of Trewyn – and the views from it.
>
> Yours sincerely,
> John E. Milne

Although the editor of *Vogue* did not take Milne up on his proposal, his letter is in itself an important document. To its impressive list of guests one is able to add others known to have stayed at the house, among them Ronald Alley, Keeper of the modern collection at the Tate Gallery; the actor Irene Worth (a friend of Robertson); playwright and actor Noël Coward; architect Maxwell Fry; writer and performer George Melly; jazz musician Humphrey Lyttelton; and violinist and conductor Sándor Végh.[31] The film director Lindsay Anderson was another visitor. There are also rumours in St Ives that Rudolf Nureyev once stayed. Christine Farrington, who lived at Trewyn between 1964 and 1971, has provided more names to add to the list:[32] she recalls that during her time, guests included the actor Patricia Neal and her husband the writer Roald Dahl, and film director John Schlesinger. There was also the Russian writer, translator and great-niece of Pyotr Tchaikovsky, Galina von Meck, and the Carmelite friar and literary figure Brocard Sewell, described by one of his obituarists as 'a scholar, theologian, printer and brilliant connoisseur of 1890s decadence'.[33] Both stayed at the house on a number of occasions.

Yet another escapee from the north-west, Farrington first visited St Ives for a holiday in 1963, travelling down with a friend from her home in Manchester. Bewitched by the place, she decided that she wanted to live there, and so in the following year, having secured in advance a job as a waitress, she made her return. After a time she got to know Milne, who suggested that she come to live at Trewyn, where she could help run the place alongside him and his boyfriend Ivaldo Ferrari. While it is unclear how Milne and Ferrari had met, it seems that they made something of a double act, their relationship at times tempestuous. Of Ferrari, Farrington remembers him as 'very Italian, very dramatic ... a prima donna of the highest order'.[34] He did the cooking, first discussing menu ideas with Milne, who sometimes assisted in the kitchen; both were excellent cooks. Guests were able to book to have dinner at Trewyn on three evenings each week, and as Farrington recalls, 'Of course they always wanted to, because it was so much nicer than eating out in St Ives, at the time.' The actor Keith Barron and his wife Mary stayed at Trewyn on a number of occasions. Both from working-class backgrounds in Sheffield, they developed an affectionate friendship with Milne. They remembered the terrible rows he had with Ferrari and how Ferrari took charge of organising domestic matters, as Keith stated: 'He was absolutely wonderful at it ... He looked like a little Mussolini.'[35]

*

Along with Milne's loyal confidante Boots Redgrave, Brian Smith was the closest of his St Ives friends. A year or so younger than Milne, he was originally from Birmingham and had first visited the town on a holiday with friends in the 1950s, eventually settling there in 1965, when he made a living from shop work and as a part-time hairdresser. For a time he was employed at the New Craftsman, the gallery run by Janet Leach and Boots Redgrave on Fore Street. Leach recommended Smith to Hepworth, and as he later recalled, he began to work for her during the lead-up to her 1968 Tate retrospective:

> At the time, Barbara really needed someone to organise her social life. She often entertained people here [in St Ives] – other artists and gallery owners would come down from London to see her. She also travelled to London frequently, as she was a Trustee of the Tate Gallery. At one time, she thought of moving back there, but she tried it and found she couldn't work. Her inspiration was here, in the light and landscape.[36]

When Hepworth's secretary Margaret Moir retired in 1974, Smith, having taught himself to type, began to deal with her correspondence. Always reliable, courteous and discreet, he proved invaluable to Hepworth, looking after her appointments diary, taking care of visitors and accompanying her to meetings in London. He also cut Hepworth's hair. It is clear that she trusted him implicitly and became very fond of him. She bequeathed to him a house named Bri-Smith Cottage near to her studio on Barnoon Hill, where he then lived for the rest of his life. Dell Casdagli, long resident in St Ives, remembers him as incredibly loyal to Hepworth, describing how he looked after her and pushed her about in her wheelchair when she became infirm. By all accounts well liked in the town, and with many friends, he was a modest and private person who preferred to live alone. Casdagli describes him as 'A very special man – very private' and says that, although she was aware of his homosexuality, the subject never arose between them.[37]

Part of the gay circle that congregated at Trewyn, Smith sometimes joined in the fun at social gatherings. Victor Sayer got to know Smith and describes his brilliant wit and repartee, his ability to constantly induce tears of laughter, and his 'encyclopaedic mind', a quality that must have served him well in his role as Hepworth's social secretary.

6 Working Methods

Many factors informed Milne's work, among them his dialogues with other St Ives artists. A frequent cross-fertilisation of ideas was natural in such a close community, taking place in studios, pubs and cafés, and at meetings and exhibitions of the Penwith Society. In his early years in the town Milne enjoyed conversations with the likes of Peter Lanyon and Terry Frost, and with Hepworth's secretary David Lewis, husband of the St Ives painter Wilhelmina Barns-Graham. And he learned a good deal from fellow sculptor Denis Mitchell, both when working beside him in Hepworth's workshop and in the years that followed, when they continued to discuss stylistic and technical developments in each other's work. While much influenced by Hepworth, Mitchell had gone on to develop an impressive body of sculpture, distinctive in its elegance and poise. His abstract forms tend to be light in material density and often suggest organic growth and movement in nature. Mitchell made much of the potential of a single slender vertical, seen for example in his undulating *Turning Form* (1959) and *Praze* (1964), both in polished bronze. Milne's aluminium *Project* (1969) with its predominant vertical can be seen to relate to works such as these. There are other sculptures by Mitchell, sentinel-like forms such as *Gorran* (1968), that find counterparts in Milne's *Thor* (1974) and in several variations of a work entitled *Vertical Motive* (1975). Both artists were here working with essentially archetypal forms, although in their shapes and surface textures Milne's hark back to altogether darker and more primitive traditions.

Visitors from outside St Ives were also crucial in the ongoing dialogue and exchange of ideas. Among them was the sculptor Robert Adams (1917–1984), a regular presence in the town who exhibited often with the Penwith Society, of which he became a member in 1975. Adams was one of nine British artists whose work was shown at the

Venice Biennale in 1952, the year in which he also made his first visit to St Ives, where he stayed with Lewis and Barns-Graham. Milne is bound to have met him then and would have found great interest in Adams's entirely abstract carvings in stone or wood. Influenced by Brâncuși early in his career – Adams had visited his Paris studio in 1948 – at the time of his first arrival at St Ives he was affiliated with a group of English avant-garde Constructivist artists. Central among them was Victor Pasmore, who had famously taken a radical change of direction in his work in 1948 when, abandoning his much admired figurative painting, he began to make purely abstract work. Pasmore, too, had connections with St Ives, exhibiting in 1950 with the Penwith Society and becoming a member the following year.

Looking further afield, Milne was keenly aware of the work of the Japanese American sculptor Isamu Noguchi (1904–1988). Two of Noguchi's sculptures were included in *Painting and Sculpture of a Decade*, a large survey show at the Tate Gallery in 1964, and it is highly likely that Milne visited the artist's solo show at Gimpel Fils in London four years later.[1] Only weeks before that exhibition opened, Hepworth had given him a copy of a newly published monograph on Noguchi for his 37th birthday. In it she had written the following dedication:

> for dear John – sculptor & my good neighbour with every good wish for his Birthday
> Barbara, St Ives, June 1968[2]

Affinities with Noguchi's formal repertoire can be found in a number of Milne's sculptures, among them *Deimos* (1967), *October Form* (1968) and the bronze *Oracle* (1971), which bears more than a passing resemblance to Noguchi's pale brown marble *Pisa* (1966). *Oracle* relates to Milne's first visit to Delphi, hence its title. Unusual in his work, it is formed of two ovoids, the top of which has a mouth-like cavity and can be turned on a central pivot. One notes incidentally that Noguchi seems also to have exerted some influence upon Hepworth: for instance, there is a marked similarity between his *The Family* (1956–57) and her nine-part *The Family of Man* (1970).

A sculptor of great refinement whose practice extended to architectural projects, theatre, furniture and lighting design, Noguchi was yet another profoundly influenced by Brâncuşi, whose sculpture he first encountered at a show in New York in 1926. It set Noguchi, then in his early twenties, on a course from academic figuration towards modernist abstraction. In the following year, as a recipient of a Guggenheim fellowship, he travelled to Paris, where an introduction to the 51-year-old Brâncuşi led to him working for five months or so as his part-time assistant. Noguchi described the master's atelier as 'a laboratory for distilling basic shapes'.[3] Milne would have admired Noguchi's sensitivity to material and an assimilation of Eastern and Western cultural traditions learned in no small part from Brâncuşi: the art historian Carola Giedion-Welcker described the master's art as 'sculpture [that] unites the radiant formal beauty of the Mediterranean with the formal wisdom and symbolism of the East'.[4] For Milne too, Brâncuşi remained the touchstone, the single artist for whom he always retained the greatest reverence.

There was also Henry Moore. When Bryan Robertson mounted a show of his sculpture at the Whitechapel Art Gallery in November 1960, Milne travelled to London for the opening. Finding it 'really staggering', he returned to see it at least three times.[5] The show covered the sculptor's output of the previous decade, all of it in plaster or bronze. In the accompanying catalogue, Robertson described the 62-year-old Moore as 'the greatest artist to emerge in England since the death of Turner', and in commenting on the sculptor's influences wrote: 'To begin with, although alive to the ancient Mediterranean world, Moore's allegiances were with other, more grim and more ancient civilizations: Mexico and Egypt for example.'[6]

Milne, with his knowledge of ancient cultures, would have understood and appreciated this statement, as indeed he would Moore's atavistic impulses and the underlying eroticism in some of his work. He doubtless derived both sensual and intellectual pleasure from the earthy physicality of the sculptor's rough-hewn surfaces, from the works' heroic mass and weight, and the inventive synthesis of archaic forms with those of human and animal anatomy. Included at the Whitechapel were a number of Moore's small-scale relief pieces from 1955, produced as exploratory maquettes for a vast wall relief. Mostly untypical of the artist's work, they are made up of biomorphic protuberances laid out in rows or clusters, sometimes with the addition of groups of ribbed lines set in parallel so that they take on the appearance of rudimentary circuit boards or stringed instruments. One suspects that Milne was aware of these works before seeing them at first hand, as they bear striking similarities to his own *Les Baux*, a relief in bronze and wire produced in 1959. It was based on drawings made two years earlier following a visit to the medieval village of Les Baux-de-Provence in southern France, where he became fascinated by the tortuous volcanic forms of the Val d'Enfer, believed to have been Dante Alighieri's inspiration for the rocks and caves of his epic *Inferno*.[7] *Les Baux* consists of an irregular rectangle, its top edge slanting at a 20-degree angle. Structurally, it combines concise architectural shapes that suggest blanked-out apertures or portals, with roughly textured surface modelling. Again, the work appears somehow both modern and ancient; one could imagine it as cut from a far larger relief, such as those that had transfixed Milne in his student days. The charcoal drawings from which it derives are characteristically dense and granular, with sweeping radial movements tunnelling inwards to what reads as a series of steps leading to the dark unknown of an underground chamber at its centre. Such drawings are also metaphorical maps of the mind's inner workings. And here we return to Carl Jung, who himself made a series of spontaneous drawings as expressions of his psychic state, which he came to realise resembled ancient mandalas. As the Jungian analyst Anthony Stevens has written of these drawings: 'Jung began to understand these as representations of the Self, the central nucleus of the personality, which he sometimes referred to as the "archetype of archetypes". He found that his mandala drawings enabled him to give objective form to the psychic transformations that he underwent from day to day.'[8]

As for Milne, the Jungian precepts to which Franz Greenbaum had introduced him surely continued to resonate. There are insights into his production of both drawings and sculpture in a written statement he made in April 1976. It indicates a man existing in a state of great unease whose work was a hard-won form of catharsis:

> Sometimes, when I wish to express myself, in a drawing for example, the urge to release the tension is so strong that my hands tremble and

> I cannot make a steady line. This happens even in writing. Only when I am in the utmost despair, alone and beyond caring can I take up the charcoal, or pencil, and draw calmly.
>
> The results of these drawings still reflect a terrible struggle but the delineation, and sometimes even the forms, reflect serenity and ease. On the otherhand [*sic*] when I force the drawing, it looks wild and savage and uncontrolled. In this case I cannot achieve the exact result.
>
> With sculpture one does not work frenziedly, as some romantic writers would have us believe of artists in the past, hacking away until one collapses from exhaustion. Sculpture is essentially a methodical slow process, demanding the utmost thought, care, and deliberate control. One gets there in the end. Inside is the turmoil, perhaps also in the end product but between the two, and this is essential, the hands must be steadied by the will.[9]

And so turmoil was contained – in Jungian terminology 'concretised' – in Milne's sculpture, his hands steadied by his will, inner conflict subsumed within its necessarily slow and methodical processes.

*

In the 1950s, work such as Milne's remained central to contemporary sculptural practice, but by the middle of the next decade things had changed. At the forefront now were the so-called 'New Generation' sculptors, some of whose work was shown under that banner at the Whitechapel in the spring of 1965.[10] Each made entirely abstract art, radical in both form and material; it was produced not in bronze or wood but in prefabricated rods and sheets of steel, fibreglass, plastics and aluminium. Of the nine exhibitors, six were former students of Saint Martin's School of Art in London, where they had been taught by Anthony Caro (1924–2013), whose solo show in autumn 1963 – also at the Whitechapel – had proved a turning point in twentieth-century British sculpture. Caro had met Clement Greenberg in London in 1959, the same year in which the critic paid a visit to St Ives. In the following year Caro travelled to America, where he again met with Greenberg, who introduced him to artists including the sculptor David Smith (1906–1965) and the painter Kenneth Noland (1924–

2010). Both highly rated and championed by Greenberg, they had a major impact on Caro's thinking about making sculpture, and the next year saw a fundamental change in both his work and teaching methods. For the first time he created entirely abstract sculpture, constructed in welded steel. His innovation was in painting it in a uniform coat of brightly coloured industrial paint. This new approach to sculpture brought it closer to the work of Smith, and to American painters such as Noland, with whom Caro retained a friendship and dialogue. The alliance with Greenberg also continued; the critic described Caro's 'radical rejection of monolithic structure'.[11]

Dependent on line and plane as much as volume, the work of the New Generation sculptors was, like Caro's, the antithesis of monumental. It was displayed not on plinths but directly on the floor, where it established an entirely different relationship with both the viewer and the space it inhabited. And while it drew on classical formal language – of proportion, geometry, symmetry and asymmetry – its suppression of landscape or figural connotations was emphasised by unnatural colour, either painted on flatly like that of a car's bodywork or left as that intrinsic to the material itself. In short, it looked entirely new.

It is not known if Milne visited the show, but he is likely to have discussed it with Hepworth, who had. While Milne doubtless took an informed interest in the New Generation sculptors – the majority of whom, incidentally, were no more than five years his junior – his own work was not noticeably influenced as a result. He did, though, begin to produce pieces in cold cast aluminium and in fibreglass, for which he sought technical advice from the sculpture department at Falmouth School of Art. He created a number of relief works in aluminium: *Icarus* and *Wave* in 1967 – a bronze version was also made of *Wave* – and in the following year *Storm Descending* and *Storm Lifting*. In its cleanly defined shapes, the latter is stylistically closer to Jean Arp than to anything by Henry Moore. *Storm Descending* was based on watching dense black clouds through a car windscreen as they clamped down against a strip of intense white light along the rim of the horizon. The related *Storm Lifting* had its origin in a painted wood relief made ten years earlier, revisited once more in a smaller version in white fibreglass (1970). There were also plinth-based sculptures in aluminium, of which the first was *Vertical Aluminium* (1967). Comparatively light in material density, their effect is wholly different to that of polished bronze: altogether cooler, more detached. Milne returned to making work in fibreglass in a version of *Wave Form* (1972) and another relief, *Les Vagues* (The Waves, 1976). He worked, too, in stainless steel during the early 1970s, combining it with slate in his *Vertical Forms* (1974). In the mid-1960s he had shifted his focus from carving, concentrating instead on sculpting in plaster, from which editions could then be cast in bronze or aluminium. He occasionally returned to carving in wood, for example in the subtle *Vertical Form* (1977), for which he used some of the remaining Nigerian guarea that Hepworth had given to him.

*

For the greater part of his career, Milne's production of sculpture was sporadic. From the time of his arrival in St Ives, he had produced around 30 pieces by 1967; then in each of the next two years he made 13 and in the following year just four. Although he took part in many group shows during those years, he was 38 when he had his first one-person exhibition in 1969, which was late by many standards. After it came a period of intensive drawing, lasting into 1971, 'so that I almost stopped sculpting – then came back into sculpture by way of bas relief and then working in the round again'.[12]

There were various reasons for this irregularity, one of which was Rodewald's continuing financial support, so there was little pressure to earn money from selling work. Rodewald had in fact set up a trust fund for Milne with a London bank, the income from which might have been enough were it not for his overspending. Milne was also distracted by his hedonistic side, as well as his role as mine host at Trewyn, with its attendant responsibilities and social aspects. Another consideration was the issue of Milne's mental instability. He is known to have made several suicide attempts, including one in June 1960, when he spent several weeks in hospital after taking an overdose of the barbiturate Seconal, prescribed for his insomnia. This latter episode came after a highly emotional break-up with his boyfriend Ken Bryan earlier in the year. And indeed there was his continual insomnia, and the nightmares that afflicted him from early life onwards, referred to in a letter to Nixon probably written in 1964: 'The house is desperately lonely again with Ron [Lande] gone back. I *cannot* sleep alone. I have nightmares all the time, and I keep waking up all night long. I sleep with my light on – *and* the staircase light. I definitely will not spend another winter here on my own.' Hence, perhaps, his need for a housemate in the winter months.

Notwithstanding all or any of this, Milne remained deeply serious and ambitious about his work. As well as exhibiting in Cornwall during the 1960s, he also took part in several shows at the Artists International Association (AIA) Gallery in London, and in *The St Ives Group* at the Regent Street gallery of the tailor and outfitter Austin Reed. Opening in September 1968, the latter comprised work by 40 artists, among them five sculptors, the other four being Hepworth, Denis Mitchell, Paul Mount and William Redgrave. Milne showed a group of five works, including the polished bronze *Gnathos* (1967) and the swan-like *Leda* (1968) in aluminium, the most literal and unsuccessful of his mature sculptures.

Milne's output accelerated exponentially as he received more frequent requests and invitations to exhibit, both in the UK and abroad. He took on studio assistants, the first of them Chris Booth, a 19-year-old New Zealander who, not long after arriving in St Ives in 1968, had knocked on Hepworth's door to ask if he might work for her, in any capacity. Telling him she was not then able to take on students, she recommended he approach Milne next door. As Booth later wrote:

> Barbara Hepworth introduced me to John with the prospect that I assist him part-time (for no pay – my decision and, as it turns out, echoing John's former undertaking as student with BH) and maybe he would allow me to use his studio to make my own work. I was living at Anchor House, 5 Barnoon Hill, just across the road from Barbara and down the hill from Trewyn. John and I quickly became friends even though I was very much his junior (only a boy and looked much younger than my age). I worked hard for him, three mornings a week plus Saturday morning when Allan Dunn came [Dunn also helped in the studio]. John soon realised my capacity for work and offered to pay me – this meant I could give up my job as night cleaner at a local club. In the afternoons he generously allowed me to use his studio, in fact

> this became my base for creativity and he genuinely encouraged my being there.[13]

Milne's reputation was further enhanced when examples of his work entered public collections. In 1968 the ever-supportive Rodewald donated the aluminium relief *Icarus* (1967) to the Whitworth Art Gallery at the University of Manchester, then two years later the Arts Council purchased a copy of the same work from its edition of four, along with the bronze *Horus* (1969). Rodewald also presented a bronze *Gnathos* (1966) to the Tate Gallery in 1971, and in 1975 the Government Art Collection purchased *Oracle* (1971) from Marjorie Parr's London gallery. Milne's first commercial representation was with Parr, who in 1968 began to show his work at her eponymously named gallery on the King's Road in Chelsea. She had founded the gallery in 1963, and in 1969 established a second, in the premises of a former antiques shop on Wills Lane in St Ives. It was open between Easter and October, during which time Parr spent part of each month there, living in a flat above the gallery. In her absence Ivaldo Ferrari, employed as gallery manager, ran the place. Along with Milne, the exhibited artists included Hepworth, Denis Mitchell, Roger Leigh, Bernard and Janet Leach, Bryan Pearce and Patrick Heron. The selection was not confined to St Ives artists but also encompassed British artists working elsewhere, including those who exhibited at the London gallery, such as the sculptors Margaret Lovell and Peter Thursby and the painter Douglas Portway.

It was at Parr's London gallery that Milne had his first solo show in the autumn of 1969. Bryan Robertson supplied an insightful essay for its catalogue and also wrote reviews for both *The Spectator* and *Studio International*. Of these, the latter was the most sharply analytical, including as it did the following:

> Milne's images are atavistic, tough, hieratic, and quite often predatory in form. The sculptures are very tightly controlled: those with a highly-polished surface are deliberately reflective, with light as a modifying agency, and not for any decorative reason ... A dominant aspect of all the work is its animality: there is often the feeling of an invented anatomy and this applies to forms which have evolved from

> landscape as well as to the godhead or deity images, such as *Horus* and *Easter Island Form.* Milne's achievement is to have resisted the trap of the 'archaic presence', or fragment, as well as the concomitant rhetoric, or sentimentality, which occasionally conditions the impact of work in roughly the same area of awareness from Moore or Hepworth. There is a difference of generation here; and though it would be absurd to suggest that Milne has made greater sculpture than Moore or Hepworth, in some ways he has cut through and avoided the 'heroic' or pietistic factors which sometimes make it hard for younger artists to appreciate their full stature.[14]

Over the years in which Robertson stayed at Trewyn, he and Milne established a genuine friendship. Six years Milne's senior, he was to prove supportive in several ways, such as buying work from him.[15] When invited by the Arts Council to curate a show of sculptors, Robertson included Milne within an all-male group comprising Robert Downing, Kenneth Draper, Barry Flanagan, Nigel Hall, Bryan Kneale, Denis Mitchell and John Panting. Featuring sculpture and drawings selected in large part from the Arts Council's own collection, *Eight Individuals* toured to five English galleries from December 1971 to August of the following year.[16] Robertson chose Milne's *Icarus, Gnathos, Horus* and an untitled charcoal drawing of 1967. Mitchell, represented by two bronzes was, at 59, much the oldest artist in the show, with Draper and Hall, respectively 27 and 28, the youngest. Second oldest was Milne's near-contemporary Kneale (b.1930); of his four selected sculptures, two were plinth-based, one wall-mounted and the other intended to be positioned directly on the floor. Most radical were Flanagan's three pieces. Produced in 1966–67, they too were floor-based, one made from rope, the others from muslin or hessian filled with sand. Born in 1941, and a Saint Martin's student in the 1960s, Flanagan's concerns centred on experiments with freely available, very ordinary materials from which to create sculpture using the most minimal of physical interventions. Robertson's selection represented a snapshot of the diversity of contemporary practice, and what he described in the catalogue as the 'main break' between the biomorphic, landscape or hieratic forms – referring here directly to Milne and to Mitchell with their 'distancing' use of pedestals or bases on which to display the work – and the more open, less enclosed sculpture of the younger artists.[17]

Highly effective both in promoting her artists and in selling their work, Parr was instrumental in securing for Milne a retrospective at Plymouth City Art Gallery. It opened in June 1971 – Milne's great friend Richard Wattis made the opening speech – and featured around 45 sculptures and a selection of drawings. At its centre was *Variations* (1970), a large seven-part work in cold cast aluminium, displayed on a raised platform over 4.5 metres long, which was painted in a grey similar to that of the sculptural material itself (or so it would appear from black-and-white archival photographs of the installation). Each component is a variation on a curved cradling form. The seven individual units are each positioned differently and are spread out in an irregular formation, in one of many potential permutations. The platform, raised 30 centimetres or so from the floor, both contains the work and becomes integral to it, setting out the parameters of interaction with the viewer and between its seven forms. *Variations* is the closest Milne got to the New Generation sculptors; had he set it directly on the floor, it would have been entirely in keeping with their work.

While Milne's mature sculpture was often inspired by the Cornish landscape, it drew more deeply on his experiences in the three places he had most wanted to visit when young: Greece, Iran and Morocco. After his first journey to Morocco in 1967, he returned in the following year and many times thereafter, sometimes with friends, such as Ronnie Lande and Byron Temple. In a typewritten document made in the early 1970s he recorded his memories of the place, writing of its dramatic landscape with an acute sensitivity to form, surface, light and shadow:

> I rarely made notes on my numerous journeys to Morocco; it was unnecessary. The impressions of those journeys were so vivid they will always remain a part of my thoughts. For me, Morocco is predominantly the land of the desert, the sun and mountains.
>
> It was from the nine hundred years old city of Marrakech that I first began to discover the country in my travels southwards. Heading up into the Atlas mountains, a range of incomparable grandeur.

Wild, rugged[,] serene – all words which I have used before, but what are words? Great surging masses of rock topped with dazzling white snow. ...

Once over the Atlas the landscape becomes immediately desert; arid, parched and tough. There is a feeling of great spaciousness, open and free. Never anywhere have I been so aware of the feeling of liberation one can get from seeing so vast an expanse of sky. As far as the eye can see mountains rise gently in all directions. It is a landscape of many subtle colours. Browns merge into ochre, ochre into gold, gold and red, grey and green, all muted into one harmonious organic unity.

On first impression it is an uninhabited world but one becomes aware of distant buildings. Casbahs or small villages. Fortresses surrounded by crumbling walls. Always flat roofed and often with pyramid-like towers and ramparts. Sometimes constructed of local stone but more usually of mud, blending so discreetly with the landscape that they are often barely discernable [*sic*]. The textured surfaces on the weathered facades, coarse and crude in the harsh African sunlight, echo the stratas of the surrounding mountains. Vertical shafts of deep shadows intersperse the long low horizontal rooftops, ramparts, and rows of black windowless apertures. Sometimes the ruins would be those of old palaces[,] sometimes just a group of simple mud houses. ...

Then the great gorge of Todra. Cathedral-like walls of sheer rock rise precipitously on both sides of a narrow winding road. Monumental boulders are suspended precariously on the mountainsides, seemingly without support, ready to hurtle down in a tremendous landslide. Dark caverns are gouged out of the rocks, deep black and mysterious. There is every conceivable pattern and texture on these cragged (jagged?) surfaces as if some gigantic hand has taken hammer and claw to create a colossal sculpture. Powerful and intimidating, terrifying yet eternal.[18]

Milne's first visit to Iran was in 1971. Accompanied by his friend David Field, the pair went to Tehran, then to the city of Isfahan. Sited in a fertile oasis on a high plateau, the city's spectacular architecture dates from the reign of Shah Abbas the Great, who in the seventeenth century made it the capital of Persia and a centre of Islamic art and trade to rival the Ottoman Empire. Milne was awed by the architecture, particularly the centuries-old arched brick bridges over the Zayandeh River and the mosques and minarets with their dazzling blue and turquoise mosaics. Colour was everywhere: in silver-painted fluted columns, in houses of pink and blue, the earth itself cinnamon-hued.

From Isfahan the friends went to Shiraz, then onward 90 kilometres north-east to Pasargadae, the capital of the Achaemenid Empire under Cyrus the Great. Finally, they arrived at Persepolis, site of the ancient palace of Darius and Xerxes that was destroyed by Alexander the Great, where they walked through the Hall of a Hundred Columns and saw at first hand the intricately carved bas-reliefs, from which casts and fragments in the British Museum had so bewitched Milne as a student. He wrote several versions of his account of the visit to Iran, the most concise published as 'Artist's Notes' in the catalogue for his 1972 exhibition at Parr's London gallery:

> It was a brief but unforgettable journey. One night I sat for hours beneath the arches of the oldest bridge in Isfahan; something which I felt upon seeing it the previous day compelled me to return. It was a feeling, obsessive and hypnotic, about the interlocking structure of the arches and tunnel forms through which the waters of the river pounded. There was no explanation, but later, when back in England I showed photographs of this place to various friends, they said 'Ah, that is where so many of your ideas stem from; it is almost a prototype of some of your drawings'. But the drawings referred to were executed fifteen to twenty years before. It was like breaking a dream.
>
> Climbing up the great blocks of stone which form the tomb of Cyrus the Great, and sitting *inside* that simple cave-like monument, constructed over two and a half thousand years ago for the founder of the Persian Empire, I again felt this sense of mystery and intense awe. It was very, very, silent, and one looks out from that dark cavern, down and across the vast empty plains surrounded by a savage wall of gigantic mountains into an intensely blue sky broken only by the movements of a passing eagle or stork.
>
> From there I arrived, at last, at Persepolis ... I looked up the vast staircases hewn out of the mountainside which lead to the tombs of the Kings and, with reverence, at finally seeing the exquisitely carved

> bas reliefs which I had known as a student only from photographs and visits to the British Museum, but which had made such a profound impression upon me when I first embarked upon a career as a sculptor. I was overwhelmed with a feeling which connected all those past years. It was an emotion which I cannot explain, but immensely powerful and stimulating. A moment both religious and full of magic. And magic for me is present in all art.[19]

The impact of Iran on Milne's work is evident in a series of pieces clearly influenced by its architecture and landscape. Many consist of a simple shape – a dome, mound or arch – into which sometimes an aperture is set, suggesting concealed interior space. There are also small free-standing relief pieces in cold cast bronze, such as *Sha Abbas*, that draw upon Islamic architectural forms. Several of them featured in his 1972 exhibition, including *Landscape (Isfahan)*, *Cyrus*, *Darius*, the standing profiled figure of *Persian Monolith*, and the 15-centimetre-high *Persepolis* in patinated bronze. All were made in the year of his exhibition, with the exception of the monumental *Persepolis II* – Milne's largest work – which was produced the following year.

*

A man of innate intelligence, Milne was in many ways an autodidact. He read widely, and in a list of books that meant the most to him, he included André Gide's journals and the prose-poem *The Fruits of the Earth* (1897). There was also Jan Morris's autobiographical *Conundrum*. First published in 1974, it is an extraordinary account of the transgender author's quest for what she defined as the 'escape from maleness into womanhood'. There is a mystical element in Morris's story, connected to her sensitivity to place and to a wanderlust resulting in some degree from her earlier professional life as a foreign correspondent. In a passage to which Milne will have related, she wrote: 'I spent half my life travelling in foreign places ... I have only lately recognized that incessant wandering as an outer expression of my inner journey.'[20]

As was often his habit when reading, Milne wrote down several quotations from *Conundrum* in a notebook. Other books from which he transcribed selected passages include Yukio Mishima's *Forbidden Colours* (1951), Henry Miller's *Black Spring* (1936), James Baldwin's *Nobody Knows My Name* (1961) and part of an interview with the film director Ingmar Bergman, in which he says, 'I think all artists have an impatience of the soul to find out things about reality and themselves. They never feel "now I am completed".'

Other favourite titles were Virginia Woolf's *To the Lighthouse* (1927), André Maurois's *Proust: Portrait of a Genius* (1950) and Antoine de Saint-Exupéry's autobiographical *Wind, Sand and Stars* (1939). The Saint-Exupéry fascinated Milne in its descriptions of the desert and of flight; the author was an aviator whose plane crashed down in the Libyan Desert in 1936, during an attempt to break the record for flights from Paris to Saigon. *Wind, Sand and Stars* contains an account of the crash and of the writer's subsequent miraculous survival. Its narrative is imbued with a brand of philosophising that Milne would have found compelling. From it he made the following transcription:

> And yet we know the joys we could not possibly have known elsewhere. I shall never be able to express clearly whence comes this pleasure men take from *Aridity*, but always and everywhere I have seen men attach themselves more stubbornly to barren lands than to any other. Men will die for a calcined, leafless, stony mountain. The nomads will defend to the death their great store of sand as if it were a treasure of gold dust. And we, my comrades and I, we too have loved the desert to the point of feeling that it was there we had lived the best years of our lives.[21]

Saint-Exupéry loved the desert; indeed, his myth was forged there. He died in 1944 while in his early forties, when his aeroplane crashed into the sea, never to be found. This, too, became interwoven with his myth as a romantic heroic figure. As for Milne's own love of the desert, Paul Hodin used a telling phrase about his compulsion to return to that part of North Africa when he described him as 'a mesmerised pilgrim'.[22]

In much of Milne's work there is a characteristic earthiness that very much reflects the man himself, for he was energised by the sensate. He luxuriated in the heat and colour of northern Africa, and that of the Mediterranean, where representations of the male physique in antiquity found intoxicating echoes in the bronzed men and youths of contemporary life. The intensity of light he encountered in those places resulted in an enhanced perception of form and surface that brought the sensations of sight and touch vividly closer. While Milne was drawn to the desert for aesthetic and spiritual reasons, also intrinsic to the allure of Morocco were the opportunities it presented for him to have sex with young men. The charged atmosphere of the place, with its permissive attitudes to sex and sexuality, was liberating for homosexuals, and from the 1950s onwards many were magnetised by it. Among them were the writers Jean Genet, André Gide, William Burroughs, Allen Ginsberg, Tennessee Williams, Truman Capote, Gore Vidal and the English playwright Joe Orton and his artist partner Kenneth Halliwell, who were often accompanied by their friend the actor Kenneth Williams. For some gay men it was also a place of self-imposed exile. Richard Blake Brown's friend Rupert Croft-Cooke and his secretary-companion Joseph Alexander had decamped to Tangier in 1954 upon their release from prison, having both been convicted of gross indecency on dubious grounds. Croft-Cooke wrote of his experiences in his book *The Verdict of You All* (1955), an eloquent and very human account of his arrest and imprisonment for six months at Wormwood Scrubs and Brixton, related in a tone of restrained anger and ridicule. He and Alexander remained in Tangier for 14 years.

In notebooks kept during visits to Agadir in southern Morocco in 1975 and 1976, Milne wrote evocatively of his impressions of the region's geography, his sexual encounters and use of hashish. Some of his notes were written in French; what follows are selected extracts:

> Agadir 15/4/75
>
> Do I feel *so* different. Yes – Is it the 'hash' – perhaps. And to be so far away from grey, leaden, skies and problems. But the 'hash'. It could also be that I am laying [*sic*] in the hot sand under a blazing sun next to the naked body of my lover. Warm caressing hands, and then the 'hash'. My body is burning – *beautiful* sensation. No cares – nothing matters except being here, *now* ...

> I swim. The pool is warm, after the sea, but artificial like all the people around me. Gone is my lover. Washed away is the sand and the water of the pool is sterile. Still, the sun burns, my body is glowing and there will be tomorrow.

> Agadir 17/4/75
> Last night aggression and anger (Hotel de Paris avec KEBIR). Returned via the park and met KABIA. Quelle tendresse. Amour que je n'ai reçu pas dans beaucoup des anneés. La bouche me baiser milles milles fois et transporte dans le ciel. We sat and [indistinct word] through the night and the night was wonderful. Full of calm, a crested moon. A stillness and the warmth of that body. I was alive and young again.

In the same entry of 17 April, Milne goes on to write of how he and Kabia had arranged to meet on the beach that day, and of how when the young man did not turn up he felt an inexplicable feeling of complete sadness: 'Back is the loneliness. The aching, yearning void. And it should have been so – different.' Underlying many of these notes from Morocco is the theme of Milne's personal isolation, and of how the momentary liberation that came with each sexual encounter reminded him also of the lack of deep and lasting intimacy that he so longed for. There is a sense too of how the very atmosphere of the place was charged with sensuality and eroticism, as in the following entries from 1975 and 1976:

> May 5th 75
> Walking in the Palmarie with Dick – après midi [Dick Bird, an old friend of Milne's who was resident in Morocco]. *Very* hot. Suddenly, sounds of distant thunder. Spattering of rain so we took shelter in a farmyard. Standing beneath the mud shelter talking to the farmer, all the animals shuffle inside to take cover from the torrential downpour. We feel strange standing in our shorts and clay covered sandals, being nuzzled by goats, sheep, cows. Heavy farm smells. As if by magic a *beautiful* young Moroccan appears. Well dressed, in this strange, biblical setting. Dark velvet jacket tight, light grey trousers. He stands close, – smiling. Dark sombre eyes looking at our faces then at our scantily clad bodies. Quickly embarrassed (and blatantly obvious from

the surging 'packet' in his trousers) he becomes confused and 'disappears' into another building. The air heavy with sexual undertones and things unspoken. The farmer invites us into the 'best' room. We take off our sandals and sit on banquettes. Naked feet on the straw covered floor. Hundreds of flies – everywhere. The atmosphere is heavy, hot and animals peer in at us from the doorway. We are offered tea but Dick declines and we sit in silence with the farmer looking, penetratingly, at our naked brown legs. On the wall, a photograph of a strikingly beautiful young man. I enquire and it is the farmer – as a soldier. Now a wizened gnarled old face and balding head. Perhaps only forty years but looking a hundred. Terrifying thought that *so* beautiful young son will, all too soon, become like his father. The storm slackens so we leave. Many happy smiles to see us off and animals, everywhere, in the mud.

The rain is increasing. In no time, we are slipping and floundering in streams that were previously paths. Down thunders the rain echoing the lightning and rumble of thunder. Heavier and heavier. We flounder on. Completely soaked. Water everywhere. Clothes clinging to our bodies and water streaming down our necks. We laugh and laugh and laugh. It is wonderful – exhilarating and liberating. After several miles we find the elegant car and whish ourselves back to hot baths and dry clothes. To a cocktail party (chez Anne Porter). Dreary, dreary, people, making silly English conversation, sipping glasses with crooked fingers. How *ghastly*. All I can think of is the afternoon – the farm – those faces – the elements – *That* is what it is all about.

Agadir, 1976

The waiters in the bar are very friendly and treat me as an old friend. I feel a sense of 'belonging' in this country. I wander back towards the hotel – through a park. The moon is full and the sky is clear and blue. I enjoy relieving myself under the eucalyptus trees looking at the sky – it is a very natural sense I am aware that someone is watching. From the shadow of the trees a young man appears. I do not want him but I need physical contact. We sit on a bench and I feign drunkenness. My cough makes things worse. Eventually we go into the trees and he makes 'love'. We part and I continue homewards. Just before the hotel, there is someone standing. I linger a moment and we greet each other.

Again, I do not want him but I feel excitement at being wanted. He is a guardian (soldier) on a building and he takes me down into the basement. It is dark and mysterious but I feel no danger. Hands caress and fondle and we kiss. He puts down a blanket on the floor and we make love. When we part we make a rendezvous for Friday when he will be on duty again. I enter the brightly lit hotel, full of western tourists overdressed, noisy and silly. I make my way across the moonlit garden by the pool, to my room. A young waiter pursues me and asks if he can come to my bed! End of evening.

Making love under the stars. A passionate dark face with gleaming teeth and large penetrating eyes. Strong dark arms and tender caressing fingers. The sound of the sea and the passionate warmth of the body. So masculine and so positive.

Lying in bed in a small arab hotel with the same lover. Our bodies completely naked and warm. The primitive room looks magically transformed by the moonlight which sifts through the half open shutters. We caress and make love, again and again. He is young and virile and wants to continue all night –

[At his hotel] I cannot sleep. The birds sing and the mountains look more lovely than ever. I long to make love, but not for sex, but because I am so happy and so bursting to express it – to Taiel, whom I shall see later in the day.

And the Atlas. Hazy now in the gold sunshine. A white drawing, faintly traced, on a blue-gold background.

After a lovely evening, I return to the hotel with a large branch of orange blossom which Taiel plucked from a tree on the road ...

25/3/76

I awake to the birds' chorus again and to a room heavy with the scent of orange blossom.

*

There is a centuries-old history of the use of covert language, symbol and metaphor to signify queerness. Some of this – in personal diaries, for example – remained private markers of transgression, made solely for their author's eyes, while others operated as coded messages for interpretation by fellow initiates. To express such concealed meanings, queer artists and writers have adopted various strategies, using particular words, vocabularies and forms of imagery. From the late Victorian era until well into the twentieth century, the idea of Arcadia was a signifier of sexual attraction between men. As the art historian Andrew Stephenson has written:

> 'Arcadianism' in the developing homoerotic vocabulary was not only a reference to the search for an earlier pastoral idyll, but rather a way of signalling same-sex desires and tastes. It acted as a form of shorthand for a set of idealised codes and cultural interests through which the newly emerged male 'homosexual' community could identify fellow kindred spirits. For some British artists and intellectuals, especially in the late nineteenth and early twentieth century, arcadianism took the explicit form of an idealisation of ancient Greece.[23]

This theme of Arcadian idyll extended – and was in fact central – to queer British neo-Romantic artists of the 1940s and 1950s, such as John Craxton (who spent many years in Crete) and John Minton. It was there, too, in Keith Vaughan's drawings and paintings of the 1940s, which were also very much associated with the neo-Romanticism of the period. A key motif for Vaughan was the male figure depicted in a landscape setting, a theme developed from his experiences working on the land as a conscientious objector during wartime. In his paintings of the male nude of the 1950s and 1960s, Vaughan often appropriated the idealised forms and postures of antiquity, thus framing his work within an established tradition that effectively legitimised its homoerotic subtext. Although many knew of or at least suspected the artist's homosexuality, such classical allusions, in paintings with titles such as *Standing Figure – Kouros* (1960) and *Ganymede* (1962), enabled those who did not wish to engage with his queerness to bypass it, as indeed the majority of contemporary critics did, in print at least. One might add that Vaughan is highly likely to have discussed the classical world with Rodewald during the years of their initial friendship in the war years: he visited Greece for the first time in 1960, when he too was bewitched by its young men.

Whereas encoded desire is comparatively obvious in figurative paintings such as Vaughan's – and, for that matter, in those of Francis Bacon, his fellow sensualist in paint – in abstract art the signs are by definition more complicated. In Marlow Moss's work there are parallels between the austerity of her paintings and sculptures and that of her own self-fashioning, both of which reflect a queer sensibility. Another queer abstract painter was the American Mark Tobey, who stayed as a guest at Trewyn for a period, probably during 1961 (he had a retrospective at the Whitechapel Art Gallery in the following year). Tobey visited the south-west of England on several occasions, having formed a lifelong and platonic friendship with Bernard Leach after their initial meeting in 1932 at Dartington Hall School in Devon, where Tobey was the resident artist. The importance of this friendship to Leach was such that, when Tobey died, he wrote that he had represented 'the profoundest influence in my life'.[24] Tobey had converted to the ecumenical Bahá'i Faith in 1918; its monotheistic doctrine, advocating a universal equivalence of all religious faiths, informed both his life and his art. He was also instrumental in Leach's acceptance of the Bahá'i Faith, which, while welcoming all people to its membership, considers homosexuality an affliction to be overcome, and so advocates celibacy among queer people. It is clear, however, that Tobey was able to find a personal accord between his faith and sexual nature, for he did not remain celibate. His partner from the early 1950s was Per Hallsten, a Swedish linguist who later became an artist. They lived together in Seattle, then later in Basel until Hallsten's death in 1965.

Tobey had developed an interest in calligraphy and East Asian art from discussions with Teng Kwei, a Chinese artist he met in Seattle during the 1920s. His knowledge developed further during a visit to Japan with Leach in 1934, when he spent a month studying Zen and calligraphy at a Zen monastery at Kyoto. He made his first truly abstract paintings a year later.

Informed by Eastern art and philosophy, the majority of Tobey's paintings are made with the water-based mediums of tempera and gouache, and are often intimate in scale. He strove to work meditatively, gradually forming edge-to-edge screens and veils of intermeshed calligraphic marks, each placed with a delicacy of precision and touch, the hand governed by subtle movements of the wrist.

One finds contained within the materiality of these paintings a metaphysical expression of that accord between spirituality and sexuality. It is defined most effectively in something Tobey said in relation to the philosophy underlying his work, published in a 1966 monograph on the artist: 'The dimension that counts for the creative person is the space he creates within himself. This inner space is much closer to the infinite than the other, and it is the privilege of a balanced mind – and the search for an equilibrium is essential – to be as aware of inner space as he is of outer space.'[25]

One wonders if Milne became aware of Tobey's statement, and indeed if the theme of balance and equilibrium was ever raised in conversations between the two of them when the American was staying at Trewyn. We know from the psychologist Marianne Jacoby's analysis that Milne was never able to achieve such unity on a personal level. Where he was able to realise equilibrium was in the formal clarity of much of his sculpture. In analysing what drove his work, we know that he drew from a young age, that Franz Greenbaum had prompted him to visualise his nightmares as a means of confronting his unconscious, and that drawing remained a means of expression deeply connected to his psyche. There is also the significance of his exposure to the natural world, in visits to the Lake District, Derbyshire and Scotland during his youth and then later, and more profoundly, in Greece. He was highly attuned to the numinous in landscape and architecture, most particularly in ancient places. While as a child he was made to attend church – he sang in the choir – in adult life he did not define himself as a religious man in the Christian sense. He was, though, a spiritual person, something that informed much of his work. The drawing made as a memorial to Käthe Schuftan is an obvious example of this, although there are many others equally infused with a sense of the human spirit. Sculpture is by definition a form of embodiment, and quite often in Milne's work the corporeal and the spiritual are effectively conjoined. Among the most powerful examples is the bronze *Credo* (1974). A work of indisputable presence, its Apollonian sensuality is heightened by its highly polished surface. The use of such high polish was learned from Brâncuși, who knew of its potential to evoke the divine (one is reminded also of the biblical idol of the golden calf). While Milne himself described *Credo* as a religious, resurging form, its two raised, claw-like shapes suggesting prayer or supplication, there is also in its intense muscularity an undeniable eroticism, and this too is a factor in its potency.

7 How to Disappear

> In the artist of all kinds I think one can detect an inherent dilemma, which belongs to the co-existence of two trends: the urgent need to communicate and the still more urgent need not to be found.[1]
> —Donald Winnicott

Milne's relationship with Hepworth was complex. The close proximity of their homes was something of a double-edged sword, for although there were undoubted compensations in being her neighbour, there were occasions too when it threw Milne's self-doubt into sharp relief. Hepworth's achievements so far eclipsed his own that looking down on her premises from the higher vantage point of Trewyn – the former stable block viewed from the manor house – must have seemed like peering through the wrong end of a telescope. Reg Singh, who in the early 1970s took over Marjorie Parr's St Ives gallery – it was renamed the Wills Lane Gallery – remembers Hepworth thus: 'She was a hard nut ... She was the art mafia of St Ives; she dominated the town ... And you saw this little woman, dressed very middle class; you never expected her to be the greatest artist in the town, or in Britain at one point.'

Hepworth could appear formidable in social situations, her hauteur surely one of her coping mechanisms to conceal shyness. Victor Sayer recalls one evening when she was due to call in for drinks at Trewyn: 'There was a sort of grandeur about her. It was almost as if the Queen Mother was coming.' And Milne's friend Lesley Hassey, who stayed at Trewyn on a number of occasions, states: 'I think the relationship between John and Barbara Hepworth was love–hate. Barbara complained about his parties. She was a controller, I think. Because he had worked for her, that probably meant for her that she could dictate.'

Hassey also recalls Milne saying to her one evening, undoubtedly after he had had a few drinks: 'Darling, everybody else has fairies at the bottom of the garden – I've got fucking Barbara!'[2]

But for all of this, Hepworth remained immensely significant to Milne, as was later manifest in his memorial sculpture to her. She believed in him as an artist and perhaps saw in his sculpture something of a continuation of her own concerns: that he had in effect taken up the baton.

Hepworth suffered ill health during the last ten years of her life. In 1965, the year she was made a Dame of the British Empire and appointed as the first female Trustee of the Tate Gallery, she was diagnosed with cancer of the tongue; her visits to London for meetings at the Tate were often combined with seeing her specialist at the nearby Westminster Hospital.[3] As well as the cancer, which continued to make her unwell, Hepworth endured permanent mobility problems after she broke her femur during a trip to the Scilly Isles in June 1967. Earlier that same year, at her request, Milne's friend Ronald (Ronnie) Lande had taken her on as a private medical patient. Already on friendly terms from Lande's visits to St Ives, their friendship deepened, and they went to London restaurants together, he sometimes accompanying her to events at the Tate and elsewhere.

Having been constantly engaged in the daily discipline of work that was fundamental to her being, Hepworth had for years paid insufficient attention to her physical health, a factor that became a concern for many of those close to her. Bryan Robertson visited St Ives in the autumn of 1965, and the following January sent Hepworth one of his teasing yet serious letters, in which he alluded to his unease at her loss of weight:

> I really just want to say that I think you are a very beautiful, wise, courageous, alarmingly intelligent, and superb woman (your sculpture has possibilities, too) and I was so pleased, glad, and delighted to see you working better and fractionally more solid. It all disappears when you stand sideways, of course; but front or back view is distinctly encouraging; on a clear day, with spectacles, I can *see* you. So please slap back those blasted egg custards (or better, mildly alcoholic egg nogs – have you tried the drink called Avocaat? It's a Dutch (mild)

> egg nog, and an occasional nip is as good as a wink). As Ogden Nash said about babies: 'A little talcum is always walcum' ...
>
> Keep well. Have another sponge finger with cream. Try quince preserve from that good grocers.[4]

On 9 January 1973, the day before Hepworth's 70th birthday, *The Times* published an article about her.[5] Titled 'Keeping Up the Fight and the Work', it was based on an interview undertaken in St Ives. The unnamed author reported:

> Still an active, prolific sculptor of excellence, she has been spending the weeks leading up to her birthday working out how many pieces she can create in the next 10 years.
>
> That, at least, is what she told me at the beginning of our five-hour interview. 'Every year is more marvellous than the last', she said.
>
> Later on, the optimism began to wear thin. 'I'm glad to reach 70', she said ... 'I didn't think I would. You came here for a birthday interview and what you may be writing is my obituary.'

The writer made mention that, although Hepworth lived alone, she was supported by a domestic and professional staff of eight, and entertained around 1,000 visitors each year, so her life was not a reclusive one. The article described the 'large and amazingly disorderly bed-sitter' in which she lived, with books, clothes, pictures and sculptures on and around her bed:

> 'I don't really care about comfort', she explained. 'I've always lived for my work. If I do a new work I like to put it in front of me and consider it.'
>
> For the first part of the interview we sat on two modern, black swivel chairs in front of an electric fire. Bottles of drink for entertaining visitors stood on the floor next to her. On doctor's orders, the only liquor she is allowed is whisky.

In fact, Hepworth was by now addicted to whisky, and her health also undermined from chain-smoking cigarettes. Michael Hunt believes that Janet Leach, 'a big mate of Barbara Hepworth's ... taught her how to drink'. Hepworth was not entirely new to alcohol, though, and like many of her generation had smoked from young adulthood onwards. The writer Leo Walmsley, who knew her in the 1920s when she was a student at the Royal College of Art, wrote of her smoking 'fags' and drinking whisky then. He recalled her saying: 'What damned good stuff whisky is. Do you think I could have another?'[6] But while Hepworth did not start to drink heavily until later on in life, Leach was a longer-term alcoholic, and it seems that Hepworth's addiction developed after the two became close friends and began to drink together. They met almost every day and talked often over the telephone. In Emmanuel Cooper's biography of Leach he wrote of how Hepworth, aware of her friend's bisexuality, became concerned that people might suspect them of having a lesbian relationship, and so sought legal advice and distanced herself from Leach, for a time at least.[7] Their friendship remained, however, and they spoke on the telephone when Hepworth went to bed at night, taking her regular sleeping tablet and smoking a last cigarette before the tablet took effect.

*

On 1 February 1975 Richard Wattis died suddenly from a heart attack while in a London restaurant. He was 62. Milne, for whom he had been a great friend for many years, was terribly upset at the news. But the defining blow came a few months later.

> *The author's diary, Wednesday 21st May 1975*
> Sculptor Barbara Hepworth died in a fire at her home last night in Cornwall.

It is uncertain if Hepworth and Leach had talked over the phone on the night Hepworth died. Perhaps her cigarette fell from her hand as she became drowsy from the effect of her sleeping tablet. As the fire took hold, sheets of polythene, used as protective coverings for wood-carvings, added fuel to the blaze. Hepworth's son-in-law Alan Bowness described how the fire 'completely blackened the whole place ... [It was] absolutely appalling, really, the smell and blackness of the fire.'[8]

A report on Hepworth's death covered most of the front page of the *St Ives Times and Echo* on 23 May. Under the heading 'Sculptor Found Dead in Bedroom Blaze', it included a graphic account of how her night nurse, Mrs McMinn, having ensured that Hepworth was safely in bed at 9.55pm, then went to sleep in the adjoining room. Getting up after 11pm to use the bathroom, she smelled what she thought was burning plastic: 'I went into her room and saw she was on fire. The whole of the bed was on fire. I couldn't get to the telephone because that was also on fire. She was in bed. I could see her in bed but I couldn't possibly get near her. I ran across the road to her secretary and he called the police.'[9]

Later that year, after hearing evidence from 12 witnesses, the coroner at the inquest into Hepworth's death recorded a verdict of accidental death. He commended efforts by a police constable and by Peter Lethbridge, a local schoolteacher, who had both made repeated attempts to enter Hepworth's smoke-filled room; Lethbridge, in a state of near collapse, had had to be rescued. Fire brigade officers concluded that the fire was probably caused by a cigarette or piece of lighted paper igniting combustible material.[10]

Following as it did the deaths of Bryan Wynter and Roger Hilton a few months earlier, Hepworth's demise meant that the imperial phase of St Ives art was effectively over. Patrick Heron wrote movingly of her for *The Observer* newspaper, in an article published within days of her death:

> No one who knew her could fail to recognise the consuming passion for her art; she was consumed by the ambition to get it out and put it over; by a single-mindedness which cost her many of the profounder human comforts most of us simply cannot do without: and finally, she was consumed by a sense of loneliness in her old age, confronted by the increasingly imprisoning infirmity which neither her achievements, her courage nor her remarkable will could overcome.
>
> To enter that increasingly cluttered studio into which she had by degrees been forced to withdraw completely in the past year or two – a room once white and empty and immaculate, but now serving as living room, bedroom, studio and office – was to enter the presence of

> a woman both formidable and enormously sensitive; both withdrawn and touchingly warm, by turns.[11]

The Dutch art critic Abraham Marie Hammacher was a close friend of Hepworth's. He published a monograph on her work in 1968, and 19 years later, in a revised edition, he added a final chapter, entitled 'The Exit'. There he wrote of how Hepworth's mobility progressively worsened and of her increasing ill health, and how in her later years, even on the occasions when she was confined to her sickbed, she had devised ways of keeping a check on the work of her assistants: 'She did not give in.' Hammacher wrote too of his final visit to St Ives a few weeks before Hepworth's death:

> Suddenly she was living in the past in a way that I had not seen in her before. She yielded unrestrainedly to unreal longings, their origins locked away in memories, and tried to imagine them as having a future.
>
> ... Events such as the end of her marriage to Ben Nicholson in 1951, or the death of her pilot son Paul in 1953, went on to weigh on her destiny. To disappear supposes a possible return; in her mind doors never closed.[12]

The shock of Hepworth's death and its circumstances – a horrible echo of Paul Skeaping's death – left family and friends bereft. Milne was profoundly distressed, and his fragile psychological balance tipped over, as Singh recalls: 'He idolised her. When she died, when she was burned to death, he was absolutely devastated ... He was knocking at her door, because he'd heard that it had happened in the night or the morning, and he was round there trying to find out what had happened and everything. But he was quite devastated.' Singh remembers that, as though to dowse his torment, Milne went into the sea, from which he had to be dragged to safety by friends: 'Just blind despair, you know.'

Paul Hodin made reference to this episode in his book about Milne, when he wrote: 'And John Milne knows how death tastes. He was very near it once when the unextinguishable memory of his master's burned body drove him half unconscious into the sea from where he was to be rescued, wounded and exhausted.'[13] In fact, this published account differs from the initial draft, for Milne had asked Hodin to remove part of his second sentence. The unedited version read thus: 'He was very near it once when he slashed the wrist of his left hand and he nearly died on that occasion when the unextinguishable memory of his master's burned body drove him half unconscious into the sea from where he was rescued, wounded and exhausted.'[14]

Hepworth's death continued to haunt Milne. In a letter written in August 1975, he apologised to Hodin for not turning up at a party, telling him that he had been going through a 'bad patch':

> It is very complicated and I will not bore you with the details but I have been mentally unwell and I can only think that is a delayed reaction to Barbara's death. Twice this week I have found myself in the sea in the middle of the night, and on Tuesday I awoke in Penzance hospital with fourteen stitches in my leg and no idea how, or why, it happened. The rest of the time I am perfectly alright and, until yesterday afternoon, I was convinced that I would come to the party. Then I began to feel 'strange' again and the last thing I wanted to do was to upset what I am sure must have been a very gay gathering.[15]

At the same time as all of this was happening, Milne's professional success was gathering pace both in the UK and abroad. In May 1974 he had a one-person show at Austin Reed Ströms, a department store in Gothenburg, Sweden, organised with the assistance of Marjorie Parr, whose ongoing relationship with Austin Reed resulted in its sponsorship of exhibitions for a number of her artists. Milne's association with the company had begun with his inclusion in its 1968 St Ives Group show, which was then followed with two further shows of St Ives artists, at the 1969 Bath Festival and three years later at the company's London gallery. Milne took part in all of them. His Gothenburg show comprised 32 sculptures and 11 reliefs, with an extract from Robertson's essay from the first London exhibition printed in the catalogue. Milne also began to establish himself in the United States and in Canada, where he featured in a mixed show at the Allan Edwardes Gallery, Vancouver, in October 1974. In that same month, Parr – constantly devoted, both professionally and personally, to Milne – gave him a third show at her London gallery, this time of nearly 40 sculptures, with one, the huge, arched, cold cast bronze *Persepolis II* (1973), displayed in the nearby rectory garden of St Luke's, Chelsea. In a piece published in the magazine *Arts Review*, the artist and critic Denis Bowen described Milne's 'way of creating an equilibrium of forces and tensions making his work silent containers of pure energy in poise and counterpoise. Both the largest and the smallest pieces in the show are likewise charged with a modulated monumentality and strength.'[16]

Among the 'silent containers of pure energy' were *Credo* (1974), *Turning Form* and *Megalith II*, which, after *Persepolis II*, was the second largest sculpture in the show. Along with the patinated bronze *Draa* (1974), which is similar in form to *Persepolis II*, these constitute the biggest sculptures within Milne's entire output (the seven-part *Variations* is another matter, as its overall dimensions result from the sum of its constituents, including the substantial platform upon which they are set).

Sculpture continued to take on new forms during the 1970s. It was the decade of the body itself as sculpture, of conceptualism and minimalism, and the media furore around the Tate Gallery's acquisition of the American sculptor Carl Andre's *Equivalent VIII* (1966), a minimalist work consisting of 120 unadorned firebricks laid out on the floor in a rectangular arrangement.[17] Never an innovator in the wider sense, Milne in his forties developed the sculptural language he had established in the 1950s, and within it the recurrent themes of growth, transition and metamorphosis. His drive was towards a greater symbiosis of formal clarity, essence and meaning. This is particularly effective in works such as the aforementioned *Credo* and the related *Resurgence* (1976), also in polished bronze. In some of Milne's later sculptures, the theme of anthropomorphism persists. Largely influenced by Surrealism, this can be seen in the work of numerous twentieth-century British artists, including Henry Moore and Graham Sutherland. The anthropomorphic element in Milne's sculpture is evident in pieces such as *Syrinx* (1976), its title like many of his others derived from classical mythology (Syrinx: an Arcadian tree nymph; a musical instrument made from reeds). The dynamism of the work stems from its sense of animated solidity and burgeoning growth, and from the negative shapes both within and around its lower and upper forms. It arises also from Milne's often utilised contrast of patinated and polished bronze, the latter in the claw-like upper section, where it is as though a layer has been peeled back to reveal its glossy underside.

Megalith II was not the gift to St Ives that Milne first proposed, for he had originally offered *Credo*, with the idea that it be housed in St Ives Parish Church, where Hepworth's *Madonna and Child* (1954), her memorial to her son Paul, is also sited. In a secret ballot held during a parish meeting in November 1975, the church initially approved this first proposal, which suggested that *Credo* would be placed over the door at the west end of the baptistery. However, in the following February the idea was rejected after the vicar had been told by the diocesan advisory committee of a regulation stipulating that a memorial of the kind offered could not be established until at least five years after the death of the person it commemorated.[18]

Following his initial optimism at the confirmation that *Credo* would be sited in the church, Milne now despaired at its rejection, writing on the morning of 7 February in his diary:

> There have always been tunnels tunnels with some light, far away in the distance. Last year (Barbara) put out that light. It lasted for a long time. There was a flash, and CRÉDO was to be my thank you because suddenly I realised that the long dark tunnel had been opened and there was light (fire?) space and direction.[19] That sculpture had *got* to be placed where *we* knew it belonged. There have been many months of problems, and the darkness descended again. Every night I wanted to give up again. Something was pushing me on. Yesterday Douglas Freeman [the vicar of St Ives Parish Church] came to tell me that Crédo could not be accepted into its home for five years. I hated the church for its petty regulations and again I cannot sleep. I *need* a solution ... In all her years of 'encouraging' me to work, Barbara (I believed) had selfish reasons. Now I feel I was wrong and she is *pushing* me on – now – no waiting. No time to wait. Those new sculptures must be finished ...

Approval was finally granted for *Megalith II* to be sited in Trewyn Gardens in April 1976, the same month in which the Barbara Hepworth Museum first opened its doors to the public. In Hepworth's will she had asked her executors to consider the idea of establishing a permanent exhibition of her work in her studio and garden, and after her death they offered the house and garden, together with the collection of sculpture displayed there, as an outright gift to the nation. The museum opened on 12 April, with Brian Smith as its curator, a role he was given at the request of Hepworth's family. There were over 14,000 visitors to the museum in its first 12 months. *Megalith II* was officially unveiled at a ceremony that December.

*

In January 1976, Milne was interviewed for Westward TV on the occasion of his inclusion in a forthcoming group show in Dubai.[20] The interview, from which there exists a clip of a few minutes' duration, was filmed in the sitting room at Trewyn, where Milne, wearing a pale grey polo-neck sweater, is seated on a red Harry Bertoia 'Bird' chair.[21] His neatly trimmed hair is now receding at the temples, his face a little puffy and cheeks reddened. He talks of his travels in Iran and Morocco, of how these journeys have influenced his work, and mentions his recent shows in Sweden and London. Behind him on the hessian-covered wall hangs Keith Vaughan's painting *Two Figures in Sequence (5th Assembly)*, and as the camera pans around the room one sees several of Milne's sculptures displayed along with a Janet Leach pot, and some rounded pebbles from the beach set on a shelf among them. The public face Milne presents during the interview is that of a witty, modest and sophisticated man. Watching the segment of film, and listening to Milne's refined speaking voice, one is struck by how untypical it is of a man from his social or geographical background, for there is a complete lack of northern accent. After watching the clip, David Lindsay responded thus to the question of Milne's lack of accent: 'That voice just couldn't have emerged naturally. It lacks any trace of his origin and must have been the result of training.'[22] There is nothing on record to suggest that Milne made a conscious effort to alter his voice. It may be that over the years a natural refinement of speech became accentuated, so that like Hepworth he retained no trace of regional accent.

Milne did not attend the show in Dubai, but during his final two years he continued to travel abroad, more so in fact than ever before. There were further restorative visits to Morocco and several professional trips to America, where he had a number of critically and commercially successful exhibitions. In May 1976 he made his first visit to New York, where he was included in a show of nine British artists at Genesis Galleries. He flew out to America and stayed at Byron Temple's apartment in Brooklyn, where, alone one evening, he typed the following:

> NEW YORK. MAY 12th, 1976. FIRST IMPRESSIONS
> I am sitting – alone – (Byron has telephoned from Lambertville that he is 'fucked out' 'exhausted' and will not be returning home tonight).[23] I am having dinner in his room on the seventeenth floor. A soft, elegant, glass lamp on the table, Californian wine beside me, Mozart playing in the background (Piano concerto No. 24).
>
> Have I come all this way to be alone ... There is no *need* to be alone. Out there is the 'City of Night'.[24] Clubs, bars, baths; all full of crazy lonely people. This is all on tap; or I could pick up the telephone, but no ... there is no point. It is probably good to have a rest from all that. All the past nights have been a frenetic round of 'rocky horror shows' of that kind. I cannot walk alone in Brooklyn. Black is beautiful ... but very dangerous; white people are not loved here.
>
> The room is full of Byron. Pots everywhere; the dish from which I have just eaten, the jug which holds the heavily scented night stock ... grey and blue ... textures everywhere. Shelves lined with his books, magazines, and more pots. Big pots, small pots, souvenirs from Peru, students' gifts. Byron's pots.
>
> A tall brown, ceramic figure stands on my left on a plain wooden stool. A work by a student. It has a 'mummy-like' appearance, yet it is also a pot. It has a contorted face; we have seen many expressions like that in the past few nights in 'haunted' bars. Dead, yet (just) alive. The mouth small and ugly, the eyes half closed. It gives off a puzzled, depraved, 'what is it all about' feeling. The fat body is ugly too; shapeless and deformed like so much that we have seen.

> Ahead, a huge horizontal window framing the Manhattan skyline. Deep blue and purple (a backcloth from Hollywood). Aircraft gently and quietly cross the velvet sky over the vast panorama of skyscrapers. From there they do not scrape the sky, they are beneath me. Millions of lights in towers of every proportion. In front of this, leaning on the glass, are two Reliefs; 'SHA ABBAS' and 'MARRAKECH'. Thousands of years between the sculpture and the background; yet they are of today. They are more calm, more beautiful, serene, and quietly composed. Yet there is some magic out there. If, suddenly, all the lights were to go out (as they will one day) it would be like Dante's 'Inferno'. It will be, it is inevitable. It is mad, crazy, insane and megolamaniac. All the buildings expressing the biggest display of sheer vulgarity and visual horror. Each striving to outdo its neighbour; a little bit higher, more ornate (that horror of a gold 'Prometheus' in the Rockefeller Plaza). Even the Empire State building has now given way to the two slim and elegant towers of the World Trade Center. Seen from below they are visually very exciting. Two modern mountains of stone and glass, soaring, like giant phalluses into the blue sky. Not the blue skies of Isfahan or Shiraz, for here is all pollution, but nonetheless a sky!
>
> Claustrophia [*sic*] in the jungles of Manhattan. Yet, looking down from the top of the Empire State building there is an atmosphere. It is one of absurdity, of impossibility. What are they doing, those buildings, and what are they trying to say? Or *tried* to say, because they have been a long time 'dead'. It is an atmosphere of death and total unreality. It is surrealist and quietly mysterious ...

The year 1977 proved to be Milne's most successful as an exhibiting artist, with group shows in Cornwall, Manchester, London and, for a second time, at Genesis Galleries, New York. There were also solo shows: in May at the Lad Lane Gallery, Dublin (sculpture and drawings), and in June at Saltram House, a National Trust property in Devon, where large sculptures were displayed in the gardens, with smaller works in the orangery. In October, Milne travelled to Philadelphia for the opening of his show with the Benjamin Mangel Gallery, at which, as he reported to Hodin, 'Everything was sold on the first day! My head is spinning.'[25]

When he was in America Milne visited California, where he had met with Bob Speaker, director of Gallery Rose in Los Angeles, who invited him to have a show there. Back at Trewyn in mid-December, Milne wrote to Speaker, updating him on recent hectic events. He reported how, while en route from California to New York that October, he had been introduced by a friend – probably Temple – to a gallery owner in Louisville, who had offered him a show, suggesting it commence in November:

> It was not until half way through negotiations that I realised she meant *this* November! It was then October 31st. Well, with the aid of the telephone and air-freight, my returning to England to see what was happening in my foundries, I flew back (on Concorde via Washington) and the show opened on the 20th. By the end of the first week, sales were good and I was also made an 'Honorary Citizen of Louisville', complete with a gold key from the mayor plus an 'Honorary life member of The Canadian Federation of Artists' by the director of a Museum in Vancouver. Things certainly happen quickly on your side of the Atlantic.[26]

The show was at Allen House Galleries. It received a favourable local press report, illustrated with a photograph of a smartly attired Milne at the opening, at which Temple and Isabel, who travelled from her home in Canada, had joined him.

*

For years Milne had found St Ives particularly oppressive during the winter months, which is when he sought solace overseas. As time wore on, and certainly after Hepworth's death, his sense of isolation became further intensified. Friends moved away: after four years living in St Ives, Alan and Valerie Lowndes had moved to nearby Halsetown, but then, in the wake of the departure of other friends such as Terry Frost, in 1970 they left Cornwall and set up home in Gloucestershire. Ever more desperate, Milne tried to persuade Cosmo Rodewald to buy somewhere for him to live and work in London, where he would feel more connected to the art scene and be closer to friends such as Ronnie Lande. Rodewald refused, but suggested instead that he might move to live at a property he had bought, part of a large house close to the River Ouse at Lewes in Sussex, 15 kilometres so from Brighton. Rodewald had acquired the place as a second home before retiring from his teaching post in September 1976. It was during that same month that Milne wrote to Temple in America, informing him that the owner of the adjoining east wing of the building had announced that he wanted to sell. With this in mind, Milne proposed to Temple that he might like to join him there, setting up studios and workshops, assuming that planning permission was possible at what he described as a 'scheduled' historic building. All of this hinged on conversations they had had about Temple returning to England on a more permanent basis. It is clear from Temple's letter of reply dated 20 September that his finances were somewhat precarious, in part because he was in the process of trying to divorce Katherine. He went on, his words suggesting that Milne had strong feelings for him:

> Now the not so easy part – yes I still want to come to England to live BUT I feel I would be giving up what I worked so hard to establish for myself here [at Lambertville] and to re-establish would take years over there ... The best I think is to let you re-locate to your best advantage and possibly in the time ahead with you or near your new location I could establish a small part time studio. Living with you would be bliss BUT I know myself that I would probably be having little flings such as Ross or Mr X, Y, or Z and that would only hurt you and that is something I do not wish to do; I do love you John, but not in a physical way – I have tried to be as honest as I know how – what else can I say? I just can not see my way clear to come over in the coming months.[27]

Towards the end of October Milne replied, thanking Temple for his 'long and "honest" letter', before going on to write:

> Regarding a move to England, I had not realised that you had so many financial commitments but it was *my* intention to raise the capital to purchase a property that we could *share* in a physical sense. For you had repeatedly told me that you wanted to return to England and that you (as I myself) did not like undertaking such an upheaval *alone*.
> I was never under the impression that you 'loved me in a physical way',

> and naturally I realise that there will always (?) be little 'flings like Ross etc.' But I thought that we had sorted out that aspect during our long talks in Marrakech, New York and when you left here last.[28]

One wonders how Milne imagined he might raise the money to buy the property, given that he was often substantially in debt. Thwarted in his desire to live in London, and unwilling or perhaps unable to move to Lewes alone, the shadows continued to encroach. David Lindsay recalls that Rodewald, by now jaded with Milne's requests for money so that he could have sculptures cast in bronze, would receive telephone calls from him in the middle of the night, in which Milne would plead for help: 'He was in a desperate state, very pissed, very emotional ... In the end he became a very neurotic drunk – he really needed medical treatment I think.'

In his later years Milne was reliant not only on alcohol but also on drugs. He had long taken prescription drugs for depression, but this was different. Referring to Milne's growing success as an artist and its attendant pressures, Michael Hunt has stated: 'It was probably a bit too much for him. He then started to go to the States and was into drugs in a big way. Heavier than marijuana certainly ... John was psychologically and emotionally insecure and as his work developed he was not able to keep up.'

In the months leading up to his death in June 1978, Milne wrote a number of letters to Paul Hodin. He reported at the end of January that he and his assistants (Richard Dubieniec, Alan Dunn and Tommy Rowe) were busy with new works, that he had many ideas for more, and that sculptures were currently in the process of being cast at the foundry. Temple, he wrote, had left St Ives following a recent stay, but in a new development was to return in September, to work once more at the Leach Pottery for a year or so. He asked if Hodin had any news from Wolfgang Fischer of Fischer Fine Art – he had offered to talk to him about showing Milne's work – and if not, requested he ask at Gimpel Fils when the opportunity arose. In February he reported that Rodewald was coming to spend a weekend at Trewyn. Then, on 16 April, in what was probably his final letter to Hodin, he included the following:

> I too am sorry that we did not see more of each other when you were in Cornwall but, for some time now, I have been unwell. Last week I had one of many confused spells and fell down the staircase (I look as though I have had an encounter with Cassius Clay) but am hoping that everything will go as planned and I will take the night train to London tonight to help arrange the exhibition.[29]

The exhibition to which Milne referred was his show at the Gilbert Parr Gallery, which opened on 21 April; included alongside Milne's work was a group of Temple's pots. David Gilbert had taken over Marjorie Parr's business in 1974 and a few years later renamed it the Gilbert Parr Gallery. Milne was not entirely happy with Gilbert as his dealer, hence his wish for an approach to Fischer Fine Art. Illustrated in a black-and-white photograph on the cover of the show's catalogue cover was the patinated and polished bronze *Birdsong* (1975), its organic upward thrust an interpretation of the cacophony of the dawn chorus he had written of in Marrakesh. Printed inside the catalogue were a series of 'Notes by the artist', from which these two are taken:

> Often, in the middle of the night, because I am tormented by dreams and cannot sleep, I am in my sitting room, in complete silence, surrounded by my sculptures. Surrounded, that is, by my life. Torments, struggles, travels, loves, and above all, by darkness and light. It is all a mystery to me. How did they all come to be here?
>
> I am a dreamer. I search for a solution in my dreams, and the solutions are in my sculpture.[30]

*

Milne died at home on the afternoon of Saturday 24 June, the day after his 47th birthday. His funeral took place on the following Friday at St Ives Parish Church and at Penmount Crematorium in Truro. It was reported in the local newspaper, which noted the principal mourners along with a long list of those also in attendance. It mentioned that his mother was unable to attend: she was in fact seriously ill and died on 12 July; she had not been told of her son's death. The Milne family was represented by Milne's sisters Audrey and Jean, by Marguerite McWilliams, and an aunt. Among other mourners were Ken Bryan, Isabel Milne, Brian Smith, Boots Redgrave, Cosmo Rodewald, Richard Dubieniec, Stanley Sellers, Peter Kinnear, Janet Leach, John Wells, Charles Breaker, Mr and Mrs Denis Mitchell, Reg and Patricia Singh, Paul Feiler, Tony O'Malley, Wilhelmina Barns-Graham (representing the Newlyn Society of Artists) and a representative from the Arts Council. There were many floral tributes, including from Milne's family; the Erskine family; Marjorie Parr; Katherine Dowd, 'To a friend for over 30 years'; David Lindsay and his partner Antonio Martinez; Neville Rawlinson and his partner Richard Gardner; Heather Jameson and her children Julia and Peter; and Bernard and Janet Leach. There were flowers too from Ivaldo Ferrari – 'With deepest love' – who after life in St Ives had returned to Italy, living at first in Milan and later in Reggio Emilia.

On 3 July, *The Times* published an article by E H Ramsden in which, referring to Milne's premature death, she stated: 'the art world has unquestionably sustained a major loss'. In summing up, she wrote:

> As if impelled by an inner compulsion, Milne always travelled extensively, since it was in landscape that he found the spring of his inspiration and thence that he sought to render in sculptural form the essence of his intense experience of the natural world, and to do so, not in imitative, but in equivalent terms. But being, as he was, an artist of acute sensibility, too acute perhaps for his own contentment, it now seems almost as if he were burnt out by a consuming creativity that left him no peace.

Those who knew of his previous suicide attempts may have assumed that Milne had taken his own life, but his death was accidental, a fact established during the subsequent inquest and reported by the *St Ives Times and Echo and the Hayle Times* on 11 August 1978:

> SCULPTOR JOHN MILNE DIED ACCIDENTALLY
> Sculptor John Erskine Milne of Trewyn, St Ives, died accidentally at his home on June 24 as a result of an overdose of drugs – a combination of alcohol and barbiturates – the Deputy Coroner for West Cornwall Mr Derrick Pepperell decided at a Carbis Bay inquest on Tuesday.

The day before he was found dead, lying face down at the foot of a flight of stairs, he had celebrated his 47th birthday at dinner with friends and was in a happy mood, the coroner was told.

Mr Pepperell had heard medical evidence that Mr Milne was an insomniac and a chronic depressive. He had attempted suicide in the past, by drugs and by drowning.

OVERWORKING

But the coroner said there was no evidence whatever that he took his own life intentionally. He may well have been confused at the time.

Evidence was given by the Cornwall County Pathologist, Dr Frederick Hocking, who said death was due to alcohol and barbiturate poisoning. Tests showed a blood alcohol level of 151 milligrams in 100 millilitres. There were no injuries to suggest a fall downstairs.

Dr WHM Jewell said Mr Milne had been his patient since 1973. He was a chronic depressive and he had been overworking. He had a number of business worries which were causing him some anxiety.

MANY WARNINGS

On a number of occasions he had been admitted to the West Cornwall Hospital after attempting suicide, and had been treated by a psychiatrist on a number of occasions.

Dr Jewell added that Mr Milne had been prescribed barbiturate drugs for many years and was currently being prescribed Tuinal and Valium.

'Many times I warned him about the danger of mixing alcohol with barbiturates and he was also warned by my predecessor and his psychiatrist', said Dr Jewell.

'He was a man with a number of personal problems and these contributed to his chronic depression.'

Mrs Mary Redgrave of Heather Cottage Nancledra, who had known Mr Milne for 25 years, said Mr Milne telephoned her at 3pm on June 24 and asked her to go up to his house.

He told her he had taken two tablets and had also drunk whiskey. She helped him upstairs to bed. He was 'a bit unsteady and fairly confused, like someone who was a bit drunk. He insisted that he had taken only two tablets.'

Mrs Redgrave added that she arranged to return two hours later

> and when she did she found Mr Milne still in his dressing gown, lying at the foot of the stairs. Ambulance men tried unsuccessfully to revive him.
>
> Mr Brian Gordon Smith of 3, Barnoon Hill, who was telephoned by Mrs Redgrave, and went to Mr Milne's house, said the three of them had celebrated Mr Milne's birthday and Mr Milne had seemed 'very happy'.
>
> Mr Smith said he had seen Mr Milne at lunch time the following day. He said he was still trying to wake up.
>
> Police Cons. Brian Davies told the coroner that he had found nothing suspicious in the house and no note left by Mr Milne.

Milne died intestate, and so Trewyn went to his sisters Jean and Audrey, who then sold the house in 1980. Richard Dubieniec recalls that in the aftermath of Milne's death:

> There were a few days of hectic activity after John's death and before his sisters' arrival, sanitising his homosexual history and losing evidence that might prove embarrassing to them. I wasn't directly involved, but was aware. One or two of his friends were 'clearing up' at Trewyn, while I did a stock take and inventory of work and editions.[31]

One assumes that Brian Smith, given his closeness to Milne, was one of those involved in clearing material from the house; Boots Redgrave was likely to have joined him. On 12 July Smith sent a letter to Chris Booth in New Zealand, written on the headed notepaper of the Barbara Hepworth Museum:

> Dear Chris,
>
> I have just received your letter. Thank you. I know how much of a shock the news of John's death must have been for you, even more than to us in a way, as the distance in miles makes such a sudden event seem even more unreal. But, as you know, he did die on 24th June, the day following his 47th birthday. Why, in medical terms, he died we do not yet know. As is usual in such cases there was an autopsy, and there will be an inquest, but when that will be is not yet known. In Barbara's case it was not until 2 months later. Anyway, more medical details will

only be given then. From the look of his body when I saw him which was within 2 hours of him last being seen alive by Boots – I should imagine a severe heart attack as his skin was quite blue and I believe this quick change of skin colour does indicate heart trouble. *Why* he should have a heart attack may be related to the fact that ever since I have known him and before, which is since 1956, he was always unable to sleep *naturally*, and over the years had increasingly relied on sleeping tablets to give him even a few hours of semi-consciousness. I am sure that these had weakened the heart, and in the few weeks before death he had mentioned a tingling sensation in his finger tips, and there was no doubt he was rapidly going downhill in health, and yet except on one occasion when I called the doctor, much to John's subsequent fury, he saw no doctor and refused even to discuss the fact that those who saw him the most – Boots and me – thought strongly that he was ill, and should seek medical advice and treatment. But that is now too late – just one of the many 'if onlys' which naturally come to mind at a later date.

You ask in particular about John's last year. Much work had been produced with the technical help of his full time assistant Richard [Dubieniec] (who has been a tremendous help in the past 2 weeks in sorting out the sculpture side of the estate, made particularly difficult as it appears John left no will) and Alan Dunn who I am sure you will remember, from Falmouth. He had been working every Saturday from about the time you were here until now. John had a successful exhibition – 2 in fact – in USA – one in Kentucky and the other in Philadelphia where much work was sold. Another exhibition was planned for Los Angeles in September of this year (and will still go ahead) and in April he showed in Kings Road, at what used to be Marjorie Parr's Gallery, but now under a new owner. Following the April show he went on holiday for two weeks to Morocco, but returned not having benefited from it at all. Apart from unsettled weather, an old friend of his who lived and worked in Marrakesh [identity unknown] was found murdered a couple of days after John arrived. This naturally upset John and made the remainder of the holiday rather gloomy. To try to put all this in a nutshell is difficult, but I think it comes down basically to the fact that John was becoming successful in the terms that his work was selling – he enjoyed the feeling of success – but as always that is not enough; and although he had many friends he felt he was alone, and no amount of support was enough. He was constantly wanting more out of the world and out of himself, and nothing he found satisfied that need, particularly in the emotional sense. I think in some ways he stopped caring, in the sense of '*What the Hell*', and yet at the same time knew that that was no answer. I could go into lots more detail of this kind, but the letter could become so complex and sound false that I shall stop now.

For what they are worth, and they are valid on a certain level, I enclose some Press notices, an obituary from *The Times*, and cuttings from local papers.

There's not much more to say at the moment.

...

Keep in touch, Chris. If anything more happens here I will let you know.

With my best wishes to you all,

Love, Brian[32]

For himself, Chris Booth recalls an incident when he was living in St Ives in 1969, a premonition of what followed nine years or so later:

At John's invitation I shifted from Anchor House [a property owned by Bernard Leach at which Booth stayed for a time] into Trewyn's attached apartment. Once, when my mother visited (and stayed for a week or so) from New Zealand, I put on a party for John and all our mutual friends in St Ives. It was quite an eye-opener for my Mum, who had not experienced gay culture and such noteworthies as Janet Leach ... Needless to say, being an adventurer at heart she loved it! But trauma followed after everyone had drifted home – later that night when we were all in bed I heard John plaintively calling for me from his bedroom, I went through and found him in one hell of a mental state, despairingly wanting company. My gentle platonic company calmed him; however, it probably wasn't enough (in fact was anything?). Much later that night Mum and I awoke to his desperate cry for help – we found him splayed, fallen at the bottom of the staircase in a kind of drunken stupor. He was alright, nothing was broken, so Mum and I somehow got him back up and into bed.

Horrifically this staircase incident echoed the fateful one a few years later.[33]

It is easy to think of Milne as a tragic figure in the Wildean mode, his life tracing an arc from early promise to its sadly premature end, one intimated in Marianne Jacoby's report to Paul Hodin. Did he consider himself a failure as an artist? Perhaps, though for all his self-doubt he was surely astute enough to realise that he had produced work of genuine merit. Did his work influence that of other artists? Not in any profound sense, although his formal repertoire finds certain echoes in sculpture made during the decades since his death, and he remains admired and collected. And while not of the first rank, in his 25 years or so as a mature artist he created a body of work that, at its considerable best, has a definite place in the crowded field of postwar British sculpture.

Milne's planned Los Angeles exhibition went ahead, opening on 6 October 1978 at the Gallery Rose on Santa Monica Boulevard, where it continued for a month. Titled *A Retrospective Exhibition of Sculpture and Drawings of the Late John Milne*, it was beautifully installed, in fact reverentially so, with sculpture displayed on tall plinths along the gallery walls, and baskets of chrysanthemums set between them on the floor as though in a mausoleum.

8 An Embellished Life

I wondered what had become of Julian Nixon after he left St Ives under a cloud in the summer of 1965, and imagined him continuing to drift from place to place, and from one encounter to another, as his physical charms gradually diminished. His name had first cropped up during the early stages of my research, and it eventually occurred to me that, along with Milne and Hepworth, he was in effect the third member of my narrative's central triumvirate, and that in many respects his story was equally worthy of inclusion. There were certainly times in writing this book when it seemed as though he was looking over my shoulder to make sure of what he considered his rightful place among its pages.

The trail had petered out with Nixon's letter to Richard Blake Brown in which he announced he was moving to live with Reg Moon at Henley-in-Arden 'more or less indefinitely'. There were some references to his subsequent life: in his own diary, in Brown's journals and the odd note, but nothing that went beyond the late 1960s. A couple of people who had known him long ago said they had heard he had died, but knew nothing more. Then eventually a new avenue opened up, yielding information about Nixon's life in the years after his departure from St Ives. It resulted from a correspondence with Moon's daughter Carey. From what she was able to outline, Nixon's life became less itinerant after leaving Cornwall in the mid-1960s, and he spent many of his remaining years in Warwickshire: at Henley-in-Arden, then at Stratford and finally at Leamington Spa, all three towns within a 40-kilometre radius. Reg and his wife Mag had moved to Henley in 1960, setting up the Torquil Pottery and opening the Gallery Upstairs, where they sold ceramics, Scandinavian glass and tableware. On first arrival, Nixon did indeed live with the family, working as their au pair and bringing his skills as an entertainer to bear in looking after the eight-year-old Carey and her younger brother Paul. After several months he moved to an address on the town's High Street. His subsequent employments included a self-catering business and work for a local manufacturing company, after which he set up a small restaurant, which made little or no profit, for as ever he enjoyed the role of mine host but was ill-equipped to deal with the monetary aspects.

Carey put me in touch with Robert Harbin, who with his partner Patrick had known Nixon during his Leamington Spa years. She also introduced me to their mutual friend Peter Durkin, who had lived on and off in the town with Nixon during the final 26 years of his life. He remembers him thus:

> Julian was a very obvious gay man, quite camp. He always wore very colourful clothes and had large, very expressive hands – and this voice that carried. He would be unaware of the effect he had on other people – he had been flamboyant for so long. He had a remarkable presence, a wonderful way of enchanting people. He was an enchanter ... His stories were embroidered, but there was always some truth in them.[1]

Harbin has this to say of Nixon's time in Leamington Spa, or 'Royal Leamington Spa' as he would have had it: 'He had a rather embellished life here. You never knew if he was telling the exact truth. He lived like a lord but was in fact penniless.'[2]

It has often struck me that one could write a novel about Nixon: a rake's progress, both tragicomic and vaguely sinister, and replete with rococo flourishes. During the 1980s Nixon continued to describe himself as an author. But, if truth be told, he was his own work of fiction, and among the verifiable episodes in his life are many that could have come from the type of melodramatic, sometimes tawdry tales he himself might have penned (and in fact did, in his unpublished 'autobiography'). He told Durkin that he had married three times, but added that in reality he was only married twice, describing Mary, the widowed fiancée who died in 1961, as wife number one. His first actual marriage was to Olive Garfield, heiress to an engineering firm and many years older than Nixon, and like him a heavy drinker. Their wedding took place on New Year's Eve 1967, and Nixon's mother Maureen joined them on their honeymoon. Olive took Nixon around Europe – he was, says Durkin, 'a kept pretty boy' – and in Gozo had him committed to a psychiatric institution, from which his mother then had to deal with his release. The marriage was annulled in September 1972, perhaps a short time before Olive died; the exact circumstances are uncertain. It had been a wholly negative experience for them both, and there is no indication that Nixon received any form of inheritance. His second wife, meanwhile, was a woman working in Dubai who had become pregnant, and whose mother asked Nixon to marry her so that she was legitimate in the eyes of the law and could continue working in Dubai. For this he was given a payment of £4,000, as he subsequently announced to a gathering of friends invited to join him for champagne and food at a party at which he was attired in one of the Arabic djellaba gowns he often wore in later years.

Durkin has various documents that belonged to Nixon. Among them is a writ issued by Bristol High Court in March 1970 that shows that Nixon had tried to take Milne to court, claiming damages for 'alienation of affection' of a young man who had recently done some work in Milne's garden.[3] Nixon had again visited St Ives a year or so before, when he stayed once more at Trewyn, very probably with the young man in question.[4] Attached to the writ is a rather convoluted statement by Nixon in which he outlines the details of his claim. He writes that Milne has 'purposely and knowingly seduced Mr Robert Day into his bed, and away from the Plaintiff with whom Mr Day had been living for the last ten months as his lover'. He stipulates that, as a result, he has 'lost the necessary labour force and goodwill' of Day 'that would have enabled the Plaintiff to purchase a business in St Ives, which is not possible physically or financially to run without the aid of Mr Day'. Nixon states that the estimated loss is in the region of £6,000, together with potential earnings from the business venture. Then, in a line reminiscent of the more fanciful flights of *Tapestry of Innocence*, he writes: 'Further the Plaintiff has been deprived of the love and companionship of Mr Day which he was led to believe would last "forever". I claim damages for this at the Court's discretions.' He then, quite unbelievably given that he has himself described Day as his lover, adds: 'Further that Mr Milne has contravened the Sexual Offences Act of 1967 by having sexual relations with a minor

Mr Robert Day, on Mr Day's own admission.' Added to Nixon's signature on the legal document was the declaration that he was acting on his own account. His claim was for up to £10,000 plus costs.

There is no indication that the case went any further; it may well have been thrown out of court. But Nixon – acting on his own account and without legal representation – had evidently sensed, not for the first time, an opportunity to make money by pursuing a desperate and misguided course of action. Whether or not he was sincere in his ambition to set up a business in St Ives is unclear; in any event it is unlikely that his friendship with Milne survived beyond this point.

*

Nixon continued to write to Richard Blake Brown and occasionally visited him in Bristol. Brown had visited Henley-in-Arden in June 1966, when with Nixon he was invited to lunch with Olive, the future Mrs Nixon, at her large house just outside the town. In his journal Brown described her as the 'invisible – patroness in [Nixon's] catering business ... [she is] v. nice, if a trifle pressingly – affected. – She has been a lone widow for six years.' She appears in his journal again not long after this first encounter: 'Olive (over 50) is a highly strung widow with grey-white hair and make-up, who is charming if just a shade affected, but possibly habitually rather than intentionally.'[5]

Reading between the lines, it is clear that Brown's apparent dislike was tied up with his knowledge that Olive had laid claim to Nixon. In the ensuing months, as the date of his marriage drew closer, Nixon became uncommunicative and evasive towards Brown. Feeling abandoned, Brown wrote on 2 December 1967 in his journal: 'And now Brothy has – disappeared – Broke or lazy? It's all very baffling! He writes to tell me not to worry; but what else can I do when I love him as much as I do?' Then, during a visit to Brown in January, Nixon came clean and communication was partly restored, although Brown, who was becoming increasingly unwell with arthritis and suffering debilitating vertigo attacks and a series of nasty falls, was both hurt and bewildered: 'I miss Brothy. Why did he marry Olive? I understand *nothing*.'[6]

Brown began to doubt and distrust Nixon, and considered removing him from his will, where he was named sole executor, in favour of his friend Clive Simpson. In the end, Brown's solicitor John Bedford and Nixon were made co-executors and trustees, although Nixon, following the proposal that he and Simpson were to become joint literary executors, managed to persuade Brown that he alone should undertake that role: '2nd February 1968: Letter from Julian this morning to say he wants to be my sole literary executor. I'm sure Clive will understand instantly.'

There is mention, too, in Brown's journals of Nixon being in Gozo (Carey Moon recalls that he bought a house there at some point). It seems that Brown was invited to visit Nixon there but was now far too ill to travel. His Harley Street specialist Sir Terence Cawthorne had in February informed him that his vertigo resulted from inefficient cerebral circulation and put him on methedrine. Having become progressively weaker and sometimes unable to walk, a further fall from a vertigo attack resulted in him spending three weeks in hospital from mid-March, where tests proved him to be diabetic and he was put on insulin.

Brown died at the Bristol Royal Infirmary on 3 November 1968 at the age of 66. It was a sad ending, of which his lifelong friend the fashion designer Norman Hartnell wrote to another mutual old friend:

> It is over now and upset me considerably at the time.
>
> I can tell you that he was found one morning by the fire brigade; he was on the floor having passed out from asphyxiation because his electric fire fell over. He was suffering from chronic arthritis, diabetes and vertigo and I daresay he fell down and could not get up.
>
> The only thing is he declined considerably and seemed very old and very unhappy. He often said he was longing to pass out.
>
> I went to the funeral in Bristol which was conducted by two eminent men, the Bishop of Southwark and the Bishop of Bristol, and I only hope that Blake (I called him by that name) is at last in peace, which he certainly wasn't during these last few weeks.
>
> Yes, as one gets older, life gets sadder, and all that is left are happy memories.

The Bishop of Southwark, Mervyn Stockwood, officiated at Brown's funeral, after which Hartnell wrote to thank him: 'I did tell you briefly afterwards how much I appreciated all the things you said about our dear, good, naughty, mutual friend. In lovely and amusing words, you summed up his character, and I am sure he would have enjoyed every word you said about him.'[7]

Back in November 1964, Tom, the solicitor who had fallen for Nixon, had added a post-scriptum note to his first letter to him. It reveals Milne's opinion of Brown and the influence he had on Nixon:

> Since writing this letter I have spent a few hours with John. John blames the excessive part of your flamboyance on Richard about whom he has told me a great deal.
>
> I had assumed that Richard was a good influence but I feel that the complete opposite is the case. John told me of some of the things in Richard which you had adopted as your own – not good things.
>
> I see the influence as positively evil. I believe that Richard is using your body and soul and mind and is living vicariously through you.
>
> If you search your heart, you will know whether these conclusions are valid or not.

Told of this negative verdict, Peter Durkin both strongly refutes it and puts forward his own judgement, in which he describes Brown as:

> The most influential person in Julian's life. He was a presence – his ashes were on the bookcase. You almost sensed his presence. Richard Blake Brown significantly formed the adult Julian. He assumed the affectations Richard Blake Brown had ... [He] brought out a grandiosity in Julian that was already there, but was nurtured under his influence. The affectations were already there, waiting to be acted upon. The relationship was paternal – Richard Blake Brown was in love with Julian, and made him his godson. Julian inherited the older man's estate and literary archive.

Brown's will stipulated that any income from the sale of his papers or literary works was to be shared equally between Nixon and Simpson. Nixon took possession of Brown's papers, and after his death read through the journals and occasionally added to them a note of his own. He sold off the most financially valuable items from the archive, including letters from the writer Graham Greene and Hartnell (it is not known if Simpson benefited anything from such sales). A female friend of Nixon's then sold the remainder of Brown's papers after his death.

Nixon's mother – Durkin remembers her as a formidable *grande dame* – lived with him in Stratford and Leamington, her pension covering their basic living costs. She passed away around 1996, and towards the end of his life Nixon lived on state benefits.

Aware of Nixon's early theatrical aspirations, and stage appearances in plays such as Terence Rattigan's *The Winslow Boy* (1946), Durkin says: 'He didn't need the stage – he was always on stage ... People loved him. In Leamington we still talk about him.' It seems that ultimately Nixon's talents were as a lively and entertaining social figure, and a very good cook – 'of the Fanny Cradock type', according to Durkin – who enjoyed making meals for friends and guests. Durkin adds:

> I do feel that Julian changed. Pre-Leamington, if he were with people who were rich he assumed he was permitted to spend their money. But when he moved to Leamington and became more settled that marked a transition. His opus really was his social milieu. There is a group of friends in the Midlands today that he first brought together. We remain firm friends.

Durkin describes how Nixon would write 'very supportive letters' to friends in difficulty, which were highly sensitive and considered: 'I think he found his literary muse in those letters.' Tellingly, he also states: 'Julian had the capacity to move on. He was in the present.' Yet at the same time, he once told Durkin that he regretted ending his relationship with Stanley Sellars, with whom, incidentally, he continued to meet from time to time over the years.

Ultimately, Nixon was a survivor. Like many gay men of his generation, his life bridged great changes in legal and social attitudes to homosexuality. Subjected to vilification, criminal conviction and incarceration in his youth, he then lived through the eras of gay liberation, the devastation of AIDS and increased queer visibility.

He lived long enough, too, to see the first civil partnerships take place, just six months before he died at the age of 70 on 13 June 2006. A long-term smoker and heavy drinker, he had developed cancer and his last weeks were spent in a hospice. Many friends attended his funeral, a humanist ceremony organised by Robert Harbin and his partner.

Six years earlier, Reg Moon had written to Nixon on his 65th birthday. The letter is notable for Moon's sensitive appraisal of Milne's predicament, and for the fond reassurance he offers to his friend Nixon:

> Dear Julian,
>
> Thank you for your wonderfully enjoyable letter. I do hope you get your memories into some sort of book form.[8] I haven't had chance other than to glance at the book [Peter Davies's *The Sculpture of John Milne*, published that June]. But I do think that you are wrong to have a guilt complex about John and his work. I have letters somewhere from John and vaguely remember him saying how difficult it was to work. He had a natural hedonistic desire – which is in us all – but unlike many was able to indulge because of his unusual position brought about by many factors not least Cosmo. Whilst you were there all the people who came to visit did not do so to encourage John to work but to have a good time – which is what they had but so certainly no help to John and his work. And of course John loved it but at the back of his mind worried about not working as much as he should and not just because he needed to sell his work to live like other artists but because Cosmo had set him up believing in him and John felt guilty. And of course as an artist he wanted to 'get on' but as you say hedonism got in the way. But it wasn't your fault it was the TREWYN set up which wasn't designed for a struggling young sculptor.
>
> And yet when I glance through the book there seems to have been quite a substantial body of work over the years. I am rambling & probably not thinking it through so probably need a good lunch with you to sort it out & get things straight. XXX REG[9]

9 Light and Shadow

Thinking back, it is not inconceivable that I might have passed John Milne in the street on one of those days in August 1976, were he in town at that point. I know from Bryan Robertson's diary that he was there, perhaps again staying at Trewyn as he so often did.[1] Since that first short holiday I have returned to St Ives countless times, in all weathers and all seasons. I have been there alone in late autumn, and during the winter months when, its streets almost deserted, the atmosphere and weather of the place makes it feel less benign. It becomes easy then to imagine how one might turn in on oneself, depression seeping in like a sea fog, so that you gradually lose your bearings. As Martin Clark has written of Cornwall, 'It is a place at the edge; a place of edges; where one might lose oneself completely – voluntarily or otherwise – in an old and indifferent nature.'[2]

More often, though, I have visited with my partner David, and in August 2005 we had a week's holiday there with my mum, my sister Lydia and her young son Joe, who spent most of his days fishing from Smeaton's Pier. It was the first time Mum and Lydia had been back.

I once visited Ronnie Lande at his home in London. It was when I was working on a book about Patrick Procktor, and I was invited to look at a drawing by the artist that he had in his collection. It was late May 2009, and Dr Lande, walking slowly and with difficulty, was clearly very unwell. His partner Walther had died some years before from AIDS, and it seemed obvious that he would not live much longer either; in fact, he died in August the following year. Along with the Procktor drawing, there were in his flat several important paintings by Keith Vaughan, some Janet Leach ceramics and a number of Milne's sculptures, all of which I recognised. I was already thinking of undertaking research about Milne and mentioned this to Dr Lande, who told me that he had known him well and that he could tell me a lot about him – how they used to holiday together in Morocco and so forth. Completing the book about Procktor was, however, all-consuming, and although invited to return to talk more fully, I never made it back.

*

January 2014
My friend and fellow working-class northerner the artist Linder Sterling is in the middle of a six-month Tate St Ives residency, for which she has been given use of No. 5 Porthmeor Studios. A large, white space, its seaward-facing window blanked out to eliminate distractions, its previous inhabitants include Ben Nicholson and Patrick Heron and there exist small traces of them on the walls: in dabs of oil paint and colour notes written in pencil. Linder arranged for some young friends to come to St Ives, a group of Northern Soul dancers. They were filmed with the ballet dancer Alexander Bird, dancing in the studio to a music soundtrack provided by Linder's son Max. A month later and I am again in St Ives, having been invited to host an 'in conversation' between Linder and the Northern Ballet choreographer Kenneth Tindall, after a performance of their ballet *The Ultimate Form* at the St Ives Theatre. Premiered at the Musée d'Art Moderne de la Ville de Paris in 2013, after which it was performed at The Hepworth, Wakefield, the ballet is based on Hepworth's nine-part sculpture *The Family of Man* (1970) and has costumes by the fashion designer Richard Nicoll. Linder and Kenneth went on to devise a second ballet, *Children of the Mantic Stain*, first performed at Leeds Art Gallery in 2015. Its central characters are based on Hepworth, Milne and Nixon.

March 2015
Late morning: I interviewed Jane Val Baker about Milne and co. in the little café area at the Penwith Gallery on Back Road West. Later, at around 6pm, Linder and I went to look at St Christopher's, the house overlooking Porthmeor Beach where the Val Bakers had once

lived. Peering through the windows we could see that the place was deserted, and it appeared some building works were in progress within. I bent down, pushed open the letterbox and peeped in, and to my surprise could hear a voice inside. Linder put her ear to the letterbox too, and confirmed there was a voice coming from inside the building. Then I realised the voice was that of Jane Val Baker, and that it came from the sound recorder in my bag, which had switched itself on and was playing back the conversation I'd had with her that morning. It seemed odd and spooky, especially as I could hear Jane's voice saying 'St Christopher's' as I peered in at the uninhabited building. It was strange that the recorder should spring into life at that very point. Linder and I walked on down Porthmeor Road towards the beach. Some workmen outside another house had their radio on; Cilla Black was singing her 1960s hit 'Step Inside Love'. 'The ghosts are busy', said Linder.

April 2016

I managed to secure an invitation to an event marking the 40th anniversary of the opening of the Barbara Hepworth Museum. It took place on a Saturday evening between 6pm and 9pm.[3] The guests sat or stood in the pristine upstairs room in which Hepworth died, surrounded by her sculptures and paintings, furniture and decorative objects. Hepworth's daughter, the painter Rachel Nicholson, was in attendance, as was her granddaughter, Sophie Bowness. Following an introductory speech by Mark Osterfield, executive director of Tate St Ives, a duet – a violinist and a cellist – performed several works, including some by Bach. There was also 'The interrupted melody for "Barbara"', composed in 1951 by the sculptor's friend Priaulx Rainier, during which a young man intermittently hit the piece of stone held in his hand with a hammer, a reminder of Hepworth chipping away at her blocks of stone and marble. A film of Linder and Kenneth's ballet *The Ultimate Form* was projected onto the whitewashed wall inside the greenhouse, which served also as a bar serving refreshments. Outside in the garden, the poet Rupert M Loydell read his 'Four Poems for Barbara Hepworth', with Hepworth's six-part *Conversation with Magic Stones* (1973) as a backdrop. Walking in the garden I thought of my younger self, and of my sister, wandering around and photographing the sculpture in the heat of high summer all those years before. Dusk had long descended before the event ended on that April evening, leaving the garden veiled in shadow.

Notes

Introduction: Shadow and Light

1 Sassoon 1945, p.223.
2 Lily Barnard, painter of landscape and marine subjects, was born in Colombo, Sri Lanka (then Ceylon) and in later life worked at the Puffin Studio, St Ives. She exhibited at the Paris Salon in 1930. She died at Bromley in Kent. This information is taken from https://cornwallartists.org/cornwall-artists/lily-barnard, accessed 5 January 2022.
3 Hodin 1950, pp.113.
4 *The Art of Cornwall*, BBC4, first broadcast 2 December 2010, see www.bbc.co.uk/programmes/boowbn8o.

1 The Boy from Eccles

1 Mantel 2017.
2 For clarification: the title of Milne's sculpture is *Megalith II*. The plaque on the version in Trewyn Gardens has it as simply *Megalith*. There is a small version named *Megalith*, cast in polished bronze in an edition of nine; this is the maquette version for *Megalith II*.
3 J P Hodin's books include *Henry Moore*, Zwemmer, London, 1958; *Ben Nicholson: The Meaning of his Art*, Alec Tiranti, London, 1957; *Barbara Hepworth*, Lund Humphries, London, 1961.
4 Hodin 1977, p.67. Hodin first met Milne in the spring of 1968 at a Penwith Society exhibition, and he began to study Milne's work more closely from 1974.
5 Lesley Hassey in conversation with the author, London, 27 November 2014.
6 Marianne Jacoby, letter to J P Hodin, London, 2 February 1976. Tate Archive, London, TGA 20062.
7 Marianne Jacoby's notes are reproduced in Hodin 1977, pp.68–70.
8 Quotes by Marguerite McWilliams are taken from a telephone interview with the author, 3 September 2021.
9 Hodin 1977, p.66.
10 *Ibid.*
11 From notes made by J P Hodin in 1975 during his conversations with Milne. The notepad is in the collection of Tate Archive, London, TGA 20062.
12 Salford Royal Technical College later became the University of Salford.
13 According to Milne's 'Life chronology' in Hodin 1977, pp.60–61, he was granted a scholarship to study electrical engineering at Salford Royal Technical College in 1945, although student records held on microfiche at what is now the University of Salford show that he first enrolled at the college in the previous academic year, on the Junior Building course. It may well be that he was granted a 'special place' based on an entrance examination in April 1944; this would have resulted in full or part waiver of college fees.
14 The author is indebted to Ian Johnston at the University of Salford Library Archive for providing scans of Milne's student records.
15 Milne was '"converted" to sculpture by seeing photographs of the work of Brancusi'. See 'The Sculptor Who Loves the Sun', *Eccles and Patricroft Journal*, 10 August 1972, p.6 (author uncredited).
16 *Henry Moore: Sculpture and Drawings, 1923–1948* was assembled by Eric Westbrook, Director of Wakefield City Art Gallery and Museum, where the exhibition originated and was shown from 2 April to 21 May 1948, before travelling to Manchester.
17 The Salford exhibition dates were 21 July–17 August 1948. Lyme Hall is at Lyme Park, Disley, Cheshire. The *Seated Figure* was shown at the Manchester Academy of Fine Art's 92nd Spring Exhibition, Manchester City Art Gallery, 29 January–25 February 1951. The sculpture, listed as no.260 in the catalogue, was for sale at £28.
18 Kynaston 2007, pp.376–77.
19 *The Lancet*, 16 December 1961, p.1367. Franz Max Greenbaum (Grunbaum), 25 October 1903, Berlin–1 November 1961, Manchester.

20 In 1953, the year after Hodin interviewed Jung, he wrote *The Hell of Initiation: An Essay Prompted by a Conversation with C.G. Jung*, part of which then formed his lecture at the Institute of Contemporary Arts in February 1954. He completed his essay five years later, and then revised it in 1960 and 1967. Hodin had taken issue with Jung, having read an article on Picasso – the only writing on contemporary art the psychoanalyst ever produced – which was published in 1932 in the Swiss newspaper *Neue Zürcher Zeitung*. Hodin's essay can be found in Hodin 1972, pp.57–96.

21 From an article on Milne in the *Eccles and Patricroft Journal*, 10 August 1972, p.6.

22 Andrew Hodges, email to the author, 17 July 2019.

23 Hodges 1983, p.480.

24 John Milne, undated (1952?) postcard to Reg Moon, collection of Carey Moon.

25 Tom Driberg's Column, *Reynolds News*, 30 May 1948.

26 'more fascinated by music than realities': Hodin 1977, p.73.

27 There were in fact six branches of the Kardomah Café in Manchester. The branch Tony Warren describes was at 132 Deansgate; others were at 23 Market Place, 98 Market Street, 18 St Ann's Square, 61 Piccadilly, and 1 South Street. There were branches in 14 other towns in England and Wales, and a branch at 184 Rue de Rivoli in Paris. The Mancunian writer Howard Jacobson also wrote of the Kardomah Café in his novel *The Mighty Walzer* (1999); his description of the Market Street branch makes it sound mythological:

> The KD.
> Not K for King and D for David, but K for Kar and D for Domah.
> Kar Domah, the ancient Hebrew scholar and socialite who had urged resistance against the Romans and held out against them for thirteen years, bare-handed and in his tefillin, on an unfortified mountain top in Market Street.
> The KD.
> I'd be lying if I said I could remember the old Market Street KD with any exactitude, what shape the tables were, what colour the carpet was, whether a waiter or a waitress served us coffee, or a fabled beast that was half horse, half water serpent. I wouldn't have been any clearer on the details at the time. I wasn't really looking. Not with my eyes. You used other senses to experience the Market Street Kardomah. You took it in through your pores.

The Mighty Walzer, Vintage, London, 2000, pp.212–20. The Salford-born playwright Shelagh Delaney also spent Saturday afternoons in the Market Street branch, as mentioned in Todd 2019, p.72.

28 Warren 1991, p.77.

29 David Tucker, email to the author, 19 September 2017. Warren's cousin Roy Varndell studied at the School of Art at Salford. A report on the 1959 Industrial Art Bursaries competition in the *Journal of the Royal Society of Arts* (April 1960) lists the 21-year-old Varndell's award of a bursary of £150. His award was for carpet design, namely a 'five-colour carpet suitable for hotels and public houses', also illustrated in the report.

30 Tony Warren, interviewed by John Walding, published in 2011 by *Outnorthwest* magazine and subsequently online at 'Tony Warren MBE – A Tribute', https://lgbt.foundation/news/tony-warren-mbe-a-tribute/39, 2 March 2016.

31 See Warren 1969, p.9.

32 Warren 1991, pp.78–79.

33 *Ibid.*, p.82.

34 'I was talking to my uncle Harry about this again yesterday and he remembered the lady, Käthe Schuftan, who was a bohemian type and had "open house" events in her Manchester flat for thespian and artistic folk and Harry remembers going along once, after my dad [Reg Moon] had told him about it. Tony Warren was there (who had the original idea for *Coronation Street*), although he had a different name then. Harry recalls he was as "camp as a row of tents".' Carey Moon, email to the author, 29 February 2020. In Warren's novel, Magda Schiffer's address is Daisy Bank Road; from 1947 Käthe Schuftan herself lived at Addison Terrace on Daisy Bank Road, in Manchester's Victoria Park district.

35 Yohannan, 2015, p.17.

36 Käthe Fanny Sara Schuftan, b.1899, Breslau, d.1958, Manchester. The author

is immensely grateful to Hephzibah Yohannan, who has provided much information on Schuftan.

37 The exhibition *Entartete Kunst*, displaying works deemed to be 'an insult to German feeling', opened in Munich in 1937, after which it toured throughout Germany.

38 Paul Moritz Schuftan, born 10 November 1896, Breslau. He took up residence in the UK on 10 May 1936. His home address was at Richmond, Surrey. After surveillance, Schuftan was exempted from internment in October 1939. According to a Metropolitan Police document dated 21 September 1939, his mother Else and his maternal grandmother were then living in Twickenham; an aunt, uncle and nephew also resided in England.

39 The quote and information about Paul Schuftan's employment are taken from Stokes and Banken 2015, p.143.

40 As Hephzibah Yohannan has noted, 'It was common for individuals and families to employ domestic servants; positions were advertised on a daily basis. *The Manchester Guardian* had a section for 'Refugee Advertisements' where educated women and married couples from places such as Vienna, Prague or simply 'Austria' sought employment, stating their skills and their willingness to work.' Yohannan 2015, p.19. Käthe Schuftan received a certificate of exemption from internment following a tribunal decision; the certificate is dated 8 November 1939. In September 1947 she received a certificate of naturalisation.

41 *Collectors' Choice*, Manchester Art Gallery, 25 March–22 April 1964.

42 Jan Green, telephone conversation with the author, 7 June 2017.

43 The quotes by Ken Clay are from his 'Neville', an unpublished article emailed to the author, June 2017.

44 Quotations from Geoffrey Key are from a telephone conversation with the author, 8 June 2017.

45 Matthew Haygarth, born 21 February 1909, Bury, Lancashire. He eventually sold the Whitethorn Cottage restaurant and went with his partner Brian Oldknow to live in Malta. He died there on 4 February 1988 and is buried in Malta. The author is grateful to David Sayer for providing information on Haygarth.

46 The review of Schuftan's exhibition was published in the *Manchester Guardian*, 20 August 1951. The author was identified by the initials W.L.W.

47 Margo Ingham's year of birth is variously given as 1917 or 1918. Her obituary notice states that she died at the age of 61 (see Jackson 1978).

48 A letter dated 9 October 1951 from Salford City Art Gallery to Margo Ingham is addressed to 3 Addison Terrace, Manchester 14. At the same time, Käthe Schuftan was living at 11 Addison Terrace.

49 *Manchester Guardian*, 17 September 1943, p.8.

50 The gallery premises were at 96 Mosley Street and had previously been used for the same purpose by Lucy Wertheim. The building was later demolished to make way for redevelopment.

51 *Paintings and Drawings by L.S. Lowry*, comprising 33 oil paintings and 10 drawings, 26 October–20 November 1948.

52 The dates of the Sven Berlin show at Mid-Day Studios were 25 October to 19 November 1947.

53 From the catalogue for the *Private View of the Margo Ingham Collection*, 3 April 1979, Colin Jellicoe Gallery, Manchester.

54 Kalman and Lambirth 2003, p.11. For further information on Andras Kalman, see Whittet 1962, pp.108–10 (from which some information included here derives).

55 Quotes by Ivor Braka are from a telephone conversation with the author, 28 February 2019.

56 Documentation of the inaugural show at the Crane Gallery has not been traced. The second exhibition was *Paintings by Seven Women Artists*, 18 January–11 February 1950. The artists – in the order in which they were listed in the catalogue – were: Stella Marsden, Sine MacKinnon (Mrs Rupert Fordham), Helen Lessore (spelled Lassore in the catalogue), Cathleen Mann, Anne Carlisle, Margaret Thomas and Anne Spalding. The *Summer Exhibition* of June–July 1950, probably the sixth gallery show, included the following artists: Sir Gerald Kelly, Vanessa Bell, R O Dunlop, Dame Ethel Walker, Margaret Thomas, Duncan Grant, Matthew Smith, Henry Moore, Graham Sutherland (who had a solo show

at the gallery in 1953), Adrian Ryan, John Minton, L S Lowry, Augustus John and Jacob Epstein. Another exhibition was *Important Paintings*. The catalogue gives the dates as 27 April–19 May, although the year is not printed. The artists included: Constantin Guys, Johan Jongkind, Eugène Boudin, Édouard Vuillard, Edgar Degas, Pierre Bonnard, Pierre-Auguste Renoir, Maurice Utrillo, Maurice de Vlaminck, John Duncan Fergusson, Henryk Gotlib, Louis Marcoussis, Charles Malfray, André Derain, Yohanan Simon and Maxime Moufra.

57 The catalogue for *Five Painters* includes the following biographical information for Lowndes: 'Born 1921 in Stockport. Studied Art at night school. Painted whilst with the Army in Italy ... At present a textile designer.'

58 'the biggest influence on my life' is from a notepad entry by J P Hodin, undated but probably August 1975. Tate Archive, London, TGA 20062.

59 *Barbara Hepworth: Sculpture and Drawings* was a touring show, organised by Wakefield City Art Gallery. It was first seen at that venue, 19 May–7 July; then at York Art Gallery, 14 July–12 August; and finally at Manchester Art Gallery, 24 September–21 October 1951. The accompanying catalogue included an introduction by Patrick Heron.

60 Biographical information about Cosmo Rodewald is taken from Jackson and Sekunda 2007, pp.7–9. Rodewald was to be a benefactor of the British School at Athens, ensuring continuation of the Macmillan Studentship, a fellowship open to application from researchers engaged in advanced postgraduate or postdoctoral research at UK universities, and now known as the Macmillan-Rodewald Studentship.

61 Alistair Smith in Jackson and Sekunda 2007, p.19. Rodewald also bequeathed funds to the gallery so that it might 'purchase modern art by living artists'.

62 David Lindsay, telephone conversation with the author, 13 July 2015.

63 Westwood 1960, p.34.

64 While John Milne's student records state he was enrolled to study postgraduate sculpture during the academic year 1952–53, it appears that he left the institution at the end of the preceding academic year.

65 Katharine Hepburn and Robert Helpmann both appeared in a production of Bernard Shaw's *The Millionairess* at the New Theatre, London, 27 June–20 September 1952.

66 John Milne, undated letter to Reg Moon, collection of Carey Moon.

67 The quote by Zadkine is taken from www.zadkine.paris.fr/en/zadkine/his-teaching-sculpture/academie-de-la-grande-chaumiere-paris, accessed 30 March 2018.

68 It has not been possible to trace the dates of Milne's studies at La Grande Chaumière. There are apparently no records from the institution, as outlined in an email dated 27 May 2019 to the author from Cathy Corbett, who has researched Osip Zadkine in depth. As Corbett writes: 'The Académie seems to have been on many artists' itinerary as they passed through Paris, but there is no archive or any definitive record of who studied there. Annie Barbara, who was the long-term archivist at the Bourdelle museum before she retired a couple of years ago, told me that there were no Grande Chaumière archives. There may have been a problem with a fire at one point, but largely it is just that records don't appear to have been taken. It was not an official school, nor linked with any of the official Parisian organisations that might have kept records, and if they had lists they have disappeared. I regularly come across the names of artists who were there, but am saving the compilation of a list for a post-doc entertainment for myself.

In Zadkine's case, it is also complicated by the fact that although post-war he did teach classes there, he also taught small groups in his studio, so sometimes when students say they studied with Zadkine, they didn't get as far as the Grande Chaumière (Kenneth Noland is a case in point, often misquoted as having studied there, but in fact he just studied in Zadkine's atelier).'

69 John Milne, quoted in an undated note made by J P Hodin, 1975. Tate Archive, London, TGA 20062.

70 John Milne, postcard to Reg Moon, Athens, 1952, collection of Carey Moon.

71 Document from collection of papers related to John Milne, Tate Archive, London, TG 4/2/722.
72 *Ibid.*
73 John Milne, postcard to Reg Moon, Athens, 28 July 1952, collection of Carey Moon.

2 At Trewyn

1 Barbara Hepworth quoted in Hammacher 1968, p.117. The quote is taken from a letter from Hepworth to Hammacher dated February 1955.
2 With thanks to Sophie Bowness for insights into Hepworth's responsiveness to approaches from young artists; and for suggesting that John Milne's introduction to Hepworth may have come from David Baxandall at Manchester Art Gallery, with whom she was friendly.
3 Gardiner 1994, p.10.
4 Barbara Hepworth's assistants over the years were as follows: Denis Mitchell, 1949–59; Terry Frost, 1950–52; John Wells, 1950–51; Owen Broughton, 1951; John Milne, 1952–54; Roger Leigh, 1953–54 and 1957; Brian Wall, 1955–60; Keith Leonard, 1955–59; Tom Pierce, 1959–61; Breon O'Casey, 1959–62; Michael Broido, 1959–62; Dicon Nance, 1959–71; Tommy Rowe, 1962–64 (and 1958–62 during vacations when he was a student at the Bath Academy of Art, Corsham); Norman Stocker, 1962–75; Angela Conner, April–December 1963; and George Wilkinson, 1964–75. This list is taken from *St Ives, 1939–64*, p.124.
5 Rowe 2020, pp.7–8.
6 Bowness 2017, pp.37–39.
7 Curtis 1998, p.6.
8 Skeaping 1977, p.207. Paul Skeaping, 3 August 1929, London–13 February 1953, Thailand.
9 Gardiner 1994, p.17.
10 *Ibid.*, pp.17–18.
11 Barbara Hepworth, letter to Herbert Read, Trewyn Studio, 18 February 1953, Sir Herbert Edward Read fonds, University of Victoria Special Collections, Canada, SC100, HR/BH-152. Priaulx Rainier, b.1903, South Africa, d.1986, France.
12 Hodin 1950, pp.113–24.
13 Mellor 1987, p.16.
14 Rachel Nicholson in conversation with the author, St Ives, 11 April 2016.
15 There is also a memorial to Paul Skeaping at St Ives Parish Church: Hepworth's *Madonna and Child* (1954).
16 John Milne quoted in 'The Sculptor Who Loves the Sun', *Eccles and Patricroft Journal*, 10 August 1972, p.6 (author uncredited).
17 Rachel Nicholson, in conversation with the author, St Ives, 11 April 2016.
18 From a statement by Barbara Hepworth in Read 1952. Reprinted in Bowness 2015, p.61.
19 Read 1954.
20 Barbara Hepworth, letter to Herbert Read, December 1946, Sir Herbert Edward Read fonds, University of Victoria Special Collections, SC100, 8.61, HR/BH-98.
21 John Milne's letter and postcard to Reg Moon, collection of Carey Moon.
22 Liddell 1974; Liddell 1948, pp.187–202.
23 Information from Owen 1992. See also Byrne 2021, p.385.
24 William Redgrave had founded the St Peter's Loft School of Painting with Lanyon and Frost in 1955. All the 'regulars' listed here are artists, with the exception of the poets W S (Sydney) Graham and his partner Nessie Graham, aka Nessie Dunsmuir, and Vernon Rose, artist, writer, performer, singer and musician. Tony Shiels, letter to the author, 29 March 2016.
25 Wynne-Jones 1987, p.66.
26 Quoted in Stephens 2006, p.30.
27 *Ibid.*
28 Howarth 2019, p.5.
29 Ben Nicholson quoted in Hodin 1949, p.87.
30 Marlow Moss's three letters to Ben Nicholson (the third addressed to Mr and Mrs Nicholson) are held at the Tate Archive, London, TGA 8717/1/2/3147-3149.
31 Seuphor 1957. See Seuphor 1958 for the English translation. The quote here is from the English edition, p.228.
32 The dates of Marlow Moss's exhibitions at the Hanover Gallery were 10 November–4 December 1953, and 4 March–3 April 1958.
33 Barbara Hepworth's letter to Herbert Read (Sir Herbert Edward Read fonds,

University of Victoria Special Collections, SC100, 8.61, HR/BH – 200-201) is undated but was written towards the end of 1958. Marlow Moss has in recent years been written back into art history and included in several exhibitions. Lucy Howarth completed her PhD thesis on the artist in 2008 and has co-curated a display of her work that toured from Tate St Ives to Leeds Art Gallery, the Jerwood Gallery, and Tate Britain (2013–15). Charles Darwent also wrote about Moss substantially in Darwent 2012.

34 There is mention of John Milne's 1956 one-man exhibition at the Crane Gallery in his potted biography in the catalogue that accompanied the Penwith Society's *Tenth Anniversary Exhibition* (1960). The author has found no other reference to it.

35 Portner 1959.

36 *Eleven British Artists*, Jefferson Place Gallery, Washington DC, 29 January–27 February 1959.

37 John Milne, letter to Julian Nixon, 16 January 1963, collection of Tom Sargant. In the same letter he mentions a new Manchester club, the Rockingham, which was the first gay club to open in the UK. It was in the basement of a warehouse (since demolished) on Queen Street.

38 Quoted in Morley 2013, pp.97–98.

39 The identity of Jan is unknown. John Milne, postcard to Alan Lowndes, 1956, collection of Tom Sargant.

40 Val Baker 1959, p.22.

41 Noall 1964.

42 Many thanks to Janet Axten and staff of the St Ives Archive for information about the name Trewyn (emailed to the author 6 January 2022). In a subsequent email of 13 January 2022, Axten added: 'The name *Trewyn* had been the name of one of the Hain Line ships. The names of all the ships in the fleet (there were a lot of them, and they were actually tramp steamers and went around the world picking up cargo etc.) started with the letters *Tre*, because [St Ives shipping magnate and MP] Sir Edward Hain liked their Cornishness. Apparently, Mr Trewhella had been an early investor in the Hain shipping line, and when he came to give Brunswick House a name in 1892, he preferred something that sounded more Cornish, so he chose to use that particular name. So it was really Edward Hain who brought the name into use.'

43 Axten 1995, p.41.

44 William Redgrave quoted in Stephens 2018, p.228.

45 Following Milne's death, the Vaughan was with the Wills Lane Gallery, St Ives (then owned by Reg Singh); it was then sold to the Redfern Gallery, London. The painting is now in a private collection. See Hepworth and Massey 2012, p.111. The author recalls seeing a 1950s Soulages lithograph, likely to be the one from Trewyn, at the Wills Lane Gallery in the 1990s, during the period in which local architect Henry Gilbert owned the business. The Soulages, along with a large blue gouache by William Scott, seemed over the years to be permanent fixtures, and were perhaps there for Gilbert's own enjoyment rather than for sale. Sara Matson has noted that Patrick Heron was influenced by Soulages, whom he visited regularly at his studio in Paris. See Denison 2014, p.109.

46 Cosmo gave the property to John in a Deed of Gift dated 17 March 1965.

47 Ingham 1958.

3 Tapestry of Innocence

1 Peter Wildeblood, *Against the Law*, Weidenfeld & Nicolson, London, 1955, p.3.

2 Reg Singh, telephone conversation with the author, 7 July 2015.

3 Val Baker 1963, p.141.

4 For a fuller account of the Vince Man's Shop, see Crow 2020, pp.17–19.

5 A National Insurance card for 1958–59 records Julian's given name as John Capper Humphrey; his address at the time was Trewyn, St Ives.

6 'events *and* peoples lives': in the original letter, 'and' is written as an ampersand, and doubly underlined for emphasis.

7 *The Times*, London, Thursday 27 May 1954, p.3.

8 Higgins 1996, pp.204–05.

9 Julian Nixon, *Tapestry of Innocence*, handwritten manuscript, collection of Tom Sargant.

10 'Psychoanalysts have suggested a distorted

relationship between the boy and his parents as the main causative factor in the development of homosexuality. Freud suggested a breakdown in the Oedipus relation, Brill suggests a mother fixation and Young notes a strong attachment of the son to his mother.' Westwood, 1960, p.7. Westwood refers here to Freud's 'The Pschyogenesis of a Case of Female Homosexuality' (1920); AA Brill's 'Homoeroticism and Paranoia' (1934) and Kimball Young's 'Personality and Problems of Adjustment' (1941).

11 There exists a 147-page typescript of *Tapestry of Innocence* that includes variant emendations and notes by Richard Blake Brown. There is a 'Cast of Characters' (probably taken from Julian Nixon's original manuscript), along with a full-page synopsis written by Brown. The author of the present book has not accessed these copies; at the time of writing they are in the possession of a rare book dealer in New Jersey.

12 In what Julian Nixon described as a diary, but which is in fact a form of memoir that he began to write in August 1969, he wrote of Richard Blake Brown soon after they first met in 1957, 'whose unique friendship was already becoming the guiding force of my life'. The diary is in the collection of Professor John Cave.

13 Brown's father went on to be for many years managing director of the Westinghouse Brake & Signal Company.

14 See Pick 2019, p.34: 'Blake had invented a religious service with Croft-Cooke as acolyte in a small room of Blake's parents' house.'

15 Croft-Cooke 1966, p.93.

16 Pick 2019, p.32.

17 Quoted in Cohen 2014, p.146.

18 Croft-Cooke 1966, pp.92, 94.

19 Brown 1938, p.100.

20 *Ibid.*, p.101.

21 The manuscript of Richard Blake Brown's *The Bavarian Cousins*, his unpublished biography of Ludwig II of Bavaria, is held at the University of California Irvine.

22 Cohen 2014, p.173.

23 One example of a condemned man Richard supported was 27-year-old Miles Giffard, whom he accompanied to his execution by hanging at Horfield Prison in February 1953; Giffard had murdered his parents.

24 *Ibid.*

25 On 26 April 1959, Brown noted in his journal: 'Broth is at St Ives for the summer, opening a café, in which I heartily wish him every possible success.' In a further entry he wrote that the café was to open on Friday 15 May.

26 Val Baker 1963, p.145; the sum of £150 would be equivalent in 2022 to about £2,900.

27 Quotes by Valerie Lowndes are from a conversation with the author, Sheffield, 26 August 2015.

28 Tony Shiels, letter to the author, 29 March 2016.

29 See Tufnell 2006, p.69.

30 For example: '[Belton] had the further advantage, in the eyes of some homosexuals, of being remarkably well-endowed.' Stevens and Swan, p.427.

31 Information about Ron Belton, including the quote by Christopher Gibbs, is taken from Stevens and Swan 2021, pp.427–29.

32 'There are thirteen extant paintings that Bacon did in St Ives, numbered 59-08 to 59-16 and 60-01 to 60-04 in the *Catalogue Raisonné*; in some cases, they were probably begun in St Ives and completed in Battersea.' Art historian and Bacon expert Martin Harrison, email to the author, 19 February 2017.

33 'Lucian Freud stated that it was painted from life, with Bacon capturing Ron Belton': quoted in Harrison and Daniels 2016, p.580.

34 Francis Bacon's letters are reproduced by kind courtesy of the writer Jon Lys Turner; Turner 2016.

35 Redgrave quoted in Tufnell 2006, p.72.

36 The guest book, at one time in the possession of Julian Nixon, is now in a private collection.

4 The Playground

1 Norman Levine, letter to Alison Oldham, 21 February 2000, quoted in Oldham 2002, p.48.

2 'In the mid to late 1950s, when Bacon was spending large parts of the year there, Tangier had a distinct expatriate hierarchy

and *modus vivendi*. David Herbert, the younger son of the Earl of Pembroke, was a natural choice as the unofficial head of the British community. He had established himself in a picturesque house with an aviary, surrounded by a splendid garden, where he entertained all the passing grandees from the Windsors to Noel Coward; Ian Fleming, who had gone to Tangier to work on a book, put it in a nutshell: "David is a sort of Queen Mum."' Michael Peppiatt, *Francis Bacon: Anatomy of an Enigma*, Weidenfeld & Nicolson, London, 1996, p.170.

3 Before 1967, all male homosexual acts were illegal in Britain. The 1967 Act legalised sexual acts in England and Wales between two consenting men over the age of 21, conducted in private. Separate legislation in 1980 and 1982 would legalise homosexual acts in Scotland and Northern Ireland, respectively.

4 See Weeks 1977, p.30.

5 St Ives doctor Roger Slack referred to 'a very active lesbian pottery scene in the town' in a conversation with the writer David Whittaker, going on to say that 'when [Nancy] Wynne-Jones set up Trevaylor in the 1960s the place was overrun with gay women potters, with Boots Redgrave at the helm. Janet Leach was also in the mix.' David Whittaker, email to the author, 2 February 2017.

6 Lord Montagu, Michael Pitt-Rivers and Peter Wildeblood had faced trial at Winchester Assizes in 1954, hence John's exclamation mark. The word 'very' is elongated for emphasis.

7 Val Baker 1963, pp.68, 70.

8 'His work was briefly interrupted by a stint in the US Army as an MP stationed in England, but by the end of the 1950s Temple had gained what he felt was an adequate proficiency. He attempted to sell his pottery while supporting himself at various times as a waiter, elevator operator and technical assistant in the ceramics studio at the Art Institute of Chicago. And he had grown confident enough to write Leach asking for an apprenticeship. At Leach's invitation he traveled with a bag of pots to the University of Michigan, where the British potter was conducting a workshop. After being interviewed by Leach, he was told to come to St Ives, the Leach pottery in Cornwall.' Rob Barnard, 'Byron Temple: The Gift To Be Simple', *American Craft*, vol.51, no.4, August–September 1991, available at www.rob-barnard.com/essays/6mak/maktwo/, accessed 15 February 2018.

9 Temple's reference to working with Bernard Leach for 3 years may reflect his personal ambition to remain there for that amount of time: as previously stated, the initial agreement was that he would work at the pottery for 2 years.

10 Extracts from Byron Temple's diary are from the Emmanuel Cooper Archive, London, quoted here courtesy of David Horbury.

11 Byron Temple's letter to Bernard Leach, 2 October 1961, is in the collection of Leach's papers held at the Craft Study Centre, Farnham, Surrey, ref.4775 7/27.

12 Tony Shiels, letter to the author, 29 March 2016.

13 Michael Hunt, telephone conversation with the author, January 2014.

14 Jonathan Xavier Coudrille, email to the author, 16 March 2016. Coudrille's father was the artist and ventriloquist Francis Coudrill (1913–1989).

15 Nancy Patterson, email to the author, 15 November 2020.

16 Levine 2001, p.9.

17 See Oldham 2002, p.12.

18 *Ibid.*, p.15.

19 Levine 1970, pp.25–26.

20 Levine 1990, pp.6–17.

21 Levine 1979.

22 Levine 1961, pp.56–57.

23 *Ibid.*, p.58.

24 'Officers' is double underlined in the letter.

25 See Val Baker 1963, pp.72–73.

26 Levine 1961, p.73.

27 From William Redgrave's journals, vol.8, p.115. Quoted in Stephens 2018, p.249; date of journal entry not given.

28 Nancy Patterson, email to the author, 21 February 2020. The couple did in fact later return to St Ives.

29 Barbara Hepworth was included in the show *British Sculptors* at the Art Gallery of Toronto, 13 January–12 February 1957; *Barbara Hepworth Sculpture* was at the Montreal Museum of Fine Arts for the month of March 1957.

30 Information from Guy Milne, email to the author, 12 March 2017.

5 Le Quartier St Ives

1 Harrod 1999, p.340.
2 'Le Quartier St Ives', *The Tatler and Bystander*, 26 July 1961, pp.170–73.
3 John Milne's reference to having squatters in his greenhouse is in an undated letter to Julian Nixon: 'Other news from St Ives is that my greenhouse is full of "Beatnik", "squatters".'
4 Jonathon Xavier Coudrille, quoted in White 2013, p.54.
5 White 2013, p.56.
6 Skeaping 1977, p.72.
7 Hepworth 1970, p.7.
8 Julian Nixon mentioned Roditi's visit in a letter to Richard Blake Brown dated 31 August 1958, referring to him as 'one of our new guests'. Roditi's book *Dialogues on Art* was published by Secker & Warburg, London, in 1960; in the preamble to his piece on Hepworth (pp.90–102), Roditi writes that he stayed with John Milne at Trewyn during his visit. Roditi was incidentally yet another gay visitor to St Ives.
9 Brian Wall quoted in 'Barbara Hepworth: "Marginalised" in her Artistic Prime', *The Times*, 26 June 2015.
10 *Ibid.*
11 Quoted in Stephens 2006, p.30.
12 See Sophie Bowness, 'Introduction', in Bowness 2015, p.9.
13 The photograph was reproduced on the cover of the *Sunday Times Magazine*, 26 September 1965, with the byline 'Snowdon on the British Art Scene'.
14 Robertson, Russell and Snowdon 1965, p.43.
15 *Barbara Hepworth: A Retrospective Exhibition of Carvings and Drawings from 1927 to 1954*, Whitechapel Art Gallery, London, 8 April–6 June 1954 (catalogue preface by Bryan Robertson; introduction by David Baxandall). *Barbara Hepworth: An Exhibition of Sculpture from 1952–1962*, 10 May–8 June 1962 (catalogue essay by Bryan Robertson).
16 Bryan Robertson's letters to Barbara Hepworth are housed at the Tate Archive, London. They range in date from 1953 to 1970. The letter quoted from here is dated 17 June 1954.
17 Barbara Hepworth, letter to Bryan Robertson, 1 May 1955, Whitechapel Gallery Archive, London.
18 Bryan Robertson, letter to Barbara Hepworth, 27 October 1959, Tate Archive.
19 Bryan Robertson interviewed by Sarah Jane Checkland in 1996. See Checkland 2000, p.296.
20 *Ida Kar*, Whitechapel Art Gallery, London, March–April 1960. The catalogue's title page describes the show as 'An exhibition of portraits of artists and writers in Great Britain, France and the Soviet Union; and other photographs'.
21 Levin 2012, p.380.
22 Bryan Robertson's appointments diary for 1961 (held at the Tate Archive) shows that he and Krasner met in London on 16 June. There is nothing in the diary to suggest that the two made a trip to St Ives around the same time. The dates of Krasner's Whitechapel retrospective were 21 September–31 October 1965. Those of Frankenthaler's Whitechapel retrospective were 7 May–8 June 1969.
23 Lambirth 2019, p.226.
24 Procktor 1991, p.72.
25 Yorke 1990, p.67.
26 See Yorke 1990, pp.67–69. Yorke notes that Vaughan's first mention of Cosmo Rodewald in his journal dates from July 1941. John Lehmann published a selection of Vaughan's drawings in *Penguin New Writing*, no. 13, April–June 1942.
27 Keith Vaughan, journal entry, 27 April 1972, in Ross 1989, p.189.
28 Keith Vaughan, letter to Marjorie Jenkins, September 1955, quoted in Yorke 1990, pp.164–65.
29 John Milne, letter to Beatrice Miller, January 1972, Tate Archive, London, TGA 200823.
30 A regular Trewyn guest, film actor Richard Wattis (1912–1975) was a great friend of Milne's, part of his close gay circle; Milne was reportedly devastated when Wattis died. Keith Barron (1934–2017), Fanny Carby (1925–2002), Adrienne Corri (1930–2016) and Peter Vaughan (1923–2016) were British television and film actors. Sir Edward

Hulton (1906–1988) was co-founder and owner of the photojournalism magazine *Picture Post*.

31 The Russells, owners of Trewyn House at the time of the author's visit on 2 March 2015, mentioned Melly, Lyttelton and Végh had visited; they also stated that Princess Margaret was said to have visited the house.

32 Christine Farrington, email to the author, 28 July 2019.

33 McCarthy 2000.

34 Christine Farrington, telephone conversation with the author, 15 August 2019.

35 Keith Barron, telephone conversation with the author, 7 August 2016.

36 Brian Smith in Powell 1980, pp.34–35.

37 Dell Castagli, conversation with the author, St Ives, 11 April 2016.

6 Working Methods

1 *Painting and Sculpture of a Decade*, Tate Gallery, London, 22 April–28 June 1964. The dates of Noguchi's show at Gimpel Fils were 9 July–24 August 1968.

2 Fuller 1968.

3 Herrera 2015, p.73.

4 Giedion-Welcker 1949, p.195.

5 'I came up for the opening of the Moore exhibition at Bryan's gallery. It is really staggering. I have been back three times already, even tho' it is an awful drag getting across [to] the Whitechapel. Still, I can see why he likes the area!' John Milne, letter to Julian Nixon, 28 November 1960, collection of Tom Sargant. *Henry Moore: Sculpture, 1950–1960*, Whitechapel Art Gallery, London, November–December 1960.

6 Bryan Robertson's preface in the unpaginated catalogue accompanying *Henry Moore: Sculpture, 1950–1960*, Whitechapel Art Gallery, November–December 1960.

7 See, for example, Henry Moore's *Definitive Maquette for Bouwcentrum Wall, Rotterdam* (1955, bronze) and *Maquette No. IV Wall Relief* (1955, plaster for bronze), respectively no.36 and no.39 in the Whitechapel show catalogue.

8 Stevens 1994, p.34.

9 John Milne, statement, April 1976, typescript copy, collection Tate Archive, London, TGA 20062.

10 *The New Generation: 1965* was a show of work by nine sculptors: David Annesley, Michael Bolus, Phillip King, Roland Piché, Christopher Sanderson, Tim Scott, William Tucker, Isaac Witkin and Derrick Woodham. It was held at the Whitechapel Art Gallery, London, from March to April 1965.

11 Greenberg 1967, pp.116–17.

12 Quote from a handwritten note made by Paul Hodin during a conversation with Milne in 1975, Tate Archive, London, TGA 20062.

13 Chris Booth, email to the author, 2 September 2013.

14 Robertson 1969, p.133.

15 'Bryan Robertson was here and he bought some of my work. Very flattering; and very useful to me at the moment.' John Milne, letter to Julian Nixon, 16 June 1962. The letter was addressed to Nixon in New York.

16 The first venue for *Eight Individuals* was Derby Museum and Art Gallery, after which the show toured to Southampton City Art Gallery, Folkestone Art Centre, Billingham Art Gallery and the Graves Art Gallery, Sheffield.

17 Robertson 1971, p.7.

18 Quotations from Milne's typescript are from Forsdyke-Crofts 1998, pp.116, 118, 120. The original typescript is in the Tate Archive, London.

19 John Milne, 'Artist's Notes 1972', in *John Milne*, the catalogue for the artist's show at Marjorie Parr Gallery, London, 7–29 April 1972, n.p.

20 Morris 2001, pp.7, 88.

21 John Milne notebook, J P Hodin materials, Tate Archive, London, TGA 20062.

22 Hodin 1977, p.92.

23 Stephenson 2017, p.133.

24 Leach 1977, p.28, quoted in Balken 2017, p.78. Tobey stayed at Trewyn during either 1960 or 1961; Byron Temple, who stayed at Trewyn during 1960–62, told Emmanuel Cooper in a 1995 interview that Tobey also stayed at the house for a time while he was living there.

25 Tobey's statement appears in Schmied 1966, p.11.

7 How to Disappear

1 Donald Woods Winnicott quoted in Fraser 1984, n.p.

2 Lesley Hassey in conversation with the author, London, 27 November 2014.

3 Curtis 1998, p.22.

4 Bryan Robertson, letter to Barbara Hepworth, 20 January 1966. Tate Archive, London, TGA 20132/1/175.

5 'Keeping Up the Fight and the Work, *The Times Diary*, 9 January 1973.

6 Walmsley 1945, p.237.

7 Cooper 2006, p.92.

8 Alan Bowness in *Trewyn Studio*, a film by Helena Bonett in collaboration with Jonathan Law, 2015, 52 mins: www.youtube.com/watch?v=JYrhgQMjkNM&t=144s, accessed 17 January 2022.

9 'Sculptor Found Dead in Bedroom Blaze', *St Ives Times and Echo*, 23 May 1975.

10 Information about the inquest into Barbara Hepworth's death is taken from the *St Ives Times and Echo*, August 1975.

11 Heron 1975.

12 Hammacher 1987, pp.193–94, 197.

13 Hodin 1977, p.66.

14 Unpublished draft of Hodin's text with Milne's comments and amendments, Tate Archive, London, TGA 20062.

15 John Milne, letter to Paul Hodin, St Ives, 17 August 1975. Tate Archive, London, TGA 20062.

16 Bowen 1974.

17 Purchased by the Tate in 1972, Carl Andre's sculpture had already been exhibited twice by the time the *Sunday Times* published a contentious story about it in February 1976, which was then picked up with gusto by other newspapers. The controversy resulted from the idea that taxpayers' money had been used to buy a pile of bricks masquerading as an important work of art.

18 The initial acceptance of *Credo* by the parish council was reported on the front page of the *St Ives Times and Echo*, 7 November 1975. The follow-up report detailing the rejection of the idea was in the same newspaper, February 1976.

19 In the publications on Milne's sculpture, *Credo* is referred to without an accent; only the artist's own notes include the accent. For the purposes of this book the sculpture is referred to without the accent.

20 John Milne was interviewed by Clive Gunnell on 15 January 1976. The Dubai exhibition took place in January 1976 and featured three sculptors: John Milne, Denis Mitchell and Enzo Plazzotta. It was arranged by the Marjorie Parr Gallery.

21 The excerpt from the television interview with John Milne is held by the South West Film and Television Archive, Plymouth.

22 David Lindsay, email to the author, 17 February 2019.

23 Byron's pottery studio was at Lambertville, New Jersey, about 110 kilometres from New York.

24 'City of Night', a reference to the American writer John Rechy's novel, first published in 1963, with publication in Britain a year later. The book's theme is the American homosexual subculture and male prostitution, a subject considered highly controversial in its day.

25 John Milne, letter to Paul Hodin, 20 October 1977. Tate Archive, London, TGA 20062.

26 John Milne, letter to Bob Speaker, courtesy of Jessica Nicholls and Dickon Tyrell.

27 Byron Temple, letter to John Milne, 20 September 1976, courtesy of Victor Ktori.

28 John Milne, letter to Byron Temple, 26 October 1976, courtesy of Victor Ktori.

29 John Milne, letter to J P Hodin, 16 April 1978, Tate Archive, London, TGA 20062.

30 Catalogue of the exhibition *John Milne* at the Gilbert Parr Gallery, London, 21 April–13 May 1978.

31 Richard Dubieniec, email to the author, 26 May 2017.

32 Brian Smith, letter to Chris Booth, 12 July 1978, courtesy of Chris Booth.

33 Chris Booth, email to the author, 10 November 2013.

8 An Embellished Life

1 Peter Durkin, conversation with the author, Preston, 10 July 2019.

2 Robert Harbin, telephone conversation with the author, 2 July 2019.

3 Brian Smith's diary, held in the St Ives Archive, includes a note for 29 February 1970: 'Robert (Day?) doing garden at

Trewyn'; on 9 April Smith wrote: 'Ivaldo saw me re Julian Nixon'. There are several other references to Robert in connection with John Milne. St Ives Archive.

4 Julian's signature and a Bristol address are in the visitors' book of Marjorie Parr's St Ives gallery for the date 5 April 1969.
5 Richard Blake Brown's journal entries are dated 22 June and 23 June 1966.
6 The word 'nothing' is double underlined in Richard's original diary entry.
7 Quotations from Norman Hartnell's letters to Mrs N. Smyth and Mervyn Stockwood are taken from Pick 2019, p.432.
8 Julian had been dictating his memoirs to a female friend.
9 Reg Moon, letter to Julian Nixon, 8 July 2000, courtesy of Carey Moon.

9 Light and Shadow

1 In his 1976 appointments diary, Bryan Robertson wrote on 16 August, 'Train to Cornwall', with a line drawn from 17 to 26 August indicating that he was in Cornwall during that period. Roberton's diary is in the Tate Archive, London, TGA 200310.
2 Clark 2009, p.vii.
3 The 40th anniversary event was on 9 April 2016 at the Barbara Hepworth Museum and Sculpture Garden, St Ives.

Bibliography

Axten 1995
Janet Axten, *Gasworks to Gallery: The Story of Tate St Ives*, Janet Axten & Colin Orchard, St Ives, 1995

Balken 2017
Debra Bricker Balken, *Mark Tobey: Threading Light*, Skira Rizzoli, New York, 2017

Barnard 2002
Rob Barnard, 'Byron Temple, Romantic Pragmatist', *The Studio Potter*, August 2002, available at www.rob-barnard.com/essays/6mak/makseven/, accessed 13 June 2021

Bowen 1974
Denis Bowen, 'John Milne', *Arts Review*, 18 October 1974

Bowness 2015
Sophie Bowness (ed), *Barbara Hepworth: Writings and Conversations*, Tate Publishing, London, 2015

Bowness 2017
Sophie Bowness, *Barbara Hepworth: The Sculptor in the Studio*, Tate Publishing, London, 2017

Brown 1938
Richard Blake Brown, *Mr Prune on Cotswold* [1938], The Richards Press, London, 1941

Byrne 2021
Paula Byrne, *The Adventures of Miss Barbara Pym*, William Collins, London, 2021

Checkland 2000
Sarah Jane Checkland, *Ben Nicholson: The Vicious Circles of his Life and Art*, John Murray, London, 2000

Clark 2009
Martin Clark, *The Dark Monarch: Magic and Modernity in British Art*, exhibition catalogue, Tate St Ives, 2009

Cohen 2014
Deborah Cohen, *Family Secrets*, Penguin, London, 2014

Cooper 2006
Emmanuel Cooper, *Janet Leach: A Potter's Life*, Ceramic Review Publishing, London, 2006

Croft-Cooke 1996
Rupert Croft-Cooke, *The Wild Hills*, WH Allen, London, 1966

Crow 2020
Thomas Crow, *The Hidden Mod in Modern Art: London, 1957–1969*, Paul Mellon Centre for Studies in British Art/Yale University Press, London, 2020

Curtis 1998
Penelope Curtis, *Barbara Hepworth*, British Artists series, Tate Publishing, London, 1998

Darwent 2012
Charles Darwent, *Mondrian in London*, Double-Barrelled Books, London, 2012

Davies 2000
Peter Davies, *The Sculpture of John Milne*, Belgrave Gallery, London and St Ives, 2000

Denison 2014
Paul Denison *et al.*, *Modern Art and St Ives: International Exchanges, 1915–65*, exhibition catalogue, Tate St Ives, 2014

Forsdyke-Crofts
Lynette Forsdyke-Crofts, *Reflections of a Sculptor: The Art and Life of John Milne*, Innocom Ltd, St Ives, 1998

Fraser 1984
Ronald Fraser, *In Search of a Past*, Verso, London, 1984

Fuller 1968
R. Buckminster Fuller, *Isamu Noguchi: A Sculptor's World*, Thames & Hudson, London, 1968

Gardiner 1994
Margaret Gardiner, *Barbara Hepworth: A Memoir*, Lund Humphries, London, 1994

Giedion-Welcker 1949
Carola Giedion-Welcker, 'Constantin Brancusi', *Horizon*, vol.XIX, no.111, March 1949, pp.193–202

Greenberg 1967
Clement Greenberg, 'Anthony Caro', *Studio International*, vol.174, no.892, September 1967, pp.116–17

Hammacher 1968 / Hammacher 1987
Abraham M. Hammacher, *Barbara Hepworth*, Thames & Hudson, London, 1968, revised edition 1987

Harrison and Daniels 2016
Martin Harrison and Rebecca Daniels (eds), *Francis Bacon: Catalogue Raisonné*, 5 vols, The Estate of Francis Bacon/HENI Publishing, London, 2016

Harrod 1999
Tanya Harrod, *The Crafts in.Britain in the Twentieth Century*, Bard Graduate Center for Studies in the Decorative Arts/Yale University Press, New Haven and London, 1999

Hepworth 1970
Barbara Hepworth, *A Pictorial Autobiography*, Moonraker Press, Bradford-on-Avon, 1970

A. Hepworth and Massey 2012
Anthony Hepworth and Ian Massey, *Keith Vaughan: The Mature Oils, 1946–1977*, Sansom & Co., Bristol, 2012

Heron 1975
Patrick Heron, 'Hepworth: A Singular Passion', *The Observer*, 25 May 1975

Herrera 2015
Hayden Herrera, *Listening to Stone: The Art and Life of Isamu Noguchi*, Thames & Hudson, London, 2015

Higgins 1996
Patrick Higgins, *Heterosexual Dictatorship: Male Homosexuality in Post-War Britain*, Fourth Estate, London, 1996

Hodges 1983
Andrew Hodges, *Alan Turing: The Enigma*, Vintage, London, 1983

Hodin 1949
J P Hodin, 'Ben Nicholson', *The Cornish Review*, no.3, autumn 1949, pp.83–88

Hodin 1950
J P Hodin, 'The Cornish Renaissance', *Penguin New Writing*, vol.39, 1950, pp.113–24

Hodin 1957
J P Hodin, *Ben Nicholson: The Meaning of his Art*, Alec Tiranti, London, 1957

Hodin 1958
J P Hodin, *Henry Moore*, Zwemmer, London, 1958

Hodin 1961
J P Hodin, *Barbara Hepworth*, Lund Humphries, London, 1961

Hodin 1972
J P Hodin, *Modern Art and the Modern Mind*, The Press of Case Western Reserve University, Cleveland and London, 1972

Hodin 1977
J P Hodin, *John Milne: Sculptor*, Latimer New Dimensions, London, 1977

Howarth 2019
Lucy Howarth, *Marlow Moss*, Eiderdown Books, Arundel, 2019

Ingham 1958
Margo Ingham, 'Käthe Schuftan, Obituary', *Manchester Guardian*, 24 February 1958

Jackson 1978
Norman Jackson, 'Art World's Bubbling Margo Dies', *Manchester Evening News*, 28 March 1978

Jackson and Sekunda 2007
Alastar Jackson and Nicholas Sekunda, 'Cosmo Rodewald, 1915–2002: A Brief Biography', in Nicholas Sekunda (ed), *Corolla Cosmo Rodewald*, Foundation for the Development of Gdansk University, Gdansk, 2007, pp.7–9

Kalman and Lambirth 2003
Andras Kalman and Andrew Lambirth, *LS Lowry, Conversation Pieces: Andras Kalman in Conversation with Andrew Lambirth*, Chaucer Press, London, 2003

Kynaston 2007
David Kynaston, *Austerity Britain, 1945–51*, Bloomsbury Publishing, London, 2007

Lambirth 2019
Andrew Lambirth, *The Life of Bryan: A Celebration of Bryan Robertson*, Unicorn Press, London, 2019

Leach 1977
Bernard Leach, 'Mark Dear Mark', *World Order*, vol.11, no.3, spring 1977, pp.28–30

Levin 2012
Gail Levin, *Lee Krasner: A Biography*, William Morrow, New York, 2012

Levine 1961
Norman Levine, 'The Playground', in Norman Levine, *One Way Ticket*, Secker & Warburg, London, 1961, pp.11–75

Levine 1970
Norman Levine, *From a Seaside Town*, Macmillan, London, 1970

Levine 1979
Norman Levine, *Alan Lowndes: Paintings, 1948–1978*, exhibition catalogue, Penwith Galleries, St Ives, 1979

Levine 1990
Norman Levine, 'Soap Opera', *Encounter*, vol.74, no.3, April 1990, pp.6–17

Levine 2001
Norman Levine, 'An Autobiographical Essay', *Canadian Notes and Queries*, no.60, 2001, pp.7–19

Liddell 1948
Robert Liddell, 'Studies in Genius: VII – Cavafy', *Horizon*, vol.XVIII, no.105, September 1948, pp.187–202

Liddell 1974
Robert Liddell, *Cavafy: A Critical Biography*, Duckworth, London, 1974

Mantel 2017
Hilary Mantel, 'The Princess Myth', *The Guardian*, 26 August 2017

McCarthy 2000
Fiona McCarthy, 'Obituary of Brocard Sewell', *The Guardian*, 4 April 2000

Mellor 1987
David Mellor, *A Paradise Lost: The Neo-Romantic Imagination in Britain, 1935–55*, exhibition catalogue, Barbican Art Gallery, London, with Lund Humphries, 1987

Morley 2013
Paul Morley, *The North*, Bloomsbury Publishing, London, 2013

Morris 2001
Jan Morris, *Conundrum*, Faber & Faber, London, 2001

Noall 1964
Cyril Noall, 'Trewyn, the House that Halse Built', *St Ives Times and Echo*, 28 August 1964

Oldham 2002
Alison Oldham, *Everyone Was Working: Writers and Artists in Postwar St Ives*, Tate St Ives/ Falmouth College of Arts, Falmouth, 2002

Owen 1992
Peter Owen, 'Robert Liddell, Obituary', *The Independent*, 24 July 1992

Pick 2019
Michael Pick, *Norman Hartnell: The Biography*, Zuleika, London, 2019

Portner 1959
Leslie Judd Portner, 'Cornish Group at Jefferson Place', *Washington Post and Herald*, 1 February 1959

Powell 1980
Gillian Powell, 'The Street Where You Live: St Ives in Cornwall', *Woman and Home*, May 1980, pp.32–36

Procktor 1991
Patrick Procktor, *Self-Portrait*, Weidenfeld & Nicolson, London, 1991

Read 1952
Herbert Read (intro.), *Barbara Hepworth: Carvings and Drawings*, exhibition catalogue, Lund Humphries, London, 1952

Read 1954
Herbert Read (ed), *Collected Works of C.G. Jung*, vol.17: *Development of Personality*, Routledge & Kegan Paul, London, 1954

Robertson 1969
Bryan Robertson, 'London Commentary: John Milne's Sculpture at the Marjorie Parr Gallery from 2 to 25 October', *Studio International*, vol.178, no.915, October 1969, pp. 130–33

Robertson 1971
Bryan Robertson, *Eight Individuals*, exhibition catalogue, Arts Council of Great Britain, London, 1971

Robertson, Russell and Snowdon 1965
Bryan Robertson, John Russell and Lord Snowdon, *Private View: The Lively World of British Art*, Thomas Nelson & Sons, London, 1965

Rowe 2020
Tommy Rowe, *Tommy Rowe: Sculptor*, ebook, 2020

Sassoon 1945
Siegfried Sassoon, *Siegfried's Journey*, Faber & Faber, London, 1945

Schmied 1966
Wieland Schmied, *Mark Tobey*, Thames & Hudson, London, 1966

Seuphor 1958
Michel Seuphor, *A Dictionary of Abstract Painting*, trans. Lionel Izod, John Montague and Francis Scarfe, Methuen, London, 1958 (originally published as *Dictionnaire de la peinture abstraite*, Fernand Hazan, Paris, 1957)

Skeaping 1977
John Skeaping, *Drawn from Life: An Autobiography*, Collins, London, 1977

Stephens 2006
Chris Stephens, *Brian Wall*, Momentum Books, London, 2006

Stephens 2018
Chris Stephens, *St Ives: The Art and the Artists*, Pavilion, London, 2018

Stephenson 2017
Andrew Stephenson, 'Arcadia and Soho', in Clare Barlow (ed), *Queer British Art, 1861–1967*, exhibition catalogue, Tate Britain, London, 2017, pp.132–45

Stevens 1994
Anthony Stevens, *Jung: A Very Short Introduction*, Oxford University Press, Oxford, 1994

Stevens and Swan 2021
Mark Stevens and Annalyn Swan, *Francis Bacon: Revelations*, William Collins, London, 2021

St Ives 1996
St Ives, 1939–64: Twenty Five Years of Painting, Sculpture and Pottery, Tate Publishing, London, revised edition, 1996

Stokes and Banken 2015
Raymond G. Stokes and Ralf Banken, *Building Upon Air: A History of the International Industrial Gases Industry from the 19th to the 21st Centuries*, Cambridge University Press, Cambridge, 2015

Todd 2019
Selina Todd, *Tastes of Honey: The Making of Shelagh Delaney and a Cultural Revolution*, Chatto & Windus, London, 2019

Tufnell 2006
Ben Tufnell, *On the Very Edge of the Ocean: The Porthmeor Studios and Painting in St Ives*, Tate St Ives Research Series, Tate Publishing, London, 2006

Turner 2016
Jon Lys Turner, *The Visitors' Book: In Francis Bacon's Shadow: The Lives of Richard Chopping and Denis Wirth-Miller*, Constable, London, 2016

Val Baker 1959
Denys Val Baker, *Britain's Art Colony by the Sea*, George Ronald, London, 1959

Val Baker 1963
Denys Val Baker, *The Door is Always Open*, Phoenix House, London, 1963

Vaughan 1989
Keith Vaughan, *Journals, 1939–1977*, ed. Alan Ross, John Murray, London, 1989

Walmsley 1945
Leo Walmsley, *So Many Loves*, The Reprint Society, London, 1945 (originally published by William Collins & Co., London, 1944)

Warren 1969
Tony Warren, *I was Ena Sharples Father*, Gerald Duckworth & Co., London, 1969

Warren 1991
Tony Warren, *The Lights of Manchester*, Century, Random House, London, 1991

Weeks 1977
Jeffrey Weeks, *Coming Out: Homosexual Politics in Britain, from the Nineteenth Century to the Present*, Quartet Books, London, 1977

Westwood 1960
Gordon Westwood, *A Minority: A Report on the Life of the Male Homosexual in Great Britain*, Longmans, London, 1960

White 2013
Rupert White, *Folk in Cornwall: Music and Musicians of the Sixties Revival*, Antenna Publications, Truro, 2013

Whittet 1962
George Sorley Whittet, 'Crane Kalman Gallery', *The Studio*, vol.164, no.833, September 1962, pp.108–10

Wynne-Jones 1987
Nancy Wynne-Jones, 'W S Graham in Cornwall', *Edinburgh Review*, no.75, 1987, pp.66–69

Yohannan 2015
Hephzibah Yohannan, 'Käthe Schuftan Artist', *Halliday Review*, spring 2015, ppp.16–29

Yorke 1990
Malcolm Yorke, *Keith Vaughan: His Life and Work*, Constable, London, 1990

Image credits

p.129 (top): Photograph by Ian Massey
p.129 (bottom): Photograph by Andy Hughes
p.130 (top and bottom): Photographer unknown
p.131 (top): Courtesy of the University of Salford Library Archive
p.131 (bottom): Courtesy of Carey Moon
p.132: Courtesy of the St Ives Archive
p.133 (top and bottom): Courtesy of the St Ives Archive
p.134 (top): Courtesy of the Penwith Gallery Archive
p.134 (bottom): Courtesy of Barbara Hepworth © Bowness
p.135 (top and bottom): Courtesy of Godson & Coles, London
p.136 (top): Courtesy of the St Ives Archive
p.136 (bottom): Courtesy of Crane Kalman Gallery, London, on behalf of the Estate of Alan Lowndes
p.137 (top): Courtesy of the St Ives Archive
p.137 (bottom): Courtesy of Nancy Patterson
p.138 (top): Courtesy of the Penwith Gallery Archive
p.138 (bottom): © Estate of John Milne
p.139: Courtesy of Peter Durkin
p.140 (top): Courtesy of Tom Sargant
p.140 (bottom): © The Estate of Francis Bacon. All rights reserved/DACS 2022
p.141 (top and bottom): Courtesy of the St Ives Archive
p.142: Courtesy of the Penwith Gallery Archive
p.143 (top and bottom): Courtesy of Jessica Nicholls
p.144 (top and bottom): © National Portrait Gallery, London
p.145: © Snowdon/Trunk Archive
p.146 (top): Courtesy of The Nine British Art
p.146 (bottom): Photograph courtesy of Roseberys, reproduced by permission of the Redfern Gallery, London
p.147: © Tate
p.148: Courtesy of The Nine British Art
p.149: Photographer unknown. Courtesy of the St Ives Archive
p.150 (top): © Estate of John Milne
p.150 (bottom): Courtesy of Belgrave St Ives
p.151: Photograph by Martin Koretz. Courtesy of the Whitechapel Gallery Archive
p.152 (top and bottom): Courtesy of Belgrave St Ives
p.153 (top): Courtesy of the St Ives Archive
p.153 (bottom): Photograph by Joyce Booth, courtesy of Chris Booth
p.154 (top): Courtesy of Belgrave St Ives
p.154 (bottom): © Estate of John Milne
p.155 (top): © Estate of John Milne
p.155 (bottom): Courtesy of Bonhams, London
p.156 (top): Courtesy of Bonhams, London
p.156 (bottom): Courtesy of Mallams Auctioneers
p.157 (top): © Estate of John Milne
p.157 (bottom): © Estate of John Milne. Courtesy of Bonhams, London
p.158: 1978 exhibition catalogue
p.159 (top and bottom): Courtesy of Jessica Nicholls
p.160: Photograph by Ian Massey

Published in 2022 by Ridinghouse
46 Lexington Street
London W1F 0LP
United Kingdom
ridinghouse.co.uk

Distributed in the UK, Europe and the rest of the world by
ACC Art Books
Sandy Lane, Old Martlesham
Woodbridge, Suffolk IP12 4SD
accartbooks.com

Distributed in the United States and Canada by
ARTBOOK | D.A.P.
75 Broad Street, Suite 630
New York, New York 10004
artbook.com

Front cover: John Milne and Julian Nixon on the balcony at Trewyn, St Ives, June 1959. Courtesy of Tom Sargant

Back cover: Ida Kar, contact sheet of photographs of John Milne at Trewyn, 1961. © National Portrait Gallery, London

Publication supported by the Paul Mellon Centre for Studies in British Art

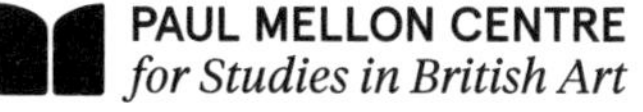

British Library Cataloguing-in-Publication Data
A full catalogue record of this book is available from the British Library.

ISBN 978 1 909932 69 2

Ridinghouse Publisher: Sophie Kullmann
Ridinghouse Senior Editor: Aimee Selby
Copyedited by Linda Schofield

Designed by Mark Thomson
Set in Chassi (Rui Abreu)

Printed in Italy by Verona Libri

Ridinghouse